History of
the Scottish Regiments

By

WILLIAM PRATT PAUL

UA
664
.P38

PUBLICATION

SECOND IMPRESSION

PUBLISHED BY M'KENZIE, VINCENT & CO. LTD., 95 BATH ST., GLASGOW
PRINTED BY GEO. OUTRAM & CO. LTD., 59/65 MITCHELL ST., GLASGOW

J. SMART

AND COMPANY

(CONTRACTORS) LTD.

BUILDING
& CIVIL
ENGINEERING
CONTRACTORS

EDINBURGH
AND
GLASGOW

Foreword

THE Erskine Paraplegic Coach and Comforts Fund, to which the proceeds of this book will be devoted, is distinct from but in no way competitive with the Princess Louise Scottish Hospital for Ex-Service Men—popularly and affectionately known as " Erskine ". The one connecting link between the two is that the Coach and Comforts Fund provides specialised services to approximately 100 paralysed ex-service men, who are, and mostly have been for years, patients in the Hospital,—a number which will soon be substantially increased by an influx from other Hospitals. These are a group who, because of the nature of their wounds, are not able to participate in many of the ongoings and enjoyments of other patients and for whom other voluntary organisations do not have appropriate facilities.

The Fund was originated twelve years ago by the late Hugh Frew and his wife, and it can be said no more truly of any one than of them that from that day they freely dedicated their lives to a cause that burdened their hearts. Mrs. Frew still takes an active personal part in the work week by week.

Throughout those years, on each Saturday and on other occasions, the Fund Bus, specially built and equipped to accommodate not only sitting but bedridden patients, has called at the hospital. Patients are taken to a football match, or other sports gathering, or theatre, or other entertainment, to a coast or country beauty spot, or to the homes and grounds of sympathetic friends. The "meal out" at the close of the outing is just that little bit that makes all the difference in the world to the patients. A small group of voluntary assistants have trained and equipped themselves to care for them during these outings.

Each week too sees its distribution of a regular quota of cigarettes, tobacco, sweets and fruits according to the individual taste of the patient, and each birthday and Christmas brings its own personal reminder. Special needs are met wherever possible whether in the shape of extra clothing, visits to or holidays at home or such like, that will give added pleasure.

Two of the cottages built in the Hospital Grounds by the Veterans' Garden Association have been leased and furnished to suit paraplegic patients to enable them to take up residence and be looked after by wives. To those who have occupied these houses the benefits and pleasure have been beyond words.

To the men the outings and visits are indeed the high-lights of their lives providing them with a " talking point " for days afterwards that is only succeeded by the anticipation of the next outing.

What can be done is dependent on voluntary subscriptions. The annual cost is between £3,000 and £4,000. The day for having to acquire a new and more up to date bus to replace the present one is drawing near and will cost around £5,000. This must also be met by voluntary subscription. Until now the many contributors have been among those who remember what those paraplegic patients did for us and how they still suffer from their wounds.

Not only is the Fund voluntary but so too is the administration of it in every way. Will you now become one more of those who are referred to on that plate on the bus " who do not forget ? "

Photograph by courtesy "Daily Mail"

HER MAJESTY THE QUEEN

COLONEL-IN-CHIEF—THE ROYAL SCOTS GREYS

THE SCOTS GUARDS AND THE ARGYLL AND SUTHERLAND HIGHLANDERS

The Royal Scots Greys

(2nd DRAGOONS) ROYAL ARMOURED CORPS

AFTER over sixteen years of foreign service in Palestine, Syria, the Western Desert, Italy, France, Belgium, Holland, Jordan, Egypt, and Cyrenaica, the Royal Scots Greys returned to the U.K. early in February, 1955. In these troubled years this world-famous Scottish regiment added many glorious epics—well in keeping with the "trooper tradition"—to an already distinguished scroll of honour.

Townsmen and country people along the banks of the Mersey paused as the strident notes of the pibroch were borne from a ship sailing up the river. The Regimental (Dismounted) March "Hielan' Laddie" was the "signature tune" of the returning Royal Scots Greys, and at Liverpool a telegram of welcome awaited them from Her Majesty The Queen, their Colonel-in-Chief.

So Scotland's "Greys" came home from the sunshine of the Middle East to the cold drab landing stage, but hearts were light when the troopers disembarked from the gangways of the "Devonshire", and at night strathspeys, reels, and the roll of drums sounded loud in Sassenach "lugs". But there was no evidence that the Sassenachs found this unpleasant, for the Celtic blood of Auld Scotia and Erin's Isle runs strong in these parts.

The Royal Scots Greys owe their origin to the religious and dynastic strife of the "Killing Time", when men sought "To prove their doctrines orthodox by Apostolic blows and knocks". Two independent troops, or companies, of dragoons were raised in Scotland on May 21, 1678. The first was commanded by Lieut.-General Thomas Dalyell, and the second by Lord Charles Murray. A third troop was added on September 23 of the same year, commanded by Mr. Francis Stuart, a private gentleman of the Life Guards.

When they first came into existence the dragoons, attired in grey uniforms, were armed with pistol, sword, musket and bayonet for service mounted or on foot. They were, in fact, mounted infantry, and operated as such. The "bluidy dragoons", as the Covenanters called them, harried the hillside religious services, or conventicles, and in 1679 they were in action, under Graham of Claverhouse, at Drumclog—where the King's troops had the worst of the exchanges—and at Bothwell Brig, under the Duke of Monmouth, which resulted in a debacle for the Covenanters. At Airds Moss, in 1680, a detachment was responsible for the slaying of Richard Cameron, "Lion of the Covenant".

Three more troops were raised in November 25, 1681, and the six units were regimented as the Royal Regiment of (Scots) Dragoons under the command of Lieut.-General Thomas Dalyell, of The Binns, Midlothian. This martinet was described by Sir Walter Scott— "bald head, with a beard to his girdle", as he sat in Hell with the Laird of Redgauntlet.

"Tam" Dalyell (or Dalziel) was a former Royalist exile and a soldier of fortune who had organised and disciplined the troops of the Czar of Russia, and led them against the Poles, Turks, and Tartars. He had been imprisoned in the Tower of London, but escaped. Fearless and ruthless, he was a bitter persecutor of the Covenanters, who said he was in league with the Devil. They believed bullets bounced off him. His treatment of prisoners was barbaric.

The Scottish dragoons took part in the suppression of Argyll's Rising in 1685, experiencing a sharp clash with the rebels near Dumbarton. They were employed against the MacDonalds of Keppoch, and overwhelmed the clansmen on the Braes of Gilroy. The Scots dragoons later defeated the rebellious Highlanders at Culnakells, and were in action again at Haughs of Cromdale in 1690, before proceeding to the relief of Abergeldie Castle and Inverness. The regiment about this time was known as the Scots Regiment of White Horses and the Grey Dragoons.

The Scots dragoons were despatched to Holland in 1694, and took part in operations in Belgium, around Ghent, Dixmude, and Ypres, but in this short campaign against the French the regiment had little opportunity to distinguish itself. The "Greys" were again in

Flanders in 1702, taking part in the sieges of Venloo, Roermond, and Stevensweert, and the capture of Lille.

Moving across the Rhine, they were present at the siege and capture of Bonn and Limburg. In this War of the Spanish Succession the dragoons at Schellenberg fought a spirited dismounted action in assisting the infantry to assault and carry the fortified heights. During the campaign a squadron served as escort to the Commander-in-Chief, the Duke of Marlborough, an ancestor of Sir Winston Churchill.

At Blenheim, in August, 1704, the Scots dragoons charged impetuously, and several infantry battalions and cavalry formations surrendered with their colours and drums. Here the Scots dragoon regiment earned its first battle-honour.

At Maastricht, in the following year, they took part in a shattering cavalry charge. Fifty enemy squadrons were overwhelmed and many surrendered with their colours and drums. At Ramillies, in May, 1706, the Scots dragoons slashed through the infantry to engage and rout the famous Regiment du Roi, which capitulated with its colours. It was during the Battle of Ramillies that a trooper of the Scots dragoons, after being wounded, was found to be a woman. She was Dublin-born Christian Davies, or " Mother Ross ". In the ranks of the Scottish regiment she was seeking her husband.

After the Union of the Parliaments of England and Scotland in 1707 the regiment took the title of the Royal Regiment of North British Dragoons in 1708. As such the regiment participated in the Battle of Oudenarde (1708). Here the Scots hurled back the infantry and entered on a ruthless pursuit of the demoralised French.

At Malplaquet, in 1709, the Scots crossed swords again with the elite Household Cavalry of France. They had to give way before the surge and press of superior numbers, but, rallying, they charged driving the enemy from the field in disorder. Later the Scots dragoons participated in the siege and capture of Mons.

In 1713 proof was adduced that the Scots dragoons had crossed the Border in June, 1685, when only one regiment of dragoons had been established in England. As a result the regiment in 1713 was designated the 2nd or Royal North British Regiment of Dragoons.

Returning to the homeland the Scots dragoons operated in their original role—enforcing law and order. During the 1715 Jacobite, or Mar Rising, the regiment severely punished the rebels at Dunfermline. They were also in action at Kinross, and later participated in the indecisive clash at Sheriffmuir. In 1719 they assisted in suppressing the minor Jacobite rising with a sharp engagement with the rebels and their Spanish allies at Glenshiel.

From 1719 until 1742 the regiment was quartered in various parts of England. In 1737 the Scots operated against the Kentish smugglers, and the following year they were employed in quelling riotous outbreaks in Dorset and Wiltshire.

Back in Flanders during the War of the Austrian Succession, the Scots were severely tested at Dettingen, in 1743. They routed the French Cuirassiers and captured a standard from their old enemies, the Household Cavalry of France. King George II was present at this incident and he highly praised the Scots dragoons for their skill at arms.

The Scottish regiment in their headlong charge at Fontenoy, in 1745, were heavily enfiladed by the French cannon, and their onslaught was repulsed after initial success against the infantry. At Raucoux the British suffered another setback, though the Scottish cavalrymen drove back the French infantry before retiring across the Meuse. Another reverse followed at Leffeldt. The Scots charged and captured several cavalry standards, but penetrating too far, came under a concentrated fire from forces lying in ambush.

The regiment returned to England in 1748, and for some ten years the dragoons were stationed in several parts of the country. A light troop, formed in 1755, to take part in what would now be termed Commando operations—then known as " Prussian exercises "—landed near St. Malo in 1758, and destroyed the port and fired several French ships. Later similar attacks were carried out at Cherbourg, and in the Bay of St. Lunaire.

At the outbreak of the Seven Years' War the Scottish dragoons returned to Flanders. At Bergen, in 1759, the British were forced to retire, but at Minden and Warburg the Scottish troopers had opportunities to distinguish themselves. Two squadrons made a dramatic charge at Zierenburg and chased several squadrons of French Dragoons back to the gates of the town.

In 1763 the regiment returned to England. This year drummers were dispensed with in the dragoons and trumpeters were introduced in

their place. For thirty years the Scots dragoons were stationed in England, but in 1793 they were again dispatched to the Continent.

Campaigning against the French, the Scottish dragoon regiment was employed at the siege of Valenciennes, in covering the siege of Dunkirk, and at the siege of Landrecies. In 1794 they took part in the Battle of Willems. In this engagement the Scots dragoons broke and destroyed an enemy square. The following year the regiment was brought back to the South of England to face the threatened French invasion, which did not materialise.

June 18, 1815—The Battle of Waterloo— and a day of glory for the "Greys". The Dutch-Belgian brigade retreated after a heavy French bombardment followed by a massed attack by the enemy infantry. At the critical moment the Union Brigade, which included the Scots dragoons, came up. They advanced over ground held by the Gordon Highlanders. The Gordons, pipes skirling, were preparing to attack when they had to make way for their Scottish comrades.

As the "Greys" passed there were shouts of "Scotland For Ever!" from both regiments, and the Scottish cavalry and infantry charged together, many Gordons hanging on to the stirrups of the dragoons—an episode since immortalised in the picture by Lady Butler. Within a few hectic minutes the ground ahead was strewn with French infantrymen and their equipment, and some 3,000 prisoners were being shepherded to the rear.

The Scots dragoons charged again to "mac siccar", shattering the infantry, rushing the guns and putting about 40 of them out of action, and cutting down the gunners. After spiking or overturning the guns they rode on, slashing through the enemy. The trumpets sounded the rally, but the call went unheard in the din of battle.

The charging Scots got on to a hill from which Napoleon had just moved, and it was then the Emperor is said to have exclaimed: "Ah ces terribles chevaux gris!" Sadly depleted in numbers they hacked their way through French Cuirassiers and Polish Lancers on the ride back to effect a junction with the Royal Dragoons who had charged to their assistance.

One of the survivors of this epic was Sergeant Charles Ewart—a Dumfriesshire man—who brought back in triumph the Imperial Eagle standard of the 45th Regiment of Invincibles. Noticing the standard-bearer had become detached from the escort, Sergeant Ewart closed with the bearer and cut him down. He was then attacked by several Frenchmen in quick succession, but he overcame his assailants, and when help arrived the sergeant was ordered to the rear so that his valuable trophy would be safe.

The eagle of the 45th Invincibles later became the regimental badge of the "Greys", and earned for them the nickname of "The Bird-catchers". The Scottish regiment took part in several charges and was awarded "Waterloo" as a battle-honour. After the conflict the "Greys" could barely muster one squadron, but nevertheless bore themselves with elan and dash in the victorious march on Paris. When peace came the Scots dragoons returned to England early in 1816, and until the outbreak of the Crimean War were stationed in various parts of the U.K.

By this time their battle-honours were listed as follows: Blenheim, Ramillies, Oudenarde, Malplaquet, Dettingen, Warburg, Willems, Waterloo. The regiment arrived in the Crimea after the Battle of Alma, and soon had a brush with the Russians. In October 1854, during the Allied advance southwards to capture Balaclava, the Scots caught up with the enemy rearguard and there was a brisk skirmish in a wood, which hastened the Russian retiral.

A few days later a Turkish force on an exposed hill position—known as the Causeway Heights—near Balaclava, received a severe pounding from the Russian artillery. The badly shaken Turks, now expecting a massed enemy attack, retired precipitately, and a squadron of the "Greys" was sent to cover their retreat.

A formation of some 3,000 Russian cavalry moved along the heights, and the Heavy Brigade—The Royal Dragoons, "Greys", Inniskillings, and Dragoon Guards—moved forward to engage. With only a few hundred yards separating them from the enemy, the British cavalry coolly performed a drill movement to get proper alignment. The Russians halted and watched the parade-ground precision of the Union Brigade lining up, then the enemy began changing their formation so that a charge would completely envelop the British cavalry.

At this moment the "Charge" was sounded by the Union Brigade trumpeters, and a storm of steel and horse-flesh broke over the enemy. The crashing impact of the British charge piled the Russians against each other, and they could not make proper use of their lances and swords.

9

Turning, the Union Brigade cut their way back. Responding to the call, "Rally The Greys", the Scots dragoons charged once more into the reeling, confused press of Russian horsemen, with the remainder of the brigade thundering alongside them. The Russian force was cut to pieces, and when some British guns engaged, the enemy cavalry disintegrated and fled from the field.

On its way back the Heavy Brigade was ordered to support the historic Charge of the Light Brigade. The troopers rode hard after the "Gallant Six Hundred", through the drifting, swirling battery smoke into the bullet-swept valley dominated by the rumbling, flashing Russian cannon. The Scots were in the vortex of the fray, and stormed in among the milling mass of Cossacks waiting to ambush and annihilate the survivors of the Light Brigade.

For his gallantry that day, October 25, 1854, Sergeant-Major Grieve won the "Grey's" first Victoria Cross. Private Ramage was also awarded this coveted decoration for valour. General Sir Colin Campbell personally congratulated the Scottish regiment on their timely support of the Light Brigade at Balaclava. The regiment was in reserve at the Battle of Inkerman. At the close of the Crimean War in 1856, with new battle-honours awarded for Balaclava and the Siege of Sevastopol, the regiment sailed for England. In 1877 the title of The Royal North British Regiment of Dragoons was changed to the 2nd Dragoons (Royal Scots Greys).

The Scottish cavalrymen participated in the Egyptian Campaign. Forming part of a mobile desert column speeding to the aid of General Gordon, trapped at Khartoum, they fought a series of sharp water-hole skirmishes, and at Abu Klea, in January, 1895, helped to break and hurl back the frenzied charge of the Mahdi's Dervishes.

The "trooper tradition" was well maintained in the open fighting during the South African War. The "Greys" earned special commendation in the dramatic dash through the Boers to the relief of Kimberley.

Lord Roberts, C.-in-C., despatched General French with his cavalry—which included the "Greys"—to crash through the Boer lines to Kimberley, which was relieved in mid-February, 1900. This operation took five days and entailed a four-mile gallop under heavy fire.

The "Greys" were also in the exhausting ride and battle to cut off Cronje's withdrawal at Paardeberg. Within a few days of Kimberley being relieved, French's cavalry detected the Boer retiral. They pinned him down in a successful delaying action on the bed of the Modder River until the infantry came up, and after bitter fighting Cronje surrendered at Paardeberg on February 27 with 4,000 men.

The Scottish cavalry regiment was well to the fore in the outflanking of the Boers at Bloemfontein, and in the rushing of Schapp's Kraal. They also experienced a number of minor clashes with the enemy at widely separated points along the extensive front. Khaki was adopted for general service purposes during this campaign, and the horses of the "Greys" were painted a similar shade. The Royal Scots Greys returned to their homeland with the battle-honours South Africa, 1899-1902, Relief of Kimberley, and Paardeberg.

Forming part of the British Expeditionary Force—consisting of only four Regular Army divisions—the Royal Scots Greys were rushed to the aid of the hard-pressed French resisting the massed invasion of Kaiser Wilhelm's Teuton legions.

The Kaiser mockingly referred to the British Expeditionary Force as "The Contemptible Little Army". But soon many of his elite formations were wilting and withering before the accurate concentrated fire and blood-reddened bayonets of the B.E.F.

The first clash with the success-flushed invaders of Belgium and France came near Mons, in August, 1914. Here "The Contemptible Little Army" beat off attack after attack by shoulder-to-shoulder masses of infantry, which threatened at times to engulf and surround the entire B.E.F. in a tidal wave of field grey amid the boom of artillery, the whistle, whine and crash of shells and the deadly chatter of machine-guns.

In danger of being enveloped, the B.E.F. began the grim fighting Retreat from Mons. The "Greys" successfully held up a strong enemy advance guard for several hours while the exhausted British infantry reorganised before again grappling with the Germans. Two squadrons of the "Greys", with a number of Gordon Highlanders, repeated the "Scotland For Ever" Waterloo episode on a lesser scale at battle-shattered St. Quentin.

For days, nights, and weeks it was fight, eat, march, sleep, march, march, march, and fight—and frequently "The Contemptible Little Army" fought off the field grey hordes with little or no sleep and meagre rations, and ammunition running dangerously low. The Scottish regiment, which had added glory to its record as cavalry, was now adding fresh pages to its scroll of honour as infantry amid the mud-holes and trenches of war-torn Flanders.

There was heavy fighting in the valiant autumn stand in the Cambrai-Le Cateau area, which once more held up the German advance, averted threatened encirclement, and ensured the further orderly retiral of the British Expeditionary Force. The battle-weary, exhausted B.E.F., in a great effort, hurled back the German legions from the Marne, which they then crossed to participate in a series of bitter but indecisive encounters with the enemy.

Both sides suffered severe losses in the First and Second Battle of Ypres in 1914 and 1915. Neuve Chapelle, Loos, and the Somme are also " Greys " memories of sacrifice, heroism and endurance in face of heavy enemy odds and appalling weather conditions. And still they carefully tended their horses, hoping one day to spearhead a breakthrough to initiate open warfare and harry the Germans back to the Rhine.

Arras, 1917, Cambrai, and the 1918 Retreat took a heavy toll. The fighting retiral before the massed German infantry advancing across a carpet of their own dead and wounded was reminiscent of the grim Retreat from Mons, and again the enemy was fought to a standstill after initial success. The Germans paid dearly for their gigantic offensive which ended in a shambles and utter exhaustion.

There was yet another attempt to drive the Germans out of their trenches at Amiens, in August, 1918. An advance of some 12 miles was made before the arrival of fresh German divisions forced stalemate again—but not for long—for the toils of vengeance were closing on the Kaiser's shattered armies. After bitter fighting on the Somme, along the Hindenburg Line, and the Canal du Nord, the expected breakthrough came with the resulting rapid advance to the Rhine, with thousands of demoralised Germans surrendering each day.

In the final offensive which smashed the Hindenburg Line, and in the pursuit of the defeated German Army towards Mons, the Royal Scots Greys were still in the forefront. So, after fighting over lands where their forebears had made history astride " ces terribles chevaux gris ", the " Greys " crossed the German frontier on December 1, 1918, with the guidon sent out from their homeland fluttering proudly at the head of the column. Scotland's " Greys " had started the campaign in August, 1914, as cavalry, and after distinguished service on many a glorious or stricken field they were ending it as cavalry.

The achievements of the Royal Scots Greys in World War I are interpreted in their battle-honours: Retreat from Mons, Marne, 1914, Aisne, 1914, Ypres, 1914, 1915, Arras, 1917; Amiens, Somme, 1918, Hindenburg Line, Pursuit to Mons, France and Flanders, 1914-18.

After the war the Royal Scots Greys were sent overseas in 1920, serving for seven years in India, Egypt, and Palestine. On returning to the U.K. they made their famous " March Through Scotland " in 1934. In the far-reaching Army reforms of 1937 the proposal to convert the " Greys "—Scotland's only Regular cavalry regiment—to a mechanised role aroused such a storm of protest that the authorities had to amend their plans.

The Scottish regiment left Britain in 1938 for service in Palestine, where they operated with success against the Arab and Jewish terrorists. They cordoned off villages during searches and " screening " operations, and experienced many long night rides in the Jordan Valley. Frequently the Scots were following in the footsteps of the Crusaders in maintaining the peace in territory where their mobility was vital.

After the outbreak of World War II, the " Greys " took part in the short successful Syrian campaign of 1941. Then came mechanisation—prelude to some of the fiercest fighting in the regiment's long history. American Stuart tanks replaced the horses, and after six months' training the Scots Greys, as a unit of the Royal Armoured Corps, went to Egypt. It was soon to join the Eighth Army and join battle with Rommel's Afrika Korps.

But many officers and other ranks, restive to be in the fray, had already volunteered for Commando and parachute units. Lieut.-Colonel G. C. T. Keyes, V.C., distinguished son of a distinguished father—Admiral of the Fleet Lord Keyes—raised a troop of the 11th (Scottish) Commando. There was a number of Scots Greys in this troop, and with it Lieut.-Colonel Keyes proceeded to the Middle East in February, 1941. He was killed in the daring raid on Rommel's headquarters in November of the same year. The award of the Victoria Cross was posthumous.

The Scottish tank troopers drew German and Italian blood in plenty in August, 1942, at Alam Halfa. They were in the thick of the fighting at the crucial Battle of El Alamein, and spearheaded the final British advance across the Western Desert to Tripoli, with the much-vaunted Afrika Korps in full pelt retreat after taking a " bloody nose " in a series of grim encounters in the ebb and flow of the desert war. In a few months there came the final Nazi debacle on Cap Bon.

In the Italian campaign the " Greys " fought with great skill and tenacity in the Salerno beachhead, and were the first Allied troops to enter Naples on October 1, 1943. In the bitterly contested advance through the German-Italian " serial " defences and natural water and mountain barriers the " Greys " were often in the van. They had a prominent part in the costly Volturno battles and in the fighting advance on the Garigliano.

Returning to Britain in February, 1944, the regiment prepared to re-enter the fray on the Continent to " lift the curse of Hitler from the brows of men ". Landing on D Day plus one they were soon heavily committed at Calvary Hill, on the Odon. There was fierce fighting around Falaise, then they battled the Germans back to the Somme, Courtrai, and south of Arnhem, Roermond, and Antwerp.

They vigorously and skilfully fought their Sherman tanks forward from the beaches and battlefields of destiny in Normandy across France and into Eastern Holland, and over the Rhine to take part in the capture of Bremen, co-operating with the infantry of the 52nd (Lowland) Division in the capture of the town.

Then, for the fourth time in their history, the Royal Scots Greys crossed the German frontier after driving about 80 miles with airborne troops riding on their tanks, and were the first British troops to contact, at Wismar, on the Baltic coast, the Russians— advancing from the East. After the peace the " Greys " arrived in Luneburg, Northern Germany, with sadly depleted numbers, but their pipes were skirling defiantly to " gaur them grue."

World War II battle-honours were: Caen, Hill 112, Falaise, Venlo Pocket, Hochwald, Aller, Bremen, North-West Europe, 1944-45, Merjayun, Syria, 1941, Alam el Halfa, El Alamein, El Agheila, Nofilia, Advance on Tripoli, North Africa, 1942-43, Salerno, Battipaglia, Volturno Crossing, Italy, 1943.

In April, 1952, the Royal Scots Greys were ordered out to the Benghazi area, in Cyrenaica. In January of the following year one squadron was sent to the Canal Zone and served at Shandur and later at Bala, where the troopers stood by during the Egyptian " troubles ". In February, 1954, another squadron moved into South Jordan and was based at Maan for exercises with the famous Arab Legion in tank co-operation.

The Scots established excellent relations with the desert warriors of King Hussein, and before the " Greys " departed the Arab Legion presented them with a silver salver. Officers of the Arab Legion were made honorary members of the mess of the Royal Scots Greys, a courtesy which was reciprocated by the Arab fighting men. The Scots Greys earned high praise for the rescue of a considerable number of Arab families cut off by flood waters around Benghazi in 1954. The " Greys " departed from Catterick in mid-October, 1958, for Germany.

Scots remember other days, when, resplendent in red tunics, black bearskins, blue breeches with yellow stripes, white gauntlets and belts, the Royal Scots Greys provided escorts for the General Assembly of the Church of Scotland. Then Princes Street was gay with spring flowers, and the ancient Scottish Capital, beneath the scarred old Castle keep, recaptured something of her former glory and pageantry with the ring of spurs and curb-chains, the flash and jingle of steel, colourful, fluttering pennants, clattering hoofs, and the powerful heave and sway of horses.

The Scots Guards

THIS is the Saga of The Scots Guards. Here is blended tradition, pageantry, iron discipline, *esprit de corps*, hard training, enthusiasm, high endurance, and magnificent fighting qualities. Garbed in scarlet, and later, in khaki battle-dress, The Scots Guards, in over three centuries of existence, have written many glorious pages of British military history and added lustre to Auld Scotia's name and fame. Their battle-honours and graves cover the Continents, and their graves cluster close at the outposts of Empire.

The second oldest Scottish regiment, The Scots Guards were raised by the Marquis of Argyll in 1639 as a guard for King Charles I, and to carry out the orders of the Scottish Privy Council and enforce the Covenant in the turbulent Highlands. The Covenanters formed the dominant party in Scotland, and Charles, in his search for aid against his own rebellious Parliament, for a time wooed the Covenanters.

When the Irish Rebellion of 1642 broke out news of it was conveyed to King Charles while he was playing golf on the Leith Links. He ordered Argyll's Regiment to proceed, at a strength of 1,500 men, to Ireland, and the Scots entered a campaign of repression and butchery in which both sides behaved like barbarians.

Argyll's Regiment—formed of pikemen and musketeers—was brought back to Scotland in 1645 to fight against Montrose, but in 1646, after King Charles had surrendered, it was despatched to Carrickfergus, and remained in the North of Ireland until 1649. The strength of the regiment by this time had dwindled to about 400, and these survivors were formed into the Irish Companies.

While the Scots regiment was serving in Ireland the Roundheads triumphed in the Civil War, and King Charles was executed. Within a week Charles II was proclaimed King in Edinburgh. In this period of bitter strife Argyll's Regiment had in turn fought for Charles I against the Irish, and then against his supporters in Scotland, before becoming the bodyguard of Charles II. In 1650 the Irish Companies became His Majestie's Footte Regiment Of His Lyffe Guards, commanded by Argyll's son, Lord Lorne.

The regiment was in action at the Battle of Dunbar, in 1650, against Cromwell's forces. Here it clashed with Monk's (or Monck's) Regiment—later to become the Coldstream Guards. The Scots, under General Leslie, were routed, but among those who stood firm were the men of The Scots Guards. Once again the Scottish regiment of Guards fought on a stricken field—at the Battle of Worcester, in 1651. In Charles II's disastrous defeat the regiment came near to annihilation, and for about ten years little was heard of it.

But, with the Restoration of the Monarchy, in 1660, came the birth of the Regular Army. The Scottish regiment of Guards was resuscitated. Two companies were raised in 1661 to garrison Edinburgh and Dumbarton Castles, and in 1662 four companies were added to form a regiment consisting of " His Majestie's Own Company " and five others. This regiment has had a continuous existence up to the present day.

Duties performed between 1661 and 1685 were mainly of a police character—guarding the coast of Fife against the Dutch, garrisoning the Bass Rock, and dealing with religious uprisings in the West. The regiment was in action at Rullion Green, in 1666, and at Bothwell Brig, in 1679. In 1677 selected personnel were trained in " grenade casting ", and a Grenadier Company was formed in 1682.

Styled the Scotch Guards, the regiment was moved south in 1685 during Monmouth's Rebellion, but the order was cancelled on his defeat at Sedgemoor. At this time the regiment was at a strength of 14 companies, seven of which were stationed in Scotland.

After the accession of James VII seven companies were sent to London. They embarked at Leith in April, 1686, and by the end of May were encamped on Hounslow Heath, where they were brigaded with the two English regiments of foot guards—the Grenadier Guards and the Coldstream Guards. Thus the Brigade of Guards came into existence. As the Scots were last to arrive they earned the nickname of " The Kiddies ".

The Scottish companies returned to Edinburgh in March, 1687, but, owing to James's unpopularity, eight companies were sent to London the following year, and the remainder soon arrived in the English capital. On the Revolution the regiment declared for William of Orange, and was divided into two battalions. The 1st was despatched to the Continent in furtherance of the Grand Alliance against Louis XIV. The 2nd Battalion joined the 1st early in 1691, also embarking at Leith. In this campaign the Scottish Guards regiment was heavily engaged at Steenkirk, and won its first battle-honour—Namur, in 1695—and returned to the homeland in 1697.

In 1704 a Highland Company was raised and added to the establishment, performing duties in Scotland. Later this formation joined the other companies in London and relinquished its Highland garb. By the Union of Scotland and England in 1707 the strength of the regiment was 17 companies. Now the regiment became known as The Scotch Regiment of Foot Guards and The Regiment of Scots Guards. In 1712, however, it was designated The 3rd Regiment of Foot Guards.

Soon after the Union the other Scottish Household units moved to London—two troops of Life Guards—or Horse Guards, and Horse Grenadier Guards. The tradition of these formations are now in the safe keeping of the present-day Household Cavalry.

The first Battalion of The Third Regiment of Foot Guards embarked at Leith for Spain in 1709, and served with the ill-fated force which was compelled to surrender at Brihuega in 1710. A detachment of the 3rd Guards took part in the raid on Vigo, in 1719.

Both battalions participated in the War of the Austrian Succession, from 1742 to 1748, and were in the hard fighting at Dettingen and Fontenoy, being awarded the former as a battle-honour. In the Seven Years' War, from 1756 to 1763, the regiment was represented in several expeditions to the coast of France. The 2nd Battalion served in Germany. Returning to London on the signing of peace the guardsmen were much in request by the authorities, and rendered effective assistance in the Wilkes Riots of 1768, 1769, and 1771.

Early in 1776, during the American War of Independence, a composite Guards battalion was assembled, the 3rd Guards providing two of the ten companies required. From 1776 until 1781 the Scots served against the American Colonist forces and also furnished men to serve as Marines. Their principal action in this campaign was at Brandywine Creek. At home, in 1780, their comrades of the 3rd Guards

were engaged in preserving law and order in London during the Gordon Riots.

After the French Revolution relations with France rapidly deteriorated, and in 1793 war was declared on the Republic. The only troops immediately available were the Guards, and a battalion from each of the three regiments were despatched to Holland unaccompanied by transport or ammunition reserve. The Guards were heavily engaged at Lincelles and Valenciennes.

A light infantry company had been added to each battalion of the Guards in 1793, the value of such formations having been discovered during the American War. In 1798 these light companies were employed in a raid on the Bruges Canal.

On the outbreak of the Irish Rebellion of 1798, a brigade, composed of the three 1st Battalions of the Guards, was sent to Ireland and operated there until 1799. In the same year another expedition to Holland was launched but fared no better than the first, due to lack of material, bad organisation, and indifferent leadership. The Guards supplied two brigades.

In the successful campaign against the French in Egypt in 1801, the 1st Battalion formed part of the Guards Brigade, which was one of the first to land at Aboukir Bay. So the Sphinx superscribed " Egypt " came to be added to the battle-honours of The Scots Guards, who also acquitted themselves valiantly at Alexandria.

The 1st Battalion of the 3rd Regiment of Foot Guards was with the expeditions sent to Hanover in 1805, and to Copenhagen in 1807. In 1809 they took part in the unfortunate Walcheren expedition. Included in the force was brigade of the 3rd Guards, the 2nd Battalion contributing two companies. This expedition proved a costly and disastrous failure, disease decimating the ranks without a shot being fired.

The Guards earned further renown in the Peninsular War (1808-1814), at Talavera, Busaco, Barrosa, Fuentes d'Onor, in the defence lines of Torres Vedras, at Salamanaca, Burgos, Ciudad Rodrigo, and Nive. The 1st Scots Guards, during Sir John Moore's fighting retreat to Corruna, turned and gave battle to the pursuing French, keeping them at a safe distance while the evacuation operation was successfully carried out under cover of darkness. Sir John Moore's body was borne from the field by men of the Guards.

Back in Holland early in March, 1814, three companies of the 2nd Battalion of the 3rd

Guards took part in the unsuccessful assault on Bergen-op-Zoom. These companies later rejoined the battalion at Antwerp. The following year the Guards faced the storm of shot and steel unleashed on them by Napoleon at Hougoumont Chateau during the Battle of Waterloo on June 18, 1815.

The Chateau was an advanced position in front of two Guards brigades, and was at first held by the Light Companies of all the Guards regiments, commanded by Lieut.-Colonel Macdonell, of the Coldstream Guards. Reinforcements sent in included the 2nd Battalion of Scotland's 3rd Guards.

The buildings and gardens had been hastily prepared for defence, and when the French tidal wave rolled in against Wellington's main forces it became of vital importance.

Hougoumont was attacked by division after division of the enemy. The Chateau, the chapel, and the stables were set on fire by the French artillery in an attempt to make the position untenable. But the Guards held on.

Then, getting closer, the French and British were soon attacking and counter-attacking over the gardens, the orchards, and in the adjoining woods. At one stage enemy pressure was very severe, and the gates of the main yard were opened to let in a small party of the hard-pressed 3rd Guards. Sergeant Fraser, who was in command, stayed behind to give covering fire as his men reached safety, and he was the last to return. The sergeant only got back by dragging a French colonel from his horse, charging through the enemy, and riding in, after which he rallied his comrades.

As the gates were being closed a French officer attacked the structure with an axe, and he and a number of his men poured into the courtyard. The position was desperate. But Lieut.-Colonel Macdonell and several of his Coldstreamers, and Sergeants Fraser, Brice, MacGregor, and Alston, and Private Lister, of the 3rd Guards, rushed the gates and succeeded in closing them against the oncoming enemy. The French were trapped, and in a short sharp engagement they were soon overpowered.

The Duke of Wellington declared that the outcome of the battle depended on the closing of the Hougoumont gates. As a result of the magnificent stand of the Guards, Napoleon had to hurl a whole Corps against the position, and so was unable to provide Marshal Ney with enough infantry to attempt a breakthrough at the crisis of the battle.

The Waterloo Medal was awarded to every soldier who took part in the battle, but Sergeant Fraser received an honour unique in military history. A special medal was struck for him in recognition of his heroism at the Hougoumont gates. Survivors of the 2nd Battalion of Scotland's 3rd Guards regiment accompanied the army on its march to Paris and formed part of the Allied occupation forces. The battalion re-crossed the Channel in 1818 with " Waterloo " added to the Guards' long list of battle-honours.

In the years of peace which followed the Napoleonic Wars the army was drastically reduced, and the establishment of the 3rd Guards was fixed at 16 companies instead of 20. In 1824 the 1st Battalion arrived in Dublin for a tour of duty, and in 1826 the guardsmen were ordered to Manchester to suppress industrial unrest there. In the same year a Guards Brigade—of which six companies of the 3rd Guards formed part—was despatched to Portugal to preserve peace between that country and Spain. This brigade returned home in 1828.

After the accession of William IV, in 1830, the regiment was given a national title, and from June, 1831, became known as The Scots Fusilier Guards. In two attempts on Queen Victoria's life soldiers of the regiment assisted in arresting her assailants. For his part in frustrating the 1840 attempt, Private McLerie was rewarded with a commission, and later became Inspector-General of Constabulary in South Australia. The guardsman who went to the Queen's assistance in 1842, Private Allan, also received promotion.

For the campaign in the Crimea a Guards Brigade was assembled which included the 1st Scots Fusilier Guards. Though plagued by cholera and dysentery, The Scots Fusilier Guards were to fight one of the regiment's greatest battles on the banks of the fast-flowing, treacherous River Alma.

On September 20, 1854, the sun winked and danced across the shining barrels of the Russian guns in the Great Redoubt on the southern bank. The Scots Fusilier Guards were in support of the Light Division, with the Coldstream Guards on their left and the Grenadier Guards on their right. In their centre the Colours flew proudly in the breeze.

The bugles sounded shrill and clear, and the curtain went up on a glory day for the Scottish regiment. The Light Division crossed the Alma, and advanced up the steep slope towards the Great Redoubt, which they took, but a powerful Russian force attacked, trapping them in the

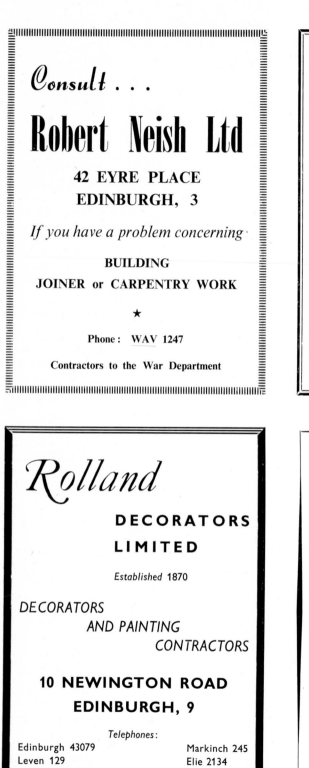

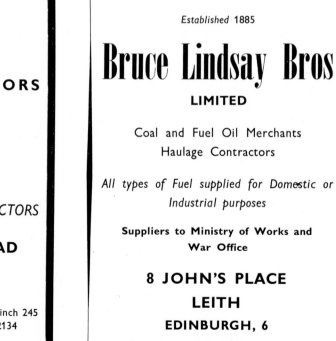

gun emplacements. Pressure of numbers told, and the Light Division was ejected from the redoubt and pressed back to the Alma.

The crisis in the battle came, and the Guards were ordered to attack. The scarlet-clad ranks advanced, and forded the river, the guardsmen wading through up to the armpits in water, and enduring a hurricane of shot. Forming up on the other bank, they continued to press forward as the hard-pressed Light Division grimly held on.

Seeing the Colours of The Scots Fusilier Guards appearing, the Light Division assumed they were being relieved by the entire Guards Brigade, and there was a confused retiral, which left the Scots to oppose the massed Russian counter-attacking formations. Although fighting against heavy odds, the Scots forced their way to within about 30 yards of the Great Redoubt when a horseman rode up—whose identity was never established—and ordered a withdrawal.

Down the hill from the so nearly won redoubt went the Guards, still fighting furiously. It was soon observed that The Coldstream Guards and the Grenadier Guards were still advancing on either flank. The Scots Fusilier Guards rallied, and again attacked the press of Russian infantry swarming after them in the retiral.

But, as the Colour party had led the attack, it was in the rear during the withdrawal, and when the advance re-commenced it was surrounded. Carrying the Queen's Colour was Lieutenant Robert James Lindsay, while Lieutenant Thistlethwayte bore the Regimental Colour. Around them were Colour-Sergeants McKechnie, Lane, Bryce, and McLeod.

The Colour party was in dire extremities— a scarlet islet lapped by the rising Russian tide. Sergeant Lane was killed, then Sergeant McKechnie, then Sergeant McLeod. But the colours continued to flaunt defiantly amid the surge and sway of the close-packed Russians.

The trapped escort was whittled down still further until there was only one N.C.O. and a few guardsmen left battling around their bullet-riddled Colours. For a few hectic minutes it seemed inevitable that the gallant defenders of the Queen's Colour and the Regimental Colour would be shot or bayoneted and the Colours of the 1st Scots Fusilier Guards borne off in triumph by the enemy. Yet, only a few yards away, the first ranks of the regiment were fighting desperately over their own and the Russian dead and wounded to link up with the Colour party.

One by one the members of the Colour escort went down before the Russian bullets and bayonets. Then Private Reynolds charged in among the Russians. With his clubbed rifle he kept them at bay, then, with a rousing cheer The Scots Fusilier Guards broke into the Russian circle with their blood-red bayonets— and once more the Colour party became the rallying point in an unbroken line of Scots Fusilier Guards, who continued the advance and drove the Russians out of the Great Redoubt.

Of the Colour party which fought so heroically only one remained unscathed—Lieutenant Lindsay (later Lord Wantage). But the Queen's Colour which he bore was holed by bullets in 24 places and the pike was shot in half. When the Victoria Cross was instituted in 1856 crosses were awarded to Lieutenant Lindsay, Colour-Sergeant James McKechnie, of Paisley, Sergeant John Knox, of Glasgow, and Private William Reynolds, of Edinburgh, for their gallant stand by the Colours at Alma.

Several weeks later, on Guy Fawke's day, The Scots Fusilier Guards again crossed bayonets with the Russians when two dense columns of the Czar's infantry made a determined attempt to surprise, surround, and destroy several British divisions in their rest camps.

The Russian columns advanced out of a morning fog and came within an ace of success. Every man who could hold a rifle and bayonet was thrown into the confused fighting—grooms, cooks, orderlies, bandsmen, officers' servants, and the walking sick and wounded.

Inkerman was a desperate battle of bayonets and clubbed rifles. The fighting quickly resolved itself into a series of grim struggles in which detached and sometimes officerless parties of soldiers fought without cohesion or control. The British came near to being engulfed by the Russian masses of infantry, but after several hours of grisly hand-to-hand fighting the enemy was beaten back with heavy losses, and many prisoners were taken. This confused shambles in the early morning mist, in which men fought not knowing what was happening a few yards on either side of them, soon became known as the " Soldiers' Battle ". A remarkable achievement was the uphill bayonet charge of The Scots Fusilier Guards after all night duty and a " double " of over a mile.

The Scots Fusilier Guards were heavily engaged at Sevastopol, and returned from the Crimea with the battle-honours, Alma, Inkerman, Sevastopol. Colour-Sergeant James Craig won the Victoria Cross for his gallantry at Sevastopol. On rising tension between the United States and Britain, the 2nd Battalion proceeded to Canada in 1861, remaining there until 1864. In 1877 Queen Victoria named the regiment The Scots Guards. Guards battalions were reduced from ten to eight companies in the Army reforms of 1881.

The 1st Battalion of The Scots Guards was included in the Guards Brigade during the Nile, or Egyptian Campaign, of 1882. They operated in defence of the Sweet Water Canal, and were in action at Tel-el-Kebir. The Scots Guards, forming part of a Guards Camel Regiment in 1884, clashed with the Mahdi's fanatical Dervishes at Abu Kru and Abu Klea in 1885, during their strenuous but unsuccessful forced march with a desert column to the relief of General Gordon at Khartoum.

The "Fuzzy Wuzzies" broke into the square, but none got out. On the fall of Khartoum a Guards Brigade, which incorporated the 2nd Battalion The Scots Guards, was sent to Suakin. This force was involved in the difficult rearguard action at Hasheen. For its part in the bitterly fought open desert campaign the Scottish regiment was awarded the battle-honours Tel-el-Kebir, Egypt, 1882, Suakin.

From 1899 until 1902 the two battalions of The Scots Guards saw much active service during the South African War. The guardsmen earned high praise for their sterling fighting qualities, endurance in defence or attack, fortitude in privations, and great marching capacity. They took part in Lord Methuen's fighting advance to the relief of Kimberley, campaigning on the rolling veldt against a brave but elusive foe.

Principal actions against the Boers were at Belmont, Enslin, Magersfontein, and on the Modder River. Battle-honours won were Modder River, South Africa, 1899-1902. A third battalion was raised in 1899, but after serving at home it was disbanded in 1906.

Lieutenant G. A. Boyd-Rochfort in the trenches at La Bassee in September, 1915 saw a German trench-mortar bomb land on the side of the parapet of the communication trench in which he was standing. Nearby was a working party of the 1st Battalion. The lieutenant could have stepped round a corner to safety, but he had no thought of this. He shouted a warning to the men, ran over, picked up the bomb, and hurled it clear of the parapet, saving the lives of the working party.

Sergeant John ("Fighting Jock") McAulay, D.C.M., of the 1st Battalion, took command and rallied his company at Fontaine Notre Dame, in January, 1918, after all the officers and warrant officers had become casualties. He led his men forward, and then noticing an enemy attack developing on the left, he took two men and beat the Germans back with machine-gun fire.

Though under heavy fire he picked up his mortally wounded company commander and carried him a considerable distance to safety. Twice Sergeant McAulay was knocked down by shell bursts, but he rose and struggled back with the dying officer. Twice he was intercepted by Germans, but each time he closed with and killed the enemy. As Inspector McAulay of the City of Glasgow Police he later bore his medals and scars into an honoured retirement. A native of Kinghorn, John McAulay was a miner before joining the police.

In the Somme holocaust in October, 1916, at Ginchy, Lance-Sergeant Fred McNess, of the 1st Battalion, led his men through a concentrated artillery and machine-gun barrage. Though severely wounded, he threw his bombs at the enemy until he was utterly exhausted by loss of blood.

One day at St. Python in late 1918 the streets were raked with machine-gun fire and enemy marksmen were installed at vantage points. Lance-Sergeant Harry B. Wood, of the 2nd Battalion, on his platoon sergeant being killed, carried a large piece of masonry out into the open. He got down behind it and ordered his men to work their way across while he kept them covered by engaging the German snipers.

Private J. Mackenzie, also of the 2nd Battalion, at Rouges Bancs, in December, 1915, saw a stretcher party give up trying to rescue a wounded man lying in front of the German trenches. He went out alone, and, under heavy fire, succeeded in bringing him to safety. Later in the day Private Mackenzie was killed, the citation states, " whilst in the performance of a similar act of gallant conduct."

Lieutenant Boyd-Rochfort, Sergeant McAulay, Lance-Sergeant McNess, Lance-Sergeant Wood, and Private Mackenzie were awarded the Victoria Cross.

This generation still remembers The Scots Guards " soldiering it out " in the mud of France and Flanders. The 1st Battalion of The Scots Guards entered the conflict as part of the British Expeditionary Force in August, 1914, near Mons. The B.E.F's great fighting withdrawal, battling every inch of the way against the massed German invaders of Belgium, is now history—much of it Guards history.

In the Cambrai-Le Cateau area the hard-pressed B.E.F. turned and grappled with the enemy, and again escaped threatened encirclement and annihilation with a fighting retiral to new positions during which a heavy toll was taken of the Germans. The field-grey enemy masses were driven back from the Marne by the exhausted and sadly depleted B.E.F., which then advanced to the Aisne.

In the First Battle of Ypres, in November, 1914, the 2nd Battalion of The Scots Guards hammered the much-vaunted Prussian Guards at Nonnebosschen Wood. But glory's price was dearly paid, for the battalion came out at company strength. There was ghastly fighting around Ghent, Ypres, Givenchy, The Triangle and Brickstacks, Neuve Chapelle, Festubert, Rue du Bois, Loos, on the Somme, and at Cambrai. The bitterly contested advance through the gun-bristling Hindenburg line defences to final victory was an unforgettable saga of heroism, iron discipline, and self-sacrifice well in keeping with the Guards' tradition.

It was during 1915 that the Guards Division was formed—soon to be regarded by the German General Staff as one of the most formidable divisions in the Allied Armies. The 3rd Battalion was re-formed to act as a feeder to battalions in the field, but it was again disbanded in 1919. Principal battle-honours of The Scots Guards in the First World War were—Retreat from Mons, Marne, 1914, Aisne, 1914, Ypres, 1914, 1917, Festubert, 1915, Loos, Somme, 1916, 1918, Cambrai, 1917, 1918, Hindenburg Line, France and Flanders, 1914-18.

The 1st and 2nd Battalions The Scots Guards returned to London from Cologne in March, 1919. In the spring of 1927 the 2nd Battalion was ordered to China, and saw service at Hong Kong, Canton, and Shanghai during one of China's numerous civil wars. It returned home early in 1929.

The 1st Battalion arrived in Egypt in November, 1935, and returned in December the following year. Their despatch to the Land of the Pharaohs was a result of mounting international tension over Italy's designs on Abyssinia. The battalion served at Alexandria and Cairo, and at Mersa Matruh—in the Western Desert.

The 2nd Battalion experienced a short stay in Palestine. In September, 1936, it disembarked at Haifa. An Arab revolt was then under way, but the situation quickly improved. The battalion returned to the U.K. in December of the same year.

The 2nd Scots Guards departed for Egypt in mid-November, 1938, for what was originally intended to be a routine tour of two years' duty. Survivors of the battalion did not see home again until April, 1944.

The 5th (Special Reserve) Battalion, Scots Guards, was formed early in 1940. It was decided to include a British unit trained in ski and winter warfare in an Allied force to be despatched to assist Finland against Russia. This was to be the role of the 5th (S.R.) Battalion —which soon became known as " The Snowballers ".

In March " The Snowballers " arrived in France and trained in the shadows cast by Mont Blanc. A battalion of Chasseurs Alpins at Chamonix were their trainers and hosts. But on an armistice being concluded between Finland and Russia, its dispersal was ordered.

The 1st Battalion, Scots Guards, formed part of the 24th Guards Brigade in Norway in April, 1950. The guardsmen disembarked at Harstad and moved forward on Mo to engage the rapidly advancing Germans, who had heavy numerical and air superiority.

In the ensuing unequal fighting, and the retreat to Bodö, the battalion was hard pressed, and it arrived at Borkenes, some ten miles from Harstad. Early in June it was evacuated and sailed for the Clyde—starting point for this ill-fated expedition. A popular song of that period ran " There will come another day ". The Scots Guards laboured unstintingly, trained hard, and fought grimly for its dawn.

First in the field in North Africa was the 2nd Battalion, which had arrived in Egypt in December, 1938. It moved out from Cairo in August, 1939, and went into the Matruh defences. In March, 1940, the battalion was relieved and then experienced a spell of garrison duty in Cairo and was later employed on the A.A. defence of the Suez Canal.

Early in 1941 the battalion again went into the Western Desert and formed part of the 22nd Guards Brigade. It operated at Matruh and Sidi Barrani, and in Halfaya Pass and the Musaid " Triangle ".

The men of the 2nd had several sharp clashes with enemy armour and infantry, and came under air attack. At the beginning of July,

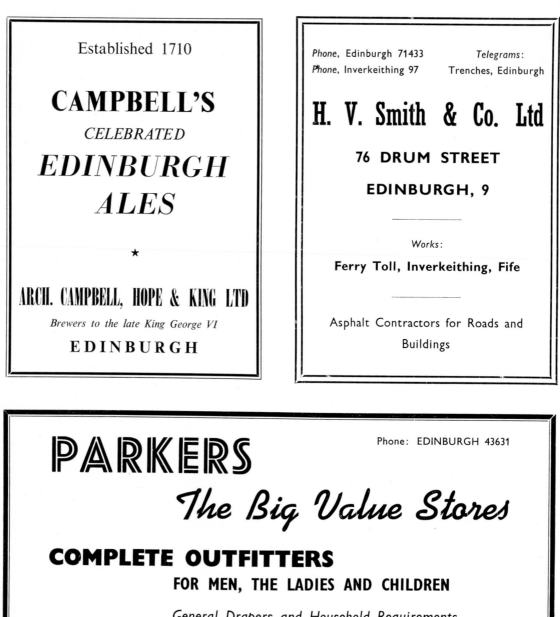

1941, the 2nd was converted into a motor battalion, and as part of the 22nd Guards (Motor) Brigade, was soon heavily engaged in the fluctuating mobile war across the Western Desert. They were the quarry as the British retired before German and Italian numerical, armoured, and air superiority, but, when reinforcements of men and tanks arrived they became the hunters, and played a leading role in the pursuit and final defeat of " Desert Fox " Rommel.

In November, 1941, the motorised battalion took part in General Cunningham's bitterly opposed advance, which relieved Tobruk and drove the enemy back to Agheila. It had to make a hasty withdrawal to the Gazala Line when Rommel launched his powerful offensive in January, 1942. In the Battle of Gazala, in June, the battalion suffered heavy losses at Knightsbridge, where it held on to its positions for over two weeks in the teeth of massed Axis armoured thrusts and under heavy air attack.

At Rigel Ridge, to the north-west of Knightsbridge, the companies and anti-tank platoons were overrun by the massed armour of the 21st Panzer Division. In this maelstrom of lumbering tanks, death-spitting guns, and churning, blinding sand, the battalion was so grievously depleted that the survivors were amalgamated in a composite battalion with the 3rd Coldstream Guards, and spent July in the Alamein defences—the Eighth Army's " last ditch " in front of Alexandria. The battalion was later withdrawn to the Delta, and in September, with the remainder of the 201st Guards Brigade, was despatched to Syria to re-form and train.

After the Battle of Alamein the 2nd Battalion again entered the conflict. An approach march of over 2,000 miles was made in 23 days along the North African shore to bring the Scots Guards—with their vital 6-pounder anti-tank guns—into contact with the enemy at Medenine, in Southern Tunisia.

Their revenge on the 21st Panzers came here on March 6, 1943. Slowly the early morning fog lifted exposing the lines of German tanks as they heaved and rolled up out of the valleys and lumbered towards the British positions. The anti-tank gunners of The Scots Guards let them come well into the trap they had laid, then opened fire at close range.

Soon the ridge was ablaze with Axis armoured fighting vehicles. The Germans fled in confusion, leaving the charred remains of 52 tanks on the battlefield. Rommel lost about one-third of his armour and never recovered from the debacle at Medenine. The battalion received the immediate congratulations of General Montgomery on its " magnificent performance ".

There followed patrolling of the Mareth Line, and early in April The Scots Guards provided support fire for the 51st (Highland) Division's attack on Wadi Akarit. After operating around Enfidaville in May, the 201st Guards (Motor) Brigade was switched from the Eighth Army to the First Army, and The Scots Guards were soon campaigning in the Medjez sector.

The battalion took part in the advance on Tunis and in the victory parade through the town. The Germans and Italians were surrendering in thousands as The Scots Guards battalion ended its active service in this theatre of war by advancing across the neck of the Cape Bon peninsula to Hammamet. In August the 2nd Battalion moved back to Tripoli. Here the 201st Guards Brigade became the 3rd Brigade of the 56th (London) Division, part of X Corps, and the battalion reverted to its old infantry role before entering the conflict in Italy.

No saga of the 2nd Battalion would be complete without mention of the part played by patrols of the Long Range Desert Group. These highly mobile units were formed in December, 1940, by volunteers from the 2nd Battalion Scots Guards and the 3rd Battalion Coldstream Guards. The L.R.D.G. was disbanded when the North African campaign ended.

There was a dashing raid on Murzuk Fort, in south-west Libya, in January, 1941. A patrol crossed the entire Western Desert, Libya, and northern French Equatorial Africa and assisted Colonel Leclerc's Free French column in its attack on Kufra Oasis. Starting out from Hon Oasis, in Tripolitania, a patrol crossed Southern Tunisia, by-passed the Mareth Line, beat off two attacks by Arabs, entered Algeria, and established the first contact between the First and Eighth Armies.

Patrols of the L.R.D.G. temporarily cut several of Rommel's supply arteries through the desert, and their sudden raiding and sabotage forays proved a thorn in the flesh of the enemy. These will o' the wisp units penetrated far into enemy territory and kept an unending vigil which resulted in vital intelligence being sent back to Middle East Command concerning

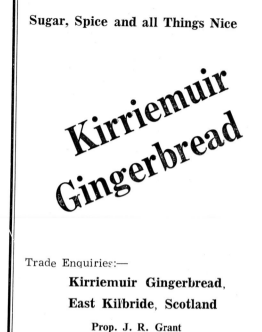

enemy movements, dispositions, strength, etc. Night and day it went on, and enemy airfields and transport received priority attention.

The 1st Battalion Scots Guards, forming part of the 24th Guards Brigade of the 1st Infantry Division, sailed from the Clyde on March 1, 1943, arriving at Algiers on March 9. The battalion entered the First Army's line at Medjez-el-Bab on the 20th. After a month of bitter fighting in the hills of the Medjez salient came the grim clash with the enemy on the slopes and ridges of Djebel Bou Aoukaz on April 27.

The guardsmen suffered heavy losses as a result of intense mortaring, machine-gun fire, and sniping, and at one point their advance was checked by the accurate ranging of a machine-gun and an 88 mm. gun. Lieutenant (Temporary Captain) Lord Lyell, of Kirriemuir, Angus, collected several of his men—Lance-Sergeant Robertson, Lance-Corporal Lawrie, and Guardsmen Chisholm and Porter—and led them out into the open under fire.

Lord Lyell reached the machine-gun post, which he destroyed by hurling a grenade. But all the members of his small party had become casualties, though two wounded guardsmen continued to give him covering fire. Lord Lyell then ran at the 88, moving so quickly that the gunners had only time to fire one more shot before he went berserk among them with the bayonet. Lord Lyell quickly accounted for most of the crew before he was overpowered and killed.

The few survivors hastily left the gun pit, and in doing so three more of them were shot by Lance-Corporal Lawrie. Both guns silenced, the advance was resumed up the bullet-swept slope to the summit of Djebel Bou Akouaz. For this and other acts of gallantry in this onslaught of The Scots Guards, Lord Lyell was awarded the Victoria Cross.

The hard-fought campaign among the hills and ridges resulted in the opening up of the road to Tunis. In May came news of the Axis collapse in North Africa. Thousands of prisoners and captured tanks and vehicles poured back from the front. The men of the 1st, like their comrades of the 2nd, made a brave show in the Allied victory parade through Tunis on May 19. In camp at Hammamet in the autumn, the 1st Battalion prepared for another call, which was to take it from Bizerta to Italy in December.

On September 9, 1943, the 2nd Battalion, with the 201st Guards Brigade, took part in the initial landing in the Bay of Salerno. The Scots Guards were soon under accurate concentrated fire in the desperate stand against the German armour and infantry to hold the narrow foothold gained by the Fifth Army. The fury of the enemy counter-attacks spent, the battalion moved north to cross the Volturno river, near Capua, in October. Then on and on, up and up, and over the high forbidding ridges to the mountain village of Rocchetta.

" Sunny Italy " before long became a joke—in bad form—with the Guards. They shivered as they crossed the icy rivers and windswept mountain barriers which the Germans used as defence lines. The demolished state of the approach roads added to the many problems of this nightmarish campaign fought out in atrocious weather conditions. The Scots Guards advanced through the gaunt, stark, crumbling ruins of towns and villages to exposed positions under intense shelling, machine-gunning and sniping, often with little or no sleep, and frequently on short rations due to transport and supply difficulties. But their fighting qualities were never impaired.

On November 7, the 2nd Battalion, under a murderous fire, scrambled over the rocks and boulders in the attack on Monte Camino. Casualties were severe, and a second assault had to be launched a month later. The enemy was blasted out of his strong defence features and commenced to withdraw. In mid-January, 1944, the battalion was transferred to the mouth of the Garigliano river, on the west coast, and after crossing, it spent two months of rain and shelling on the ridges around Minturno.

In March the 2nd Scots Guards left the snow-capped mountains behind them as they descended into the valleys already brightening with the advent of spring. It was the first stage of a journey back to the homeland before the final death-grapple with the Germans across the English Channel. But the battalion left behind more than half its strength as reinforcements for the 1st Scots Guards.

The 1st Battalion, in the 24th Guards Brigade, crossed to Taranto, disembarking on December 7, 1943. On January 22, 1944, the battalion was locked in battle during the Fifth Army's amphibious assault on Anzio. Here, for six ghastly weeks, The Scots Guards participated in grim fluctuating beachhead fighting, suffering severe casualties. In March the 1st was withdrawn and reorganised at Sorrento.

The 1st Battalion re-entered the line in April at Castel di Sangro, in the Central Apennines, and advanced through Cassino, Rome and Orvieto, then over the hills to Florence. The 1st joined the 6th South African Armoured Division in May. In the bitterly contested drive from the Tiber to the Arno there were sharp clashes with the enemy at Sarteano Ridge, La Foce, Castel di Brolio and on Monte San Michele.

In the autumn advance the battalion encountered stiff opposition on Monte Catarleto, Poggio, Monte Alcino and Monte Termine. The Scots Guards endured a winter of privations in the mountains, on the southern slopes of Monte Sole, some 18 miles from Bologna. In March, 1945, the 1st Battalion was transferred to the 56th (London) Division, serving with the Eighth Army.

With this formation the battalion fought with distinction in the final offensive, skirting the shores of Lake Comacchio and breaking through the Argenta Gap, to pursue the shattered German forces towards the River Po. Numerous prisoners from elite German regiments were taken, also considerable quantities of equipment abandoned by the enemy in his flight from the avenging tanks, guns, infantry and air power of the Allies. But nevertheless there were brisk engagements fought out on the Valetta Canal, Fossa Marina and Scolo Val d'Albero.

Soon the 1st Battalion Scots Guards had fired the last shots in the Italian campaign. The German capitulation came early in May, and The Scots Guards entered Trieste, remaining for two and a half years to maintain an uneasy peace between Marshal Tito's forces and the Italians. Trieste was handed over to the Italians in mid-September, 1947, and the 1st Battalion left for home at the end of the month.

A new and independent company—S Company—was formed from Scots Guards reinforcements at Rotondi in March, 1944, and served with the 2nd Battalion The Coldstream Guards, in the 1st Guards Brigade. In the spring S Company fought forward with the 6th British Armoured Division from the ruins of Cassino to Monte Piccolo and Monte Lignano to the left bank of the Tiber, then on through Perugia and Arezzo. By August S Company was on the Arno. It spent the winter in grim conditions in the mountains, distinguishing itself in the desperate fighting on the slopes of Monte Battaglia and Monte Penzola.

In March, 1945, at Spoleto, S Company joined the 1st Battalion The Scots Guards on the Eighth Army front, and was in at the "kill" in the final onslaught, skirmishing along the shores of Lake Comacchio, breaking through the Argenta Gap, and taking part in the pursuit of the fleeing Germans to the River Po. Two and a half years were spent maintaining peace in Trieste, and at the end of September, 1947, The Scots Guards turned their faces towards home.

Three battalions of The Scots Guards served in Field Marshal Montgomery's armies which fought from the Normandy beachheads to the Baltic. In June, 1944, X Company, the surviving unit of the 4th Battalion, was the first to be engaged. The 4th Battalion, raised in September, 1941, was disbanded in October, 1943, officers and other ranks reinforcing other Scots Guards formations.

In Normandy X Company campaigned alongside the Irish and Welsh Guards battalions of the Guards Armoured Division. This "Celtic Alliance" battled forward from the Bocage country across France and into the Low Countries to victory. Disembarking at Arromanches on June 23, X Company moved on to Caen and Bayeux. After a defensive role, the formation went over to the attack in July, and, following the breakthrough, experienced a series of sharp engagements at La Bayeud, Cagny, Courteil, Maisoncelles, Montchamp, Estry, and Sourdevalle.

The Germans retreated across the Seine, and, operations over in Normandy, X Company moved on to Arras before taking part in the great armoured dash into Belgium to liberate Brussels early in September. But X Company was soon on the move again, mopping up resistance on the Louvain road, and advancing through a hail of fire at Beringen, on the Albert Canal.

At Hechtel—X Company's most successful engagement in its short "life"—The Scots Guards inflicted heavy casualties on the enemy. The company was next in the picture guarding Aamsche Bridge, and in November took over the defence of Nijmegen Bridge. Its last action was at Bönninghardt in March, 1945. X Company was disbanded about a week later at Malden and absorbed into the 2nd Battalion Scots Guards at Heumen.

The 3rd Battalion Scots Guards—formed in October, 1940—disembarked as part of the 6th Guards Tank Brigade at "Jig" Beach, on July 20, 1944. Mounted on heavy Churchill tanks The Scots Guards joined battle in Normandy in the hectic assault on Caumont, which ended the deadlock at Caen. After the dramatic breakthrough the advance fanned out and flowed quickly across the Norman Bocage, and the tanks of The Scots Guards were soon locked in battle at Estry, and then at Chenedolle.

Thrusting on, the 3rd Battalion entered the Low Countries in September. There was a fierce clash at Oisterwijk after which the Churchills crossed a network of canals. Pushing on past Tilburg, The Scots Guards drove for the Maas, fighting well in the peat bog battle near Heusden. There was a sharp exchange with the enemy at Beringen, after which opposition was cleared up at Peel and Birgden.

In the spring of 1945 the 3rd Battalion's tanks were the first through the Siegfried Line defences. Cleve, Goch, Schloss Calbeck, and Reyshoff fell, and The Scots Guards battled on to Winnekendonck. Their tanks were first across the Rhine, and the rapid advance continued over North Germany to Dorsten and Munster.

The Churchills of the 6th Guards Armoured Brigade thundered on from Celle to Uelzen in April, and drove hard for the Elbe. Then on to the Baltic. During a halt at Lüneberg on May 2 news was received of Hitler's death. The German surrender followed two days later. Arriving on the Baltic coast a " boarding party " from the 3rd Battalion ended the campaign by capturing a U'boat with the aid of a fishing craft.

In the 6th Armoured Brigade were The Grenadier Guards, Coldstream Guards and Scots Guards. But trust the Scot to preserve his identity. The Churchill tanks of The Scots Guards bore names such as Ben Lawers, Ben Nevis, Iona, Dee, Don, Deveron . . .

Being foot soldiers at heart, the Guards co-operated well with the " P.B.I." The 6th Guards Armoured Brigade was prominently identified with the 15th (Scottish) Division in a number of epics during the campaign on the Continent. While engaged in occupation duties the 3rd Battalion Scots Guards reverted to its traditional infantry role in June, 1945, and in February of the following year came disbandment.

Crossing to Ostend at the close of January, 1945, the 2nd Battalion Scots Guards—veterans of North Africa and Italy—entered the conflict in Germany to clear the west bank of the Rhine. The 2nd was in the 32nd Guards Brigade, serving with the Guards Armoured Division. Early in March the battalion engaged the enemy at Bönninghardt. The Scots Guards fought forward with the Cromwell tanks of

the 2nd Battalion Welsh Guards, and in this sector there was close and most effective co-operation with Scotland's 52nd (Lowland) Division.

Over the Rhine went the " Celtic " Group at the end of March, then across the Ems under heavy fire. Enemy rearguard troops made determined stands at Nordhorn, Lingen, Lengerich and Menslage, and there were losses in prising him out of his strong positions. Further water barriers were forded and there were more skirmishes with the retreating Germans at Kettenburg, Visselhövede, Ottingen, Rotenburg, Oldendorf, Badensedt, Ostertimke, Westertimke, and Kirchtimke.

The final advance of the Scots/Welsh Battle Group was made to Stade, on the Elbe, during April and May, and after the German capitulation the battalion moved on to the naval base at Cuxhaven. On May 11, men of the 2nd Scots Guards went out in four German minesweepers and took the surrender of Heligoland. Its occupation duties over, the 2nd Battalion arrived in London early in December, 1946.

In June, 1948, a state of emergency was declared in Malaya because of Communist terrorism. The War Office ordered the formation of the 2nd Guards Brigade. The battalions represented in this brigade were the 3rd Grenadier Guards, 2nd Coldstream Guards, and 2nd Scots Guards. To bring The Scots Guards up to battalion establishment the 1st Battalion of the regiment provided a large draft.

On October 4 the battalion disembarked at Singapore, and after an intensive spell of training, patrols of The Scots Guards with native trackers entered the jungles and swamps to seek out the enemy. By mid-April, 1951, when the battalion sailed for home, over 100 terrorists were killed, 11 captured, and a number wounded. Several Communist leaders fell to the guns of The Scots Guards. In July, 1953, the 2nd Battalion joined the 4th Guards Brigade in the 2nd Division in Germany.

The 1st Battalion Scots Guards was despatched to Egypt in the autumn of 1951. The battalion was flown to Cyprus in December to take an internal security role, but a few weeks later, when disorders broke out in Egypt, it was rushed back across the Mediterranean. The 1st Scots Guards left Egypt for home in December, 1954, to spend Christmas and the New Year in the traditional Scottish manner. The 1st Battalion departed for a " stint " in Germany in November, 1958.

Photograph by courtesy Associated Press

H.R.H. THE PRINCESS ROYAL

COLONEL-IN-CHIEF—THE ROYAL SCOTS

The Royal Scots

(THE ROYAL REGIMENT)

THE ROYAL SCOTS—First of Foot and Right of the Line—is the oldest regiment in the British Army, and probably the oldest fighting formation in the world. It can claim direct " descent " from the Scottish Archer Guard, which campaigned in the Crusades. The First of Foot can also trace its ancestry to the Scottish units which from medieval times fought hard and well in the service of the Kings of Bohemia, Holland, Denmark and Sweden. The regiment has several indelible links with the bands of adventurous Scots soldiers of fortune, who became permanently established in the service of France about 1420.

From these hardy experienced fighting men was formed the elite bodyguard of the French kings—The Garde du Corps Ecossais (or Garde Ecossais), and the Gendarmes Ecossais. The Royal Scots have links too with the famous Green Brigade—or Scots Brigade—which fought so heroically for Gustavus Adolphus—" Lion of the North "—in the Thirty Years' War.

John Hepburn, of Athelstaneford, East Lothian, in 1625 raised the original company—which soon became a regiment—for service with King Gustavus Adolphus of Sweden. John Hepburn, ere long, became commander of all the Scottish units in the Swedish king's army. These included Mackay's Highlanders, Stargate's Corps, and Lumsden's Musketeers—of Battle of Leipzig renown. This group became known as the Green, or Scots Brigade, and its able commander was knighted by King Gustavus Adolphus.

The collated history of The Royal Scots begins in 1632, when King Louis XIII of France empowered Sir John Hepburn to embody a regiment from the numerous independent companies of Scottish fighting men serving in the French Army. Sir John, who had taken service with the French, did so, and added a force of 1,200 men raised in Scotland as the result of an agreement between King Charles I and Louis XIII.

The Privy Council of Scotland, by warrant dated April 24, 1633, and given under King Charles's authority on March 25 that year, commissioned Sir John Hepburn to raise this force. The date has been officially accepted as the origin of the regiment which in time became The Royal Scots, and precedence among Infantry of the Line was later granted accordingly.

The Scots landed at Boulogne in August, 1633, and joined the survivors of the famous Green, or Scots Brigade, and the independent companies. Thus the Regiment d'Hebron came into being—Hepburn being a difficult word for Continental tongues.

Sir John Hepburn was killed at the siege of Saverne (Zabern), in 1636, on the eve of his promotion to Marshal of France. After the death of his brother, George, the regiment became known as Le Regiment de Douglas, or Douglas Ecossais. In 1678 it was styled Dumbarton's Regiment, its colonel, Lord George Douglas, having become the Earl of Dumbarton.

It was during its service in France that the Douglas Ecossais earned the nickname " Pontius Pilate's Bodyguard ". This came about through an argument among officers of Douglas's Regiment and the Regiment of Picardy, between whom there was keen rivalry. The French formation was raised in 1562, and was the oldest French Line regiment. Its officers were envious of the precedence—and possibly the record—of Douglas's Regiment.

The Picardy officers boasted that they were the direct descendants of the Legion which had been on duty in Jerusalem on the night of the Crucifixion. The officers of Douglas's Regiment confounded them by replying that, had they themselves been on duty at the Sepulchre, the body of Christ would never have left it, meaning that they would not have slept at their posts, as the forebears of the Regiment de Picardy evidently had.

The Regiment de Douglas remained in the service of France during the Civil War and Protectorate period in Britain, but when King Charles II regained the throne he requested King Louis XIV in 1662 to restore the regiment to him. The French king agreed, and the Douglas Ecossais arrived in England, but,

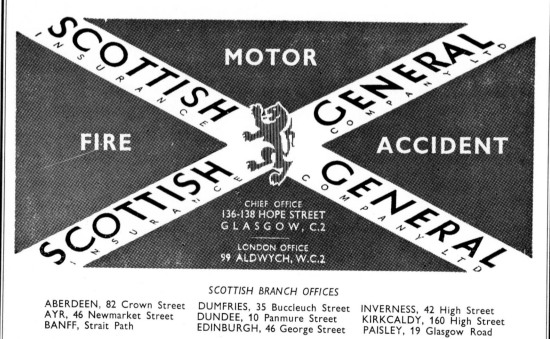

owing to the English Parliament's fear of building up a strong standing army, it was sent back to France the same year.

In the Dutch War of 1665, however, England and France found themselves on opposite sides. Permission was asked, and granted, for the return of the regiment, and in 1666 it re-crossed the Channel. There was a clash with the enemy in 1667 when Dutch fighting ships sailed into the Thames and landed forces.

The regiment served again under the French, and it was not until 1670 that it returned to British control. After a brief stay in Ireland the regiment was despatched to North Africa. In 1681 it was finally placed on the British establishment.

As Dumbarton's Regiment its 16 companies fought with distinction in the defence of Tangier against the besieging Moors from 1680 to 1684. Tangier passed to King Charles II as part of the dowry of his wife, Catherine of Braganza, and was very useful as a naval base for the despatch of punitive expeditions against pirates. At Tangier the regiment won its first battle-honour, but it was not until 1910 that the award was made.

Styled The Royal Regiment of Foot in 1684, it occupied the right of the line at the Battle of Sedgemoor, in 1685, which ended the Mon-mouth Rebellion. An officer of the regiment captured the Duke of Monmouth's standard. The regiment was organised in two battalions in 1686. In the Revolution of 1688 The Royal Regiment of Foot remained loyal to King James VII, and not until most of its officers and a number of other ranks had been removed did it finally give its allegiance to William of Orange.

The next active service was experienced on the Continent, and this in the service of King William III. At the Battle of Steenkirk, in 1692—known as Douglas's Regiment—the colours were saved by the commanding officer, Sir Robert Douglas. Seeing a Frenchman bear them off, Sir Robert felled him, but he was mortally wounded by a bullet. He had enough strength left to hurl the colours clear of the enemy before he died. In this desperate encounter, as the senior regiment, Douglas's Regiment was again in the position of honour on the right of the line. One battalion drove back four French battalions at the Battle of Landen, in 1693, and at the siege and capture of Namur, in 1695, the regiment won further renown.

In the Duke of Marlborough's campaign against the French in the War of the Spanish Succession (1702-13), the Royal Regiment of Foot was prominently identified at the battles of Schellenberg, Blenheim, Gheete River, Ramillies, Oudenarde, and Malplaquet. Blenheim, Ramillies, Oudenarde, and Malplaquet appear on the colours of the regiment.

The 1st Battalion The Royal Regiment of Foot fought with great dash against the French at the Battle of Fontenoy, in 1745. The 1st later served in Holland and raided the French coast with the Navy. After the Union of England and Scotland in 1707, the regiment had served in Ireland, and a number of Irishmen were recruited. The 2nd Battalion operated against Prince Charles's forces in the 1745 Jacobite Rising, and clashed with the Highlanders at Falkirk and Culloden.

Serving in Canada, the 2nd Battalion helped to capture Louisburg and Cape Breton Island from the French in 1758. In 1762 this battalion fought well in the assault and capture of Havanah, storming the Spanish stronghold of Moro Fort. Later the two flank companies were in action expelling a French force which had seized St. John's, Newfoundland.

The 1st Battalion remained in North America until 1763. Four companies were included in two expeditions launched against the trouble-some Cherokee Indians. The other four companies were present at the surrender by the French of Montreal. During the French wars the 1st Battalion experienced a tour of duty in the West Indies. It was engaged in sporadic skirmishing with rebellious slave labourers imported from West Africa, and not infrequently the French Royalists asked for British protection.

At San Domingo in 1794 the battalion was ravaged by tropical diseases, and at one stage could only muster about 100. In 1803 a force of 650 men was despatched to seize Dutch territory—now British Guiana—but no opposition was encountered, the Dutch later joining the British. While serving in the West Indies the battalion won the battle-honour St. Lucia.

The 1st Battalion, after its return to the homeland, took part in a lightning raid on Ostend to disrupt Napoleon's invasion preparations. This was followed by another expedition, on this occasion to Holland, in 1799.

The 2nd Battalion assisted in maintaining order in London during the Gordon riots in 1780. In 1793 it was engaged in the defence of Toulon—where Napoleon first achieved renown. After the evacuation of Toulon, men of the 2/1st were included in the force which invaded

Corsica in 1794. Here the Scottish infantrymen worked with the Navy and "muscled" heavy guns and equipment up the cliffs before taking part in the attack on Convention Redoubt. Later the 2/1st operated in Elba, after which they arrived in Lisbon.

The 2nd Battalion clashed with Napoleon's troops in the Egyptian campaign of 1801. After landing in Aboukir Bay, the "Royals" threw themselves into the fight to hold the beachhead, and drove back the French infantry. The battalion then advanced on Alexandria in the wake of the enemy retreat. At Alexandria the French were again defeated. After service in Egypt the battalion was sent to Malta, where it was severely disciplined during an unfortunate lapse in its previously unblemished record. The 2nd Battalion was later ordered to India.

The 3rd Battalion, formed during the Peninsular War, was in Sir John Moore's epic fighting retreat to Corunna in 1808-9, and afterwards served under the Duke of Wellington's command. It was in action at Busaco, Salamanca, Vittoria, and the Nive. At the siege of San Sebastian the battalion won renown, but glory's price was dearly paid in heavy casualties.

The 3rd was in the pursuit of Napoleon's forces, and was the first to enter France from Spain after fighting through the Pyrenees in the winter of 1813-14. In 1812 the regiment had been named the 1st or The Royal Scots.

Meanwhile the 1st Battalion, engaged in the American War of 1812-14, gave an excellent account of itself in the fighting at Sacketts Harbour, Sodus, Fort Niagara, Fort Erie, and Lundy's Lane. Four of its companies served in the role of marines with the Fleet.

During this period the regiment consisted of four battalions, and in the American War the 1st had many Frenchmen in its ranks, also Englishmen and Irishmen. The 4th Battalion was included in Sir Thomas Graham's expedition to Holland in 1814. This battalion suffered severely in the unsuccessful assault on the fortress of Bergen-op-Zoom.

On the renewal of the war against Napoleon, the 3rd Battalion again entered the field. It was heavily committed at Quatre Bras and Waterloo, and repulsed several determined attempts by the French cavalry to smash its squares, which stood firm against all comers. The 4th Battalion was with the force which occupied Paris. These two battalions were disbanded after peace was signed in 1815.

In India, during the Mahratta War of 1817, the 2nd Battalion—with an Indian division—was the only British formation present at the siege and capture of Nagpur, after a series of forced marches. The battalion was also involved in the fighting at Maheidpore and Talnere. In this short campaign the battalion administered a sharp lesson to the Pindaree bandits who had been giving serious trouble in Central India. In 1821 the regiment was styled the 1st or The Royal Regiment of Foot.

The 2nd Battalion next experienced service under Sir Archibald Campbell in the First Burmese War, 1824-25, taking part in the capture of the enemy's capital. For this the battle-honour "Ava" was awarded. After further service in cholera-ravaged India the battalion returned home in 1831, then moved across to Ireland. In 1836 it went to Canada. In 1837-38 the "Royals" helped to preserve order during political disturbances. Seven years later it was ordered to the West Indies.

While in the Gulf of St. Lawrence a transport carrying part of the battalion struck a rock and became a total loss. When dawn broke it was seen that the shore was not far off, and due to the fine discipline on board the entire ship's company and all the troops were brought to safety—the women and children being sent off first.

The 1st Battalion of The Royal Regiment was included in the British forces sent out to the Crimea. It was engaged at the Battle of the Alma and in the protracted siege of Sebastopol. At Inkerman the "Royals" fought like demons in the drifting morning fog against overwhelming Russian numerical superiority. After several hours of ghastly close fighting the Russian infantry masses were thrown back in confusion.

For two acts of gallantry at Sebastopol Private Joseph Prosser was awarded the regiment's first Victoria Cross. On June 16, 1855, Private Prosser left the trenches under cross-fire to pursue and bring back a soldier of another regiment in the act of deserting to the enemy. On August 11, Private Prosser left a forward trench to carry to safety a badly wounded man of the 9th Regiment. In 1855 the 2nd Battalion, joining the 1st, shared in the privations of this grim campaign.

When the Crimean War ended in 1856 the 1st sailed for India and served during the Mutiny. This battalion, while stationed at Hong Kong, formed part of Sir Hope Grant's expedition during the Chinese revolt of 1859-60. The 1st took part in the amphibious operations which led to the capture of the Taku Forts and Pekin.

In 1871 the regiment was designated the 1st or The Royal Scots, but in 1882 there was another change of name to The Royal Scots (Lothian Regiment). In 1884 the 1st Battalion was in South Africa. It was engaged against the Boers in Bechuanaland, and later operated in Zululand. A mounted infantry detachment was formed about this time which rendered excellent service in highly mobile operations.

When the South African War broke out in 1899 the 1st was stationed in Ireland and the 2nd in India. Both mobilised for service, and in this hard-fought, difficult campaign The Royal Scots gave of their best. The Royal Scots was the only regiment in which every Reservist answered his summons to duty, and a statement to this effect was made in Parliament.

Though only engaged in a number of minor actions the regiment nevertheless enhanced its already high reputation for endurance, toughness and marching powers. The 3rd Battalion (Militia) volunteered for service, and its mobility earned the nickname "The Bloody Greyhounds". A service company formed by volunteers from the affiliated Volunteer Force battalions of The Royal Scots joined the Regulars in the field. Thus, for the first time the Volunteers—who later became known as Territorials—campaigned alongside the Regulars with outstanding success.

By this time the "Royals" had a long list of battle-honours. These were:—The Sphinx, superscribed "Egypt"; Tangier, 1680; Namur, 1695; Blenheim; Ramillies; Oudenarde; Malplaquet; Louisburg; Havannah; Egmont-op-Zee; St. Lucia, 1803; Corunna; Busaco; Salamanca; Vittoria; San Sebastian; Nive; Peninsula; Niagara; Waterloo; Nagpore; Maheidpore; Ava; Alma; Inkerman; Sevastopol; Taku Forts; Pekin, 1860; South Africa, 1899-1902.

Between 1902 and 1914 the two battalions experienced tours of duty at home and in India. The 2nd Royal Scots were with the British Expeditionary Force, which landed in France in August, 1914, and soon had the advancing Germans in their sights near Mons, in Belgium. The 1st Battalion, after returning from India, sailed for France in mid-December of the same year, and entered the conflict.

Attack and counter-attack followed each other in quick succession as the fighting moved into the Cambrai-Le Cateau area. Machine-guns and rifles—in almost constant use—became too hot to fire, and bayonet crossed bayonet in bitter hand-to-hand encounters. Often it was stand firm with clubbed rifles as the German field grey legions bore down upon them.

With their blood these "bonny fechters" of The Royal Scots cemented the "Auld Alliance" between France and Scotland at La Bassee. With the B.E.F. they drove the enemy back over the Marne, and advanced to the Aisne. Then followed the Ypres holocaust, Loos, the Somme, Arras, and the Lys.

And at the end of the war on the Continent there were other calls for The Royal Scots. The 2/10th Battalion accompanied the expedition to North Russia and was engaged around Archangel, while in the Balkans men from the regiment served on the Struma. The Territorial battalions maintained the finest traditions of the "Royals" in France and Flanders, North Africa, Gallipoli, Egypt, and Palestine.

During four years of war The Royal Scots expanded to 35 battalions which gained 71 battle-honours. Six Victoria Crosses were awarded. Over 100,000 officers and other ranks served with the various battalions, and The Royal Scots had more casualties than any other Scottish regiment—11,162 killed, and over 40,000 wounded. The following battle-honours were awarded:—Le Cateau, Marne, 1914, '18, Ypres, 1915, '17, '18, Loos, Somme, 1916, '18, Arras, 1917, '18, Lys, Struma, Gallipoli, 1915-16, Palestine, 1917-18.

Near Kemmel, on December 14, 1914, during an attack on a German position, Private H. H. Robson, 2nd Battalion, left a trench under very heavy fire and rescued a wounded N.C.O. Private Robson gallantly attempted to bring another wounded man to cover, but was wounded. He continued in his efforts until hit again and rendered helpless.

For most conspicuous bravery on Hill 70, on September 26, 1915, Private R. Dunsire, 13th Battalion, went out into a storm of fire and rescued a wounded man. Another soldier, lying much nearer the German lines, was heard calling for help. Private Dunsire crawled out again and carried him back shortly before the Germans attacked across the scene of his rescues.

When his company was nearing its final objective near Frezenburg, on September 20, 1917, heavy casualties were being caused by German machine-guns and a pill-box, which had been passed by the first attacking wave. Captain H. Reynolds, M.C., 12th Battalion, reorganised his company, then proceeded alone by a series of rushes from shell-hole to shell-hole, though subjected to heavy machine-gun fire.

Captain Reynolds, on nearing the pill-box, hurled a grenade intending that it should explode inside, but the Germans had blocked up the entrance. The officer then crawled to the entrance and forced a phosphorous grenade inside, setting this strongpoint on fire. Three of the enemy were killed, and the remaining Germans surrendered with two machine-guns. Afterwards, though wounded, Captain Reynolds continued to lead his company against another objective and captured it, taking 70 prisoners and two machine-guns.

During operations at Courcelles-le-Comte, on August, 23 1918, Private H. McIver, M.M., 2nd Battalion, while acting as company runner, pursued a German for 150 yards. His quarry took refuge in a machine-gun nest. Private McIver, undaunted, jumped into the trench and shot several of the occupants and took the surrender of the remainder with two machine-guns. His bravery assisted his company forward on its objective. Private McIver carried important communications through very heavy artillery and machine-gun fire during the action.

For his fearlessness and initiative south-east of Cappelle St. Catherine, on October 15, 1918, when in charge of a Lewis gun team, Corporal R. E. Elcock, M.M., 11th Battalion, rushed his gun up to within 10 yards of the enemy guns, which were causing heavy casualties. He put both enemy guns out of action, took five prisoners, and saved the attack from being held up. Later, near the River Lys, this N.C.O. attacked an enemy machine-gun and captured the crew.

For his outstanding gallantry near Hoog-molen, on October, 22 1918, Lieutenant D. S. McGregor, 6th Battalion (attached Machine-Gun Corps), while in command of a section of machine-guns on the right flank of an assaulting battalion, concealed his guns on a limber under the bank of a sunken road. When the troops advanced they were at once subjected to a barrage of machine-gun fire from Hill 66. Lieutenant McGregor went out into " no man's land " to locate the enemy guns, and succeeding, realised it was impossible to get his own guns carried forward either by pack or by hand without considerable delay, as the ground was devoid of cover and swept by an intense and accurate fire.

Ordering his gun-teams to follow by a more covered route, Lieutenant McGregor went to the limber, got on to it, and, lying flat, told the driver to gallop forward. The driver galloped down about 600 yards of open road under a lashing fire to reach cover.

Driver, horses and limber were all hit, but Lieutenant McGregor succeeded in getting his guns into action and effectively engaged the enemy, subduing their fire and enabling the advance to be resumed. He continued to expose himself in order to direct and control the fire of his weapons until, about an hour later, he was killed while observing fire effect for the Trench Mortar Battery.

The Victoria Cross was awarded to Captain Reynolds, Lieutenant McGregor, Corporal Elcock, Private McIver, Private Robson, and Private Dunsire.

In 1918 King George V approved the appointment of H.R.H. The Princess Royal as Colonel-in-Chief of the regiment, and in 1920 its title was changed to The Royal Scots (The Royal Regiment). The regiment celebrated its tercentenary in 1933, on which occasion the pipers were authorised to wear the Royal Stewart tartan. The regiment wear trews of the Hunting Stewart tartan.

Royal interest in the regiment has been manifest on a number of occasions. Queen Victoria was proudly referred to as the " Daughter of the Regiment ". Her Majesty was born while her father, H.R.H. The Duke of Kent, was its Colonel. When Royalty is present on parade the march " The Daughter of the Regiment " is substituted for the regimental march " Dumbarton's Drums ".

In World War II The Royal Scots triumphed over early disaster. The 1st Battalion sailed with the 2nd Infantry Division to France and served around Lecelles and in the Maginot Line. When the Germans overran Belgium the battalion was rushed to Wavre, and from there commenced a fighting withdrawal to the coast. After the great German breakthrough on the Continent, the 1st Battalion at La Bassee Canal battled against overwhelming enemy air, armoured and infantry superiority, and the survivors were evacuated from Dunkirk in the dark days of June, 1940. But, after rigorous combat training, and with new weapons, the 1st Royal Scots re-appeared, eager and fighting fit, in Burma, and were engaged in that theatre of war from 1943 to 1945.

The Japanese quickly became aware of their presence in the Arakan. The Royal Scots first drew Jap blood at Donbaik in March, 1943. The battalion was locked in deadly fighting at Kohima, and later smashed through the Japanese to its relief, and then took part in the advance to Mandalay, with the enemy completely out-manoeuvred, out-fought, and in retreat. Donbaik ... Kohima ... Aradura .... Shwebo .... Mandalay. These are 1st Battalion memories—and battle-honours. As part of the 2nd Division the 1st Battalion was sent to Calcutta to equip for an amphibious operation, the object being the invasion of South Burma and the capture of Rangoon, but, on the termination of the Burma Campaign, the battalion embarked for Hong Kong. Due to political uprisings in Malaya the battalion was diverted to Singapore to assist in maintaining law and order. The 1st Royal Scots served in Malaya and Singapore until December, 1946, then returned to India. The battalion was among the last British formations to leave Pakistan in late-1947.

The 2nd Battalion was trapped after the hopeless stand at Hong Kong in 1941, and the survivors—there were not many—became prisoners of the success-flushed Japanese. But these unfortunate " Royals ", even in the years of captivity, maintained their splendid *esprit de corps* and discipline, and their courage stood up to inhuman treatment from a ruthless and barbaric foe.

Captain Douglas Ford of the 1st Battalion was tortured by his captors in an attempt to make him divulge information about a projected escape bid, but he died without incriminating his comrades. He was awarded the George Cross.

But a new 2nd Battalion The Royal Scots was soon to arise Phoenix-like from the ruins of the old. This battalion went forth and grappled with the Germans in the fierce fighting which raged on the " leg " of Italy in atrocious weather conditions in difficult terrain. The 2nd was heavily engaged in the Gothic Line battles, and also distinguished itself at Maradi and Monte Camberaldi.

After the Italian campaign was over the 2nd Battalion was moved to Trieste, as this troubled city was claimed by the Italians and Marshal Tito's Jugoslavs. The Royal Scots helped to preserve order despite tension and a number of incidents, and did not return home until December, 1948.

And, as in the 1914-18 War, the Territorial battalions of The Royal Scots added their inspiring contribution to the regiment's record. The 7/9th (Highlanders) Battalion—the " Dandy Ninth "—experienced the short 1940 campaign in France before being evacuated from Cherbourg. It re-entered the picture at the capture of Walcheren, in November, 1944. Flushing and Middleburg fell, then the Territorial " Royals " pushed on to the Maas. They battled through the Reichswald and crossed the Rhine, with the toils of vengeance closing in on the shattered Wehrmacht. The 7/9th Battalion hammered its way into Bremen in April, 1945. The 8th Battalion, in hard fighting, thrust forward from Normandy to Lubeck, on the shores of the Baltic.

The Royal Scots battalions won 38 honours in World War II. These are listed as follows:— Dyle, Defence of Escaut, St. Omer-la Bassee, Odon, Cheux, Defence of Rauray, Caen, Esquay, Mont Pincon, Aart, Nederrijn, Best, Scheldt, Flushing, Meijel, Venlo Pocket, Roer, Rhineland, Reichswald, Cleve, Goch, Rhine, Uelzen, Bremen, Artlenberg, North-West Europe, 1940, 1944-45, Gothic Line, Maradi, Monte Camberaldi, Italy, 1944-45, South-East Asia, 1941, Donbaik, Kohima, Relief of Kohima, Aradura, Shwebo, Mandalay, Burma, 1943-45.

As a result of War Office policy in reducing each Line regiment to one Regular battalion, the 1st and 2nd Battalions were amalgamated in the 1st Battalion early in 1949. So, for the first time since 1686 The Royal Scots possessed only one Regular battalion. At the beginning of 1951 the 1st Battalion left Edinburgh for Germany. The battalion came home in the spring of 1953.

In June, 1953, came another call for the " Royals "—on this occasion to serve in Korea. The battalion was moving into positions in the line when the truce was declared on July 27, 1953. The battalion operated with the 1st Commonwealth Division, but in June, 1954, it was ordered to Egypt, where the Scottish regiment was engaged in curbing terrorist activity in the Canal Zone. In September, 1955, it was performing similar duties in strife-torn Cyprus. The battalion returned home early in February, 1956.

But the 1st Battalion The Royal Scots— proud of its long association and many links with Edinburgh and the Lothians—" trooped " again in January, 1958. Then the " Royals " embarked on another tour of duty in Germany, where their forebears made history.

Photograph by courtesy Desmond O'Neill

H.R.H. PRINCESS MARGARET

COLONEL-IN-CHIEF—THE ROYAL HIGHLAND FUSILIERS

The Royal Highland Fusiliers

(PRINCESS MARGARET'S OWN GLASGOW AND AYRSHIRE REGIMENT)

THE amalgamation of The Royal Scots Fusiliers and The Highland Light Infantry became effective in January, 1959. The title decided upon was The Royal Highland Fusiliers (Princess Margaret's Own Glasgow and Ayrshire Regiment). This amalgamation, ordered by the War Office, may have begun as a marriage of convenience—some persist in calling it a "shotgun wedding"—but, like many such alliances, it is showing every sign of prospering. In 1958 sixty Highland Light Infantry recruits joined the 1st Battalion The Royal Scots Fusiliers for service in Cyprus. The Fusiliers and H.L.I. men settled down well together, a favourable augury for the future.

As each regiment involved in this fusion has a wide divergence of origin, tradition and service, the sagas of The Royal Scots Fusiliers and The Highland Light Infantry are best told separately.

THE ROYAL SCOTS FUSILIERS

The Royal Scots Fusiliers, the oldest Fusilier regiment, was raised in Scotland on September 23, 1678, when a commission was issued to the Royalist Charles Erskine, Fifth Earl of Mar. Eight companies, each of 100 men, were distributed at Musselburgh, Fisherrow, Newbigging and Dalkeith. The Earl of Mar's Regiment was originally raised to suppress the "Phanaticks"—Covenanters and Cameronians. The regiment's principal duties were to disperse hillside conventicles and arrest known Covenanters, but it also supplied troops for policing the turbulent Highlands and garrisoning the Lowland towns.

A year after its "birth" Mar's Regiment was in action against the Convenanters at Bothwell Brig. Garbed in red coats and hodden grey breeches, it was nicknamed "Mar's Grey-breeks", and this lingered for many years after the Earl and the grey breeks had both disappeared. The majority of the regiment's recruits came from rural workers in the Midland and Southern counties of Scotland, and right from the outset they proved themselves excellent military material. During the "Killing Times"

there were 10 companies stationed in Glasgow, Ayr, Stirling, Leith, Dumfries and Lanark.

In 1682 a company of 60 grenadiers was added, armed with the light musket or fusil, and it was ordered that they "be instructed in all thyngs belonging to the artillery, as gunnery, casting of hand grenadoes, and fyre workes". Three years later the whole regiment was armed with fusils. In 1685 the regiment was styled The Scotch Fuzileers.

In 1686 the Earl of Mar incurred the Royal displeasure and was relieved of his commission. He was succeeded by Thomas Buchan, his lieutenant-colonel, and for a time the regiment became known as Buchan's Regiment. A new company, raised by Kenneth MacKenzie, of Suddie, to enforce order in the Highlands, was despatched in 1688 to aid the Macintoshes against the MacDonalds of Keppoch, but this formation was decimated in the last big clan clash in Scotland, and its commander was killed.

In 1689 Buchan's Regiment operated against the Jacobites at Killiecrankie. On the Revolution, however, Thomas Buchan declared for King James, and fought in Ireland against the new dynasty. Francis Fergus O'Farrell was appointed to the command of the regiment by King William.

The Scotch Fuzileers landed in Flanders as part of the British force sent by King William III to aid the Spanish Netherlands against the French, and the regiment fought well in its first battle overseas, at Steenkirk, in 1692, and the following year, at Landen, it also acquitted itself valiantly. At Steenkirk the Scots drove back four French battalions in desperate close combat.

In 1694 a Board of General Officers, all commanding English regiments, decreed that Scottish and Irish regiments should take precedence from the time they came on to the English Establishment. Accordingly, the Scotch Fuzileers were placed 21st.

The Scottish regiment stormed the heights at Schellenburg, and advanced on Blenheim, in

1704. The Fuzileers attacked the fortified village of Blenheim, and on their assault being repulsed, they were charged by the French cavalry. The colours of the Fuzileers were lost for a brief period, then the Hessian Brigade, in support, came up and scattered the French. The colours were retrieved and returned to the Scots. The pendulum of success swung to Marlborough and the enemy suffered heavy losses, and a number of French formations surrendered on the field.

With the Buffs, the Scotch Fuzileers routed three French regiments, and alone, drove another French regiment into the marshes at Ramillies, in 1706. The regiment was not so heavily engaged at Oudenarde, in 1708, but at Malplaquet, in 1709, the Scottish regiment took part in this hard fought battle, in which they stormed the French defenceworks.

Named the 21st or North British Fuzileers in 1707, after the Union of England and Scotland, the regiment experienced a succession of siege operations at Mons, Douai, Bethune, Aire, and St. Venant, and was engaged in the capture of Bouchain in 1711. The regiment was designated the 21st or Royal North British Fuzileers in 1712.

During the 1715 Rising the regiment was engaged against the Jacobites. At Sheriffmuir the Fuzileers clashed with the adherents of the Earl of Mar—son of their first Colonel.

The Royal North British Fuzileers were on the Continent again, this time upholding the cause of Queen Maria Theresa of Austria against the French. At Dettingen, in 1743, their Colonel, Sir Andrew Agnew, was sitting down to a meal when an excited staff officer galloped up and informed him that the French were about to attack.

Sir Andrew, twelfth and last Hereditary Sheriff of Galloway, who served with the regiment for 31 years, replied: "Sir, the scoondrels will never hae the impidence to attack the Scotch Fuzileers". And he ordered the rations to be served out.

It was only when part of a chicken he was eating was knocked off his fork by a French bullet that he abandoned his calm. "Oh ay, they're in earnest noo", he admitted, and mustered his men. "My lads", he shouted, "ye see thae loons on yon hill? Weel, if ye dinna kill them they'll kill you. But dinna fire till ye see the whites o' their een".

The French Household Cavalry thundered down upon them, but Sir Andrew was equal to this crisis. "Open Ranks!" he ordered, and the Cuirassiers dashed in. "Noo, Close Ranks!" The French cavalry then entered a lane of death.

The Battle of Dettingen over and won, King George II, who was in command, could not forbear twitting the Colonel of the Fuzileers about this episode. "Sir Andrew, I saw the Cuirassiers go into your ranks", he joked.

"Oh ay, Your Majesty, but they didna get oot", came Sir Andrew's quick reply. At Dettingen his Fuzileers repulsed the French Foot Guards and shattered the Household Cavalry. Dettingen was indeed a glory day for the Fuzileers—and a gory one for the enemy.

In 1745 the Royal North British Fuzileers formed part of the "Column of Fontenoy"—two long lines of infantry which forced their way through murderous artillery cross-fire into the middle of the French position. Lacking support, the column withdrew in such good order that the enemy did not pursue.

The regiment was hurriedly recalled with other formations to meet the Jacobite challenge in 1745. The Fuzileers took part in the pursuit of Prince Charles's army from Derby. Colonel Sir Andrew Agnew's men garrisoned Blair Castle—home of the loyal Duke of Atholl. The castle was soon attacked by the Jacobite general, Lord George Murray—brother of the Duke of Atholl.

Sir Andrew and 250 of his Fuzileers held on under a hail of cannon and rifle fire, and though outnumbered and in dire extremities scorned a call to surrender. They had only a few biscuits among them when reinforcements got through to raise the siege. The regiment was present at Culloden, where the wild Highland charge broke before the cannon and musketry fire of the "Saighdearan Dearg"—redcoats.

The Royal North British Fuzileers were in action at Val, in 1747, holding a series of villages on the Allied left flank. French cavalry penetrated into the main position, and the British infantry saved the consequent retirement from developing into a rout. In 1761 the regiment was in the small ill-organised expedition which was despatched to attack the fortified Belle Isle, off the French coast.

In the spring of 1775 the Fuzileers arrived in Canada to participate in the war against the American Colonist forces. Again it was an unfortunate story of bungling and incompetence. General Burgoyne's force—which included the Fuzileers—advanced along the banks of the Hudson River, through difficult country, and was beset by snipers. There were frequent ambushes, and broken bridges and road blocks slowed down the march. There were many raids on supplies and baggage.

When General Burgoyne reached Saratoga Springs he found himself surrounded. His troops fought hard and well, but after desperate resistance—3,500 British opposing 18,000 Americans—General Burgoyne decided to surrender. The Fuzileers were among the regiments which bore the brunt of the fighting at Stillwater, and at Freeman's Farm, Saratoga in 1777, and suffered heavy losses in the fighting which preceded the surrender.

The Royal North British Fuzileers ceased to exist until the regiment was re-constituted some five years later.

The regiment re-appeared in the pages of history when it took part in the capture of the French West Indian islands of Martinique, St. Lucia, and Guadaloupe, in 1793. Yellow fever and other tropical diseases proved much more deadly than French bullets, and it was with a feeling of relief that the Fuzileers sailed from these pestilent islands in 1796. A sadly depleted regiment reached its native Scotland at the end of that year.

The Fuzileers were in Sicily in 1806, stationed at Messina. In 1809 they prevented a landing in force by the French, and over 800 of the enemy who did get ashore were taken prisoner.

A company was with General Bentinck's force which landed near Alicante, in Spain, in 1813, and was engaged in the Pass of Ordal. In 1814 the 21st was present at the capture of Genoa, where the French surrendered, and the war came to an end, Napoleon abdicating the same year.

The 2nd Battalion The Royal North British Fuzileers—raised in 1804—had its baptism of fire in the disastrous assault on the Dutch fortress of Bergen-op-Zoom, early in 1814. The fortress was strongly held by the French, but the new battalion made a great fight of it before a withdrawal was ordered. The 2nd was disbanded in 1816.

In the war with the United States the Royal North British Fuzileers was with the forces under the command of General Ross which landed in Chesapeake Bay and advanced on Washington. The American attempt to save their capital ended in a rout at Bladensburg. In retaliation for the burning of Newark and Toronto by the U.S. troops, public buildings, arsenals, and ships in the harbour were set on fire.

One company of the Fuzileers dined off a banquet which had been ordered by President Madison to celebrate the expected American victory over the " redcoats ". Crowds of civilians, many of them in evening dress, fled before the advancing British through streets lit up by blazing buildings, and the President's wife, in the nick of time, managed to save the original document of the Declaration of Independence and Gilbert Stuart's famous portrait of Washington.

In the unsuccessful attempt to capture New Orleans, in 1815, the Fuzileers stormed the American position and were the first to penetrate the defenceworks, but, through lack of scaling ladders, no further progress could be made, and casualties were high. The British and Americans clashed at New Orleans in ignorance of the fact that peace had already been signed.

The 21st Regiment returned to Europe and joined the Allied Army of Occupation in France, remaining there until 1817. During the years of peace, until the outbreak of the Crimean War, the Royal North British Fuzileers did garrison duty in the West Indies and Australia.

Taking the field again at the Battle of the Alma, in 1854, during the Crimean War, the 21st regiment added further lustre to its record. The regiment helped to drive the enemy back from the Alma, and held the key Barrier position throughout the massed Russian onslaught at Inkerman.

The Barrier was the rallying point and the most advanced position, and here the Fuzileers held on in the teeth of powerful Russian attacks, though on several occasions almost engulfed by the enemy advancing out of a thick morning fog which cloaked their strength and movements. The Fuzileers were engaged in the assault on Sebastopol in 1855, and spent a severe winter in the Crimea, experiencing a number of bitter engagements with the enemy. The regiment left the Crimea in the spring of 1856.

The 2nd Battalion was resuscitated at Paisley in 1858, and in 1877 the regiment became the 21st Foot (Royal Scots Fusiliers). In 1879 the 2nd Battalion was ordered out to Natal to deal with a Zulu rebellion. During a gale the ship in which they were sailing struck a rock near the entrance to Simon's Bay. The quartermaster ran from the wheel shouting, " All is lost ! " Rockets were fired off and boats lowered, but two recruits of the Fusiliers sprang to the wheel and held it until relieved by a seaman. The City of Paris, little the worse, then proceeded to her destination. The captain was so impressed with the cool bearing of the Fusiliers that he sent a letter of appreciation and thanks to their Colonel.

With a punitive column under Lord Chelmsford the 2nd Battalion entered Zululand and routed Cetewayo's warriors at Ulundi. At this battle the colours of the regiment were carried into action for the last time. Another troublesome chief, Sekukuni, established himself in the rocky fastness of the Eastern Transvaal. In the assault and capture of this strongpoint the Fusiliers were again engaged, and the insurrection collapsed. Thus the disaster which overtook the first British force to enter Zululand—at Isandlwhana—was avenged.

When the Transvaal Boers staged their rebellion and proclaimed the South African Republic in 1880, they surrounded small British garrisons at Pretoria, Potchefstroom and Rustenburg—all of which were held by the Fusiliers. Headquarters and half the battalion were in Pretoria, two companies at Potchefstroom, and one company at Rustenburg, while one company, equipped as mounted infantry, was divided between Pretoria and Potchefstroom.

Colonel Gildea was in command at Pretoria, and with his Fusileers, two companies of the 94th Regiment, some local volunteers and Sappers, and two 9-pounder guns he put up a spirited resistance. In several daring sorties the Boers were driven back, and ere long the enemy had to lie low and conduct a blockade.

The defence of the tiny fort at Potchefstroom by about 200 Fusiliers of C and D Companies for three months is an epic in the regiment's history. Major Winsloe's small force was under constant siege from December 20, 1880, until March 21, 1881, on which day the last food had been eaten. The Boers made several determined attacks which were thrown back with appreciable loss, the garrison's two 9-pounder guns being well handled.

The assaulting Boer commando, led by the noted Cronje, was much superior in numbers, and sickness, exposure, fatigue, hunger and casualties took a heavy toll of the defenders. Further defence being impossible, the much reduced garrison marched—or rather, staggered out—and the Boers gave them all the honours of war.

At Rustenburg E Company endured a close siege in a roofless mud fort only 25 yards square from December 27, 1880, until March 30 of the following year. The Boers made repeated determined attacks, but the garrison took on all comers, and on several occasions sallied forth to surprise the enemy. The Fusiliers were still hitting back effectively when peace was signed.

The 2nd Battalion of the regiment—which was styled The Royal Scots Fusiliers in 1881, with the same number (21)—left South Africa that year to serve in India, and for four years was on duty in the Madras Presidency. Despatched to Burma, the battalion was garrisoning the frontier stations when war broke out in 1885, and the Fusiliers were soon engaged in dealing with roving bands of dacoits (bandits) and parties of King Theebaw's warriors. This jungle campaign dragged on for almost two years in difficult conditions. The battalion was relieved in the Punjab in 1896, and the two battalions met in the same rest camp—the 2nd on its way home, and the 1st embarking on a tour of duty in the East.

In 1897 half of the 1st Battalion was ordered to Kohat, on the mountainous North West Frontier of India, to cope with a serious rising of Pathan tribesmen. Four companies of the battalion and Headquarters joined the expedition which entered Tirah, and the Fusiliers fought well in several brisk engagements during the short hard winter campaign in the hills against a cunning enemy skilled in guerilla tactics and all the tricks of surprise. As the tribesmen took no prisoners and showed no mercy to any wounded who fell into their hands, there were several hectic rearguard actions during the expedition's return down the Bara Valley.

In the autumn of 1899 the Boers declared war. At Colenso four companies of the 2nd Battalion were detailed to escort the guns. The two field batteries concerned came under an accurate and concentrated hail of fire, and the guns had to be put out of action to save them from being used by the enemy. Withdrawal attempts failed, as the Boers were closing in. At Colenso Private C. Ravenhill won the regiment's first Victoria Cross for repeated efforts to assist the withdrawal of the batteries in a blizzard of close-range fire. This award was made for acts of outstanding gallantry in the traditional role of the Fusiliers—escorting the guns.

At Pieters Hill The Royal Scots Fusiliers made their contribution to the relief of Ladysmith, which had withstood a long and exhausting siege. At Frederikstad they held firm, though at one time in danger of being surrounded, and finally repulsed the enemy. In mid-May, 1900, The Royal Scots Fusiliers were the first troops to cross the Transvaal frontier.

The battle-honours awarded to the regiment—Relief of Ladysmith, and South Africa, 1899-1902—are shared by both battalions. The 1st sent regular drafts from its station in India to the 2nd Battalion in the field. The other battle-honours of the regiment were:—Blenheim, Ramillies, Oudenarde, Malplaquet, Dettingen, Martinique, 1794, Bladensburg, Alma, Inkerman, Sevastopol, South Africa, 1879, Burma, 1885-7, Tirah.

The two battalions met at Gibraltar in 1914. The 1st, on its way home from South Africa, handed over a draft of about 300 men to the 2nd at " Gib ". On the outbreak of World War I the 1st Battalion, as part of the 9th Brigade, 3rd Division, mobilised and embarked on August 13, 1914, and by the 22nd of that month the Fusiliers were in the front line, holding the three Jemappes bridges over the Mons-Conde Canal, in Belgium.

Intense shelling and the onslaught of the massed German divisions forced back the British Expeditionary Force, and the fighting retreat from Mons began. By the end of the month the 1st Battalion was again locked in combat at Le Cateau, and after inflicting heavy casualties, the retiral continued to the Marne, where, in September, another stand was made. The Fusiliers attacked at Orly. But this time it was the German Army which was pressed back with disastrous losses.

The 1st Royal Scots Fusiliers were in the thick of the fray on the Aisne, and helped to throw back powerful enemy counter-attacks at Vailly. There was more grim fighting for the seriously depleted battalion at Herlies during the Battle of La Bassee. Meanwhile the 2nd Battalion, with the 7th Division, arrived in Belgium in mid-October in time to make history in the First Battle of Ypres at Gheluvelt.

A month later the 1st Battalion clashed with and outfought the Prussian Guards, and played an important part in frustrating the Germans in their all-out drive to capture the vital Channel ports. There followed the Battle of Neuve Chapelle, in March, 1915, with the 2nd engaged at Pietre, and later storming into the attack on Aubers Ridge. In mid-June the 1st attacked Bellewaarde Ridge, and in the Allies' autumn offensive it fought south of the Menin Road. At the Battle of Loos, in September, the 2nd Battalion suffered severely in determined attacks on the fire-spitting German trenches.

In the Battle of the Somme, in the summer of 1916, the 2nd was in the attacks on Montauban, Bazentin, Delville Wood and Guillemont, with the 1st operating on the left. There was further severe fighting for both formations during the autumn Battle of the Ancre—at Serre for the 1st, and at Flers for the 2nd.

Both battalions were in the Battle of Arras and the attack on Vimy Ridge, in the spring of 1917. The 1st captured Monchy-le-Preux, and the 2nd attacked into determined opposition near Cherisy. In July came the Third Battle of Ypres and the assault on Frezenburg, with the 2nd attacking along the Menin Road. The 1st captured Zonnebeeke in September, and this ended the outstanding service of The Royal Scots Fusiliers in the Passchendaele holocaust.

In the spring of 1918 the 1st Battalion was south of Arras, with the 2nd near St. Quentin. Long before dawn on March 21st a terrific artillery bombardment burst over the British lines. At daybreak, in shoulder-to-shoulder formation, the massed German divisions emerged out of the morning mist. The last and greatest German offensive had begun.

Undaunted, the hard-pressed 2nd Battalion threw in several spirited counter-blows, but had to give ground, the flanks having been borne back by sheer weight of numbers. The battalion retired in good order to the Somme, and was heavily engaged in the Lys fighting, at Sailly, during April, and in the enemy attack on La Bassee. In the north the 1st Battalion, locked in desperate combat, succeeded in repulsing the Germans near Arras. The battalion was again gravely depleted at La Bassee in attempting to block the enemy's steam roller advance.

Then, the German offensive spent, the 2nd attacked and captured Meteren in July, and the 1st tore into the enemy at Beaucourt, and later, at Queant. Soon the Fusiliers were battling deep into the Hindenburg Line. In late September the 2nd was operating south of Ypres, and towards the close of October the 1st fired its last shots in the attack on Vertain.

About the same time the 2nd was fighting near Courtrai, and ended its advance on October 25.

During the 1914-18 War there were 18 battalions. Including the two Regular formations, nine battalions experienced service in the field. The 4th and 5th Territorial Army Battalions served in Gallipoli, Egypt, Palestine, and France. The 6th (commanded for a time by Colonel Winston Spencer Churchill), and the 7th—both Service battalions—were engaged

in France, and amalgamated in January, 1916, owing to severe casualties. The 8th Service Battalion operated in Salonika and Bulgaria, and the 11th (Garrison) Battalion served in France.

In January, 1917, the remnants of the Ayrshire and Lanarkshire Yeomanry regiments—which had campaigned in Gallipoli, Egypt, and Palestine—and drafts from the 3rd (Special Reserve) Battalion amalgamated to form the 12th Battalion, and fought in France.

After the war the 2nd Battalion re-formed at Aldershot, and in November, 1919, left for Constantinople to form part of the Black Sea Force. The battalion was sent to Novorossisk to aid the evacuation of the British Military Mission from South Russia. The 8th Battalion also served in the Black Sea Force. The 1st Battalion served during a troubled period in Ireland.

Principal battle-honours in World War I were:—Mons, Marne, 1914, Ypres, 1914, '17, '18, Somme, 1916, '18, Arras, 1917, '18, Lys, Hindenburg Line, Doiran, 1917-18, Gallipoli, 1915-16, Palestine, 1917-18. In all, 53 battle-honours were awarded to battalions of The Royal Scots Fusiliers for outstanding service. Individual awards were:—Victoria Cross, 4; D.S.O., 29; M.C., 164; D.C.M., 141; M.M., 416; and 74 foreign decorations. A total of 5.963 officers and other ranks of The Royal Scots Fusiliers made the supreme sacrifice. The Victoria Cross was awarded to:—Second-Lieutenant J. M. Craig, in Egypt; Second-Lieutenant S. H. P. Boughey, in Palestine; Sergeant T. Caldwell, at Oudenarde; Private D. R. Lauder, in Gallipoli.

In 1921 the 2nd Battalion The Royal Scots Fusiliers was ordered to India and served for a time on the North West Frontier. For the final year in its tour of duty the battalion proceeded to Shanghai early in 1931, but its departure for the homeland had to be delayed because of the troubled situation in China. Thus the opportunity was missed of meeting the 1st Battalion at Port Said on its way out to Palestine. In the spring of 1932 the far-travelled 2nd Battalion arrived at Southampton after completing over 17 years' foreign service.

The two battalions did meet some ten years later, at Durban, in 1942, and fought alongside each other in Madagascar in May of that year. The 1st and 2nd Royal Scots Fusiliers were in the force which advanced from the landing beaches, and the two battalions battled into the narrow peninsula on which stands Antsirane, dominating the great harbour of Diego Suarez.

The British force disembarked on a beach some 12 miles farther south, and the Fusiliers pressed eastwards through thick bush towards Antsirane, about 20 miles away. On high ground enemy dugouts and machine-gun emplacements were encountered, and, after some casualties, they were "winkled out". Later the Fusiliers were swept by a hurricane of close-range fire from hidden 75's, and tank traps delayed the armour. The Fusiliers went in—bayonets against field-guns—and the bayonets triumphed.

There was determined resistance by the Vichy French forces across the base of the small peninsula. A dawn attack was launched, and for a time the Fusiliers were held up at the approaches to Antsirane by heavy machine-gun fire. At night the onslaught was renewed, and soon they were advancing through the native quarter. By midnight they had cleared the eastern part of the town, and then the Fusiliers—headed by pipers—marched up to the Governor's residence. The Japanese had been forestalled.

The 2nd Battalion had already experienced violent action in France during the disastrous days of May and June, 1940, and the Fusiliers fought desperately against great odds to cover the withdrawal to Dunkirk. The battalion was heavily engaged near Ypres, where their forebears in World War I made the sacrificial stand before the Kaiser's hordes.

The Fusiliers experienced, too, the bitter fighting which raged along the Ypres-Comines Canal. Operating south of the Somme, they turned a shattered farm near Vimy Ridge into a strongpoint and held the gaunt, crumbling, shell-torn ruins throughout 24 hours of fierce Nazi onslaughts before being completely overrun, surrounded and compelled to capitulate. Their stand allowed the battered, exhausted columns of the British Expeditionary Force to reach the evacuation beaches. The Royal Scots Fusiliers borrowed time with their blood.

After Dunkirk, the battalion was re-formed and it was not long before it was again ready for active service.

Following the short campaign in Madagascar, the 2nd Battalion was despatched to India. It was later switched by way of Iraq, to the sacred city of Qum, in Persia, to go to the aid of the Russians should the Nazis drive too deeply into the Caucasus. The alarms of war also took the battalion to Jordan, Palestine, and Egypt.

FINE CRAFTSMANSHIP

Centuries of endeavour have preceded the modern age of machines and the primitive desire to make one's flint sharper than one's neighbour's still prevails. Similarly fine craftsmanship has been the result not only of technical skill, capability, or attitude of mind alone, but by an intense desire to better the finished result. Today we accept the machines and their implications and at the same time try to impart a little of the finer sense of values that has been handed down to us through successive generations of artist craftsmen each of whom has yielded, as we hope ourselves to do, their valuable contribution to intelligent civilisation.

At Dubrien House we employ fine craftsmen, and materials, and with the aid of modern methods produce first class photography, design and engraved plates for printing. We use the knowledge gained by experience in the past to help us to this end.

Geometric Amphora from the Hellenic period (1000 BC-700 BC)

SCOTTISH STUDIOS
AND ENGRAVERS LIMITED
DUBRIEN HOUSE · 196 CLYDE STREET · GLASGOW C.I.
Tel: CITY 6961 (Three Lines)   Grams DUBRIEN, GLASGOW

On July 10, 1943, the 2nd Battalion was the first formation ashore in Sicily, landing to the east of Cassibile. The Fusiliers at once advanced to Priolo, and early in August they were operating south-west of Catania, and after its capture were engaged to the north of the town.

The 2nd Royal Scots Fusiliers were in the first landing in Italy, on September 3 of the same year. From the "toe" of the peninsula they advanced up the coastal road through Nicastro, about 70 miles from their landing point, within a week of disembarking.

The Fusiliers were in the Sangro onslaught, and took part in the attack across the blood-stained waters of the Garigliano, in mid-January, 1944. Advancing past Argento, they were soon embroiled in very hard actions in the hilly country near Minturno, where repeated German counter-attacks were thrown back. The 2nd fought hard and well in the long desperate battle to hold—and later extend—the vital Anzio beachhead. Then began the advance to the Tiber.

The 2nd Royal Scots Fusiliers made one of the longest approach marches in history—over 2000 miles from the Mediterranean, through Italy, France, Belgium, and Holland—and the Fusiliers arrived on the banks of the Elbe in time to take part in the crossing and participate in the last battles which ensured the destruction of Hitler's Wehrmacht.

Early in January, 1948, the 1st Battalion The Royal Scots Fusiliers came home from India on completing 15 years of gruelling service abroad. After operating in the brief Madagascar campaign, the Fusiliers joined battle with the Japanese in the Arakan, inflicting, and sustaining, heavy casualties in numerous engagements along this front.

The Scots operated in stifling heat, over difficult terrain, and opposed a ruthless and inhuman foe. The 1st Battalion fought with distinction wherever it served, and jungle-wise and skilled in sudden ambush and surprise attack, the Fusiliers soon proved a very sharp thorn indeed in the flesh of the Japs.

The battle honours awarded—North Arakan, Razabil, Pinwe, Shweli, Mandalay—suggest something of the ferocity of the clashes with the Emperor's troops in the Arakan and Burma. When Scot met Jap it was a fight to a finish, and the enemy was made to pay dearly for his early conquests of American, British, Dutch and French territories.

The 6th and 11th Battalions were in Normandy soon after D Day, and fought in North West Europe and Germany. The 4/5th Battalion also served creditably on the same front. Fifty battle-honours were awarded to the battalions of The Royal Scots Fusiliers for their valiant service in World War II:—Defence of Arras, Ypres-Comines Canal, Somme, 1940, Withdrawal to Seine, Odon, Fontenay le Pesnil, Cheux, Defence of Rauray, Mont Pincon, Estry, Falaise, La Vie Crossing, La Touques Crossing, Aart, Nederrijn, Best, Le Havre, Antwerp-Turnhout Canal, Scheldt, South Beveland, Lower Maas, Meijel, Venlo Pocket, Roer, Rhineland, Reichswald, Cleve, Goch, Rhine, Dreirwalde, Uelzen, Bremen, Artlenberg, North-West Europe, 1940, 1944-45, Landing in Sicily, Sicily, 1943, Sangro, Garigliano Crossing, Minturno, Anzio, Advance to Tiber, Italy, 1943-44, Madagascar, Middle East, 1942, North Arakan, Razabil, Pinwe, Shweli, Mandalay, Burma, 1944-45.

To a lad of Italian birth, Dennis Donnini, was awarded the Victoria Cross for acts of outstanding gallantry in North-West Europe, on January 18, 1945. His platoon of the 4/5 Battalion, The Royal Scots Fusiliers, serving in 156 Brigade, 52 (Lowland) Division, was attacking a strong enemy position between the rivers Roer and Maas. The Fusiliers left their trenches under concentrated machine-gun and rifle fire, and Donnini was hit in the head.

After a few minutes he recovered consciousness, and charged 30 yards down the open bullet-swept road to hurl a grenade into a window. The enemy fled through the gardens of several houses with Fusilier Donnini—bleeding from his wounds—and several of his comrades in close pursuit. He carried a wounded Fusilier to safety in a barn, then, taking a Bren gun, he went out again firing at the enemy. Once more he was wounded. He recovered and went on firing until a bullet hit the grenade he was carrying and killed him.

Donnini's self-sacrifice drew the enemy fire away from his comrades onto himself, and, as a result, the platoon was able to capture the position, accounting for 20 Germans and two machine-guns. Thus Fusilier Donnini, a former cadet, of Easington Colliery, Durham, at the age of 19, and with only seven month's service —two of which were spent overseas—won the highest award for valour in the British Army . . . . and kept a promise he had made to his mother—a miner's daughter—to win the Victoria Cross for her.

On the War Office decreeing that all infantry Line regiments must consist of one battalion, the 2nd Battalion The Royal Scots Fusiliers

was disbanded at Dortmund, Germany, early in 1948. The 1st Battalion sailed for Malaya in the spring of 1954, to take part in anti-terrorist operations.

Soon the Fusiliers were engaged with police and aircraft in the chase after Chin Peng, Secretary-General of the Malayan Communist Party, and his adherents. There were many months of hard, and sometimes unrewarding marches through dense jungle, across steaming swamps, along limestone cliffs, and airlifts into ambush positions along the mountainous Siamese border.

The 1st R.S.F. formed part of the 28th Commonwealth Independent Infantry Brigade, and for a time operated with Australian troops. The battalion quit the steamy, stifling, insect and reptile-infested green hell of the jungle and sailed for home in May, 1957, after three years' hard campaigning in Malaya.

In June, 1958, the Fusiliers were flown out to Cyprus, where they were at once engaged on internal security duties. They assisted in coping with the Eoka gunmen and bomb-slingers, and took part in patrols, searches, and round-ups, and tried to maintain peace between the turbulent Greek and Turkish communities in this strife-torn island in the sun.

The final passing-out parade of recruits of The Royal Scots Fusiliers took place at Churchill Barracks, Ayr, on October 18, 1958. And, appropriately enough, the officer in command was Second-Lieutenant F. Q. E. Agnew, a descendant of Sir Andrew Agnew, of Lochnaw, who commanded the grand old 21st of Foot at the Battle of Dettingen. Two days later, on October 20, an advance party of the 1st Battalion landed from aircraft at Blackbushe, Hampshire. The remainder of the battalion " followed through " within a week from " Trouble Island "—Cyprus.

THE HIGHLAND LIGHT INFANTRY

THE Earl of Cromarty and his son, John Mackenzie, Lord Macleod, were staunch supporters of Prince Charles Edward during the 1745 Jacobite Rising. They were taken prisoner and confined in the Tower of London, but, on account of his youth, the heir received a pardon. His title gone and his estates forfeited, John Mackenzie joined the Swedish Army, and, after 27 years' distinguished service, he rose to the rank of lieutenant-general.

Returning to England on the outbreak of the American War of Independence, John Mac-

kenzie was presented to King George III. He was well received, and the King readily accepted his offer to raise a regiment in the Highlands. John Mackenzie travelled North in 1777 and recruited 840 Highlanders in the old family estates and marched them to Elgin. Here they were joined by 240 Lowlanders, and a small party of 34, made up of Englishmen and Irishmen enlisted at Glasgow.

Initially the new regiment was numbered and named the 73rd Highland Regiment of Foot, but it was also known as Lord Macleod's Highlanders. The Mackenzie tartan was worn. A year later Lord Macleod raised a second battalion, over 600 Highlanders enlisting. This formation was commanded by his brother, the Hon. George Mackenzie. For his services John Mackenzie had his forfeited estates restored to him.

The 1st Battalion of the 73rd, though raised with the intention of reinforcing the Army in America in the war against the Colonists, was despatched to India, where the French were launching a desperate bid to regain lost territory. After a stay in the South of England the 1st Battalion of Lord Macleod's new Highland regiment arrived at Madras in January, 1780, to participate in the Carnatic campaigns.

In Southern India Sultan Haider Ali was in control of Mysore State, and it was in operations against him that the 73rd was to receive its baptism of fire. During this testing period the 73rd fought in several violent actions against great odds, particularly at Porto Novo, in 1781.

General Sir Eyre Coote had described the bagpipes as " a useless relic of the barbarous ages and not in any manner calculated to discipline troops." But after Porto Novo this " redcoat " General presented a set of silver-mounted pipes to the regiment in appreciation of the gallantry of the pipers. Another Sassenach tribute to the Gael in battle !

The flank companies of the 73rd were included in a column sent to assist a small force in dire extremities at Conjeveram. The Highlanders, though under a withering fire, succeeded in hurling back the enemy cavalry. Then ammunition blew up and the enemy closed in such overwhelming numbers that the survivors were forced to surrender. Peace was concluded with Haider Ali's son, Tippoo, in 1784.

The regimental number was changed to 71 in 1786—much to the dislike of the Highlanders. So strong was their opposition to the re-numbering that Colonel Mackenzie paraded his men. He strode down the ranks, pistol

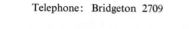
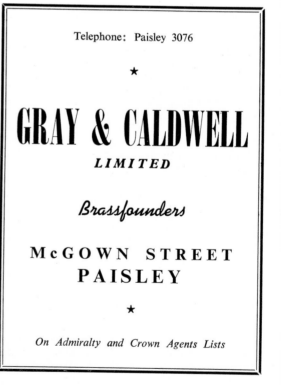

in hand, while a drummer handed out the numbers " 71 " from a bonnet. The Colonel then announced that any refusal to obey the order would have very serious and possibly sudden consequences.

In 1787 Major-General Sir Archibald Campbell, K.B., of Inverneil, Argyllshire, received a letter of service to raise the 74th Highland Regiment of Foot, and he was appointed its first Colonel. This regiment, recruited mainly in Argyllshire, was embodied at Glasgow and Dumbarton. The 71st and 74th Regiments were at a much later date to become the 1st and 2nd Battalions The Highland Light Infantry. Soon after its formation the 74th was sent to the East Indies where the wearing of the kilt had to be discontinued owing to climatic conditions.

Tippoo renewed hostilities in Mysore in 1789, and in June of that year the 74th Highlanders disembarked at Madras to join the 71st. The campaign ended in 1792 with the storming and capture of Seringapatam—the enemy stronghold. The 71st and 74th were in the forefront in the assault. In October, 1797, the 71st sailed for home after transferring a large number of men to the 74th.

The Mahratta leader, Daulat Rao Scindia of Gwailior, intrigued with other native chiefs against the British. This Mahratta confederation and its French military advisers was completely defeated in 1803 by Major-General Sir Arthur Wellesley—later the Duke of Wellington—at the Battle of Assaye, in which the 74th Highlanders had a most distinguished role.

The greatly outnumbered and gravely depleted 74th was heavily enfiladed by the enemy guns and charged by their cavalry. The Highlanders stood firm and survived both ordeals, but all their officers became casualties. The Governor-General of India ordered that special honorary colours, with a suitable device to commemorate this victory, be presented to the three British regiments which took part—a very unique and highly-prized distinction in the Army.

The 74th Regiment continued to carry this third and special colour—emblazoned with the Elephant of Assaye—until 1948, when the 2nd Battalion The Highland Light Infantry was amalgamated with the 1st Battalion. The colour is trooped on each anniversary of the battle.

The 74th was known for many years afterwards as The Assaye Regiment. The proud honour of Assaye was also commemorated in

the badge of the regiment. Indian battle-honours awarded were:—Carnatic, Sholinghur, Mysore, Hindustan, Seringapatam, Assaye. The 74th returned home in 1805, and in 1809 was taken off the Highland establishment.

The 2nd Battalion of the 73rd took part in Rodney's great action off Cape St. Vincent, in June, 1780, the Highlanders being distributed among the fighting ships and functioning as Marines. They subsequently served throughout the last 13 months of the three years' Siege of Gibraltar, when the garrison held out stubbornly against the French and Spaniards under the most severe conditions.

The Highlanders distinguished themselves in a lightning raid on a troublesome Spanish battery, which they captured. The Castle and Key superscribed " Gibraltar," with the motto " Montis Insignia Calpe " underneath, is borne on the colours. The battalion was disbanded at Stirling in 1783, after the Peace of Versailles.

In 1806 an expedition—which included the 71st Highlanders—was sent out under General Sir David Baird, a hero of Conjeveram and Seringapatam, to capture the Cape of Good Hope owing to its vital importance on the route to India. After some fighting on the Blaauberg—or Blue Mountains—the Dutch surrendered. The battle-honour Cape of Good Hope, 1806, was awarded to the 71st.

In the same year the regiment left South Africa and sailed across the South Atlantic to seize the Spanish colony of Rio De La Plata. The expedition landed and captured Buenos Aires, but after initial success the small force, through lack of support and mounting casualties, had to capitulate. Release came in 1807, and the 71st returned to duty.

Early in the 19th century Glasgow and the West of Scotland had become the 71st Regiment's recruiting area. In 1804 a second battalion was raised at Dumbarton composed almost entirely of Highlanders living in and around Glasgow. This formation became so popular in the area that it acquired the name " Glasgow Highlanders." The battalion furnished drafts to the 1st Battalion of the 71st during the Napoleonic wars, and was disbanded in 1815 after the French debacle at Waterloo.

In 1808 King George III confirmed the title " Glasgow," and the 71st was designated The Glasgow Highland Regiment. In 1809 the formation was known as the 71st (Highland Light Infantry) Regiment, and in 1810 was styled the 71st Highland Regiment (Light Infantry).

JOHN BROWN
& CO. (CLYDEBANK) LTD.
Engineering & Shipbuilding Works
CLYDEBANK, SCOTLAND

M.V. " OTAIO ". Built and Engined at Clydebank for the New Zealand Shipping Company Limited

THE Shipyard and Engine Works at CLYDEBANK which contain seven building berths and, extending over an area of 80 acres, are fully equipped to undertake the construction of Large Passenger Liners, Passenger-Cargo Liners, Cargo Vessels, Oil Tankers, Cross Channel Steamers, Geared Steam Turbines and Diesel Engines; also Gas and Water Turbines, Pressure Vessels and Equipment for the Petroleum Industry.

The 74th Regiment returned to Scotland to recruit in 1806, and the kilt was again adopted, but on being sent to Ireland in 1809 it was ordered that Highland dress must be laid aside. For 37 years its identity as a Highland regiment came very near to being lost, as the formation was simply known as the 74th Regiment.

On the reduction in the number of Highland regiments in 1809 the 71st was specially selected for service as a Light Infantry regiment. Several of these formations were included in the Duke of Wellington's famous Light Division. It was laid down that the 71st was " permitted to retain such portions of the national dress as might not be inconsistent with the duties of a Light Corps." Light Infantry were specially trained and lightly equipped to operate quickly as sharpshooters and skirmishers. The dress assumed by the 71st was similar to that worn by other Light Infantry regiments, except as to the headress, which was a diced shako. The bagpipes were retained and the pipers were kilted.

The 71st formed part of the army, commanded by the Duke of Wellington, which was despatched to aid Spain and Portugal against the French. The regiment was in the thick of the fighting at the battles of Rolica and Vimiera, as a result of which the enemy had to evacuate Portugal and the British marched into Lisbon.

At Vimiera, in 1808, Piper George Clark, of the 71st, a native of Tongue, in Sutherland, though badly wounded, sat on his knapsack and continued playing his pipes to " brosna-chadh " his comrades to victory. For his gallantry he was presented with a set of silver-mounted bagpipes by the Highland Society of London. Corporal John McKay, of the 71st, succeeded in capturing a French general. Corporal McKay was later given a commission in the West India Regiment.

Disaster having overtaken the Spanish Army, the British force under General Sir John Moore, on Christmas Day, 1808, began the tortuous 200 miles retreat to Corunna. Ill-clad, filthy, with undressed wounds and festering sores, and on short rations, the 71st marched over the Cantabrian Mountains, enduring the snow, sleety rain, mud and intense cold. The French were always at their heels, and there was no respite or shelter. The regiment fought several stiff rearguard actions which barred the enemy from annihilating the British force.

Corunna reached, it was found that the transport ships had not arrived. But discipline and the will to resist and survive were not lost, and in spite of the long hazardous, depressing retreat the tattered, starving, exhausted British turned on their pursuers and hurled them back after four hours of violent fighting, in which Sir John Moore was killed. The ships arrived and they were successfully evacuated at night, the French remaining at a respectful distance as their quarry escaped to fight another day and take a terrible vengeance.

In its first action as a Light Infantry regiment the 71st landed in Holland, as part of the unfortunate Walcheren expedition, in 1809. Some 40,000 troops were involved, but soon the force was decimated by fever, and again there was an evacuation, with over 11,000 sick.

The Light Infantry were in the thick of the fray at Busaco, in September, 1810. The French advanced in such numbers at Sobral that the 71st, which was holding a redoubt, had to give way. In their retiral, the light infantrymen had to scale a wall. An old soldier, John Rae, of Paisley, realising that he was not as agile as many of his comrades, stood his ground. He shot the first Frenchman to come up, and bayoneted two more, after which he leisurely made his withdrawal over the wall. For this action he was presented with a medal inscribed: " To John Rae for his exemplary courage and good conduct as a soldier at Sobral, 14th October, 1810 ".

Soon after Sobral the 71st and 92nd (Gordon Highlanders) made a sharp surprise attack at Arroyo Dos Molinos, capturing 1,400 prisoners and a large amount of baggage. In 1811, at the Battle of Fuentes d'Onor, the 71st and 74th Regiments joined in a combined attack. For a time the issue was in doubt, then Colonel Cadogan, commanding the 71st, gave the historic order and rally call, " Charge them down the Gallowgate, boys ! " The light infantrymen responded by driving the French at bayonet point out of the village of Fuentes. There was another bitter tussle with the French at Ciudad Rodrigo.

The scene changes to the storming of Badajos, in April, 1812, with the 71st and 74th again heavily engaged. One of the first to mount the castle wall was John McLaughlin, a piper of the 71st. Through the rattle of musketry and crash of cannon could be heard the stirring strains of the ancient Campbell air " I've Been To A Wedding In Inveraray " as Piper McLaughlin led the assault along the ramparts.

A bullet entered the bag of his pipes and the music stopped. Piper McLaughlin then seated himself on a gun-carriage and busied himself mending the damage, regardless of the shot flying all around him. Soon he again struck up his inspiring battle music. Later, at the Battle of Vittoria, Piper McLaughlin had both legs shot away by a cannon ball while he was playing beside the Colours. At his request his pipes were handed to him and he continued to play until he died.

There was stiff fighting at Salamanca, in July, 1812, and in June, 1813, at the Battle of Vittoria, the 71st and 74th further distinguished themselves. The French were routed, and lost all their artillery, baggage, stores, pay-chest, and a large number of men in casualties and prisoners. Napoleon's brother, Joseph—installed as King of Spain—narrowly escaped capture. In this battle the two regiments suffered heavy losses, including the commanding officer of the 71st, Colonel the Hon. Henry Cadogan, of Fuentes d'Onor renown, who was mortally wounded in leading a charge.

Both regiments took part in the bitter fighting in the Pyrenees, at Nivelle, Nive and Orthes, as Napoleon's battered forces were driven back into France. The Second Peninsular War, of 1810-14, ended with the capture of Toulouse, in April, 1814.

Battle-honours awarded were:—Rolica, Vimiera, Corunna, Busaco, Fuentes d'Onor, Ciudad Rodrigo, Badajos, Almaraz, Salamanca, Vittoria, Pyrenees, Nivelle, Nive, Orthes, Toulouse, Peninsula.

Napoleon escaped from Elba in February, 1815, and placed himself at the head of a formidable French army. The war-clouds again gathered over Europe, and soon the cannons roared. At Waterloo, on June 18, 1815, the 71st Regiment formed part of the famous Light Brigade of infantry which, in square formation, after concentrated artillery fire, stood firm against charge after charge by the French cavalry. It is recorded that the Duke of Wellington had to seek refuge in a square of the 71st during a furious enemy onslaught.

Napoleon, in a last bid to smash the solid unyielding British squares, sent in his renowned Old Guard. In two dense columns the enemy advanced through the drifting, swirling battle-smoke to engage the Light Infantry. The men in the compact squares poured a hail of fire into the French. The shattered columns hesitated, and at that moment the Light Infantry rushed at the enemy, their bayonets glinting. The rout of the Old Guard was complete,

and Napoleon and his staff galloped from the battlefield.

A company of the 71st claimed to have fired the last shots at Waterloo. After capturing a battery from the Imperial Guard they turned one of its guns and fired on the retreating enemy. " Waterloo " was a richly-deserved battle-honour of the 71st. After the French defeat there was a long period of peace, and the 71st and 74th Regiments served in Ireland, Canada and the West Indies. In Canada in 1838 the 71st maintained order during a period of strife between the British and French settlers. At Beauharnois they were ambushed by the French but quickly put the insurgents to flight. The French fled into the hills, and the 71st had to follow up and rescue them from the Indians.

In 1834 the 71st was granted permission to wear tartan trews, and this dress remained until the kilt was reverted to in 1948.

In the *Gazette* of November 14, 1846, the following announcement was published:—

" Her Majesty has been graciously pleased to approve the 74th Foot resuming the appellation 74th (Highland) Regiment of Foot and of its being clothed accordingly; that is, to wear the tartan trews."

The Adjutant-General directed that the tartan worn by the regiment should not be the old pattern as in use by two other regiments— the 42nd and the 93rd—but that it should be distinguished by the introduction of a white stripe. The final set used was that known as " Lamont ".

The Kaffir War, in South Africa, 1851-53, recalls an outstanding episode in the saga of the 74th—the wreck of the Birkenhead. This troopship sailed from Cove on January 7, 1852, for the Cape of Good Hope. On board were drafts from several regiments under the command of Lieut.-Colonel Seton, of the 74th. In addition to the colonel and Ensign A. C. Russell, there were 66 other ranks of the 74th. On board, too, were the wives and families of soldiers.

The Birkenhead reached Simon's Bay on February 23. Captain Salmond was ordered to proceed to Delagoa Bay and Buffalo River to land troops. The vessel left on the evening of the 25th, and shortly before 2 a.m. on the 26th, when about three miles from the coast, the Birkenhead suddenly struck a submerged rock.

The water rushed into the fore part of the ship drowning many soldiers who were asleep on the lower deck. Lieut.-Colonel Seton at once went on deck and impressed on the officers the necessity of preserving discipline. He ordered the troops to form up on both sides of the quarter-deck. The men fell in as if on parade. A party was detailed to work the pumps, another detachment to assist the sailors in lowering the boats, and a third to throw the horses overboard.

Captain Salmond, in an effort to save the Birkenhead and those on board by getting her nearer to the shore, ordered the engines to be reversed, but this only hastened the end, as the vessel again struck the rocks. Water rushed into the engine-room extinguishing the fires.

The doomed Birkenhead broke in two, and a mast and the funnel fell over the starboard side crushing many and throwing into the water soldiers who were engaged in getting a boat away. Many of them were recruits with only a few months' service, but side by side they stood at the helm to ensure the safety of the women and children. The number of boats carried was quite inadequate.

Captain Salmond announced that nothing more could be done, and advised all who could swim to jump overboard and make for the boats. But Lieut.-Colonel Seton told the men that if they did so they would swamp the boats, and he asked the troops to stand firm. Not a man moved in the silent ranks.

Then the ship began to break up, plunging scores of men into the sea. Those who could struck out for the shore, but very few reached it. Numbers of them either sank through exhaustion, were killed by sharks, dashed to death on the rocks near Point Danger, or were entangled in masses of floating seaweed.

Of the 631 on board, 438 were drowned, only 193 being saved. But not a single woman or child was lost. Lieut.-Colonel Seton, Ensign Russell, and 48 of the 66 men of the 74th perished.

Her Majesty Queen Victoria was so impressed that she erected a memorial at Chelsea Hospital. It bears the inscription:—

"This monument is erected by command of Queen Victoria to record the heroic constancy and unbroken discipline by Lt.-Col. Seton, 74th Highlanders, and the troops embarked under his command on board the Birkenhead when that vessel was wrecked off the Cape of Good Hope on 26th February, 1852, and to preserve the memory of the Officers, N.C.O.s and Men who perished on that occasion."

And the King of Prussia also erected a monument in Berlin, and ordered that the story of the loss of the Birkenhead be read at the head of every regiment in his army on three parades.

In the Kaffir War the 74th was engaged in long drawn out arduous operations against a barbaric enemy in difficult bush country. Uniforms and equipment were coloured with coffee, and this novel attempt at camouflage proved most effective. The battle-honour South Africa, 1851-2-3 was awarded to the regiment for its service in this campaign.

The 71st served in the Crimean War of 1853-55, and was present at the siege of Sevastopol. The regiment was also engaged in the occupation of the Kerch Peninsula. The battle-honour Sevastopol was granted.

In 1858 the regiment arrived in India, and for two years served with the Central Indian Field Force. It was engaged on punitive and pacification duties during the Indian Mutiny, 1857-59. The 74th was engaged in a similar role. During these operations Private Rodgers, of the 71st, was awarded the regiment's first Victoria Cross. The battle-honour Central India was awarded.

Tribal warfare on the North-West Frontier in 1863 caused serious concern, and the 71st took part in the trying Umbeyla Campaign. The regiment distinguished itself in the fighting at Crag Picquet, which it rushed and took at bayonet point.

In 1881 the 71st Highland Regiment (Light Infantry) became the 1st Battalion The Highland Light Infantry, and the 74th (Highland) Regiment became the 2nd Battalion The Highland Light Infantry. The regiment was asked if it wished to readopt the kilt, but this change was not made because the tartan trews worn signified the double distinction of being "Highland" and "Light Infantry". The tartan adopted was that of the 71st—Mackenzie.

The 2nd Battalion was engaged in suppressing a rebellion led by Arabi Pasha in Egypt. This rising, in 1882, was brought to an end at the dawn battle of Tel-el-Kebir. The 2nd Highland Light Infantry, forming part of the Highland Brigade, stormed the enemy positions with the bayonet. The gallant conduct of Lieutenant W. M. Edwards brought new honour to the former 74th with the award of the Victoria Cross. To the long list of battle-honours was added Tel-el-Kebir, Egypt, 1882.

The 2nd Battalion proceeded to India to serve with the Malakand Field Force in operations against disaffected tribes on the North-West Frontier during 1897-98. There was bitter skirmishing in the rocky defiles and gullies far beyond the Khyber and Malakand passes. The troops endured troublesome night and day sniping from tribesmen in eyries on the crags.

It was a campaign of ambush and sudden onslaught, tortuous climbs to get at sharp-shooters high up in the passes, fording thundering, boiling mountain torrents, manhandling guns, ammunition, stores and equipment, and getting across the camels, mules and horses, then up steep slopes. And to add to these rigours there were violent rainstorms and floods which carried bridges away. Each wounded man became a problem, as he had to be evacuated from the rocks under fire from snipers ensconced on the arid heights. It was a campaign in which blood and sweat mingled.

In 1898 the 1st Battalion arrived in Crete to form part of the International Army of Occupation.

The 1st Battalion, with the Highland Brigade, met with disaster under the concentrated blizzard of Boer fire on Magersfontein Hill during the dark days of the South African War. For his heroism while in charge of the stretcher parties Corporal J. Shaul was decorated with the Victoria Cross. Private Charles Kennedy also won the Victoria Cross for his gallantry in this hard-fought campaign. This soldier was later killed in Edinburgh in attempting to stop a runaway horse. Numbers of men from the Highland Brigade formed Mounted Infantry Companies for mobile operations against the enemy. Battle-honours for this campaign were South Africa, 1899-1902, Modder River.

During the First World War there were 26 battalions of The Highland Light Infantry. Fourteen served overseas, the remainder being employed as reserve battalions or garrison and holding battalions at home or abroad.

The 1st Battalion left India in August, 1914, with the Indian Expeditionary Force, and fought in Egypt, France and Mesopotamia, and entered Baghdad. The 2nd Battalion, with the 5th Infantry Brigade of the 2nd Division—forming part of the original British Expeditionary Force—landed in France in August, 1914. This battalion served on the Western Front throughout the war, and after the Armistice it was engaged in operations in North Russia around Archangel.

The 5th, 6th, and 7th Territorial Army Battalions formed the 157th, or H.L.I. Brigade,

of the 52nd (Lowland) Division, and served in Gallipoli, Egypt and Palestine. The three battalions arrived in France in time to take part in the smashing of the Hindenburg Line in the final Allied offensive which ended the war.

The 9th Territorial Battalion—The Glasgow Highlanders—was one of the first T.A. units to land in France. It served from November, 1914, for over a year in the same brigade as the 2nd Battalion, and achieved renown on the Western Front.

The 10th and 11th Service Battalions joined the 9th (Scottish) Division and served in France from May, 1915. The two battalions amalgamated in 1916 and fought on in France. The 12th Service Battalion formed part of the 15th (Scottish) Division, and operated in France from July, 1915, until the Armistice.

The 14th Service Battalion, formed at Hamilton in July, 1915, arrived in France in June, 1916, and served until the end of the war on this front. The 15th Service Battalion, raised by the Corporation of the City of Glasgow, in September, 1914, was mainly composed of Transport Department employees. This battalion arrived in France in November, 1915, and experienced service on the Western Front.

The 16th Service Battalion was formed early in September, 1914, by the Corporation of Glasgow, and was recruited mainly from former members of the Boys' Brigade. This battalion came to France in November, 1915, and fought on the Western Front throughout the war. The 17th Service Battalion was raised in September, 1914, by the Glasgow Chamber of Commerce, and landed in France a year later, serving entirely on the Western Front. The 18th Service Battalion was raised as a " Bantam " Battalion in February, 1915, by the Corporation of Glasgow. The " wee fellows " of the 18th H.L.I. served creditably in France from January, 1916, until the Armistice.

In four years of grim warfare 11,000 officers and other ranks of The Highland Light Infantry were killed. Gallantry awards were:—Victoria Cross, 7; Distinguished Service Order, 55; Military Cross, 247; Distinguished Conduct Medal, 232; Military Medal, 685.

The Victoria Cross was awarded to:— Lieutenant-Colonel W. H. Anderson, at Bois Favieres; Lieutenant W. L. Brodie, at Becelaere; Sergeant J. T. Turnbull, at Authville; Corporal D. F. Hunter, at Moeuvres; Lance-Corporal W. Angus, at Givenchy; Lance-

Corporal J. B. Hamilton, Ypres-Menin Road; Private G. Wilson, at Verneuil.

Sixty-four battle-honours were awarded to the regiment for its outstanding service on the world's war fronts:—Mons, Retreat from Mons, Marne, 1914, Aisne, 1914, Ypres, 1914, 15, 17, 18; Langemark, 1914, 17; Gheluvelt, Nonne Bosschen, Givenchy, 1914, Neuve Chapelle, St. Julien, Aubers, Festubert, 1915, Loos, Somme, 1916, 18; Albert, 1916, 18; Bazentin, Delville Wood, Pozieres, Flers-Courcelette, Le Transloy, Ancre Heights, Ancre, 1916, 18; Arras, 1917, 18; Vimy, 1917, Scarpe, 1917, 18; Arleux, Pilcken, Menin Road, Polygon Wood, Passchendaele, Cambrai, 1917, 18; St. Quentin, Bapaume, 1918, Lys, Estaires, Messines, 1918, Hazebrouck, Bailleul, Kemmel, Amiens, Drocourt-Queant, Hindenburg Line, Havrincourt, Canal Du Nord, St. Quentin Canal, Beaurevoir Courtrai, Selle, Sambre, France and Flanders, 1914, 18; Gallipoli, 1915, 16; Rumani, Egypt, 1916, Gaza, Al Mughar, Nebi Samwil, Jaffa, Palestine, 1917, 18; Tigris, 1916, Kut Al Amara, 1917, Sharquat, Mesopotamia, 1916, 18; Murmansk, 1919; Archangel, 1919.

At the outbreak of World War II the 1st Battalion The Highland Light Infantry was at Fort George, Inverness-shire, under orders for duty in Shanghai. The 2nd Battalion, after service in Palestine, was returning to the U.K.

The 1st Highland Light Infantry proceeded to France in September, 1939, as part of the Second Corps Troops, British Expeditionary Force. In May, 1940, the Corps moved into Belgium during the German invasion of the Low Countries, and from then until evacuation from Malo-les-Bains, near Dunkirk, to Ramsgate, in June, the battalion fought in the 127th Infantry Brigade of the 42nd (East Lancs.) Division, suffering heavy casualties.

The 1st H.L.I. with this division trained hard in the U.K. for the battles of destiny which lay ahead. The 42nd Division was converted to an armoured role in 1943, and the battalion then joined the 53rd (Welsh) Division in preparation for the assault on Occupied France.

By the end of June, 1944, the 1st H.L.I. was concentrated and poised for attack at Le Mare, Normandy. The battalion went into violent action in this sector on June 26th, and the Nazis were hammered back from Normandy. During August a fighting advance of 33 miles was made in seven days. The Welshmen and Scots were in Antwerp early in September, and from there the H.L.I. moved in to take part in the "corridor" operations in support of the battle at Arnhem.

The 1st H.L.I. was in the vortex of the fray in the attack on Hertogenbosch, and was also heavily engaged in the autumn fighting by the River Maas. The battalion further distinguished itself in the Ardennes during the critical "Battle of the Bulge", and in the 30 days gory fighting in the Reichswald. The 1st Battalion then took part in the final offensive, pushing rapidly forward across canals and rivers in the victorious advance into and through North-West Germany, and on VE Day the 1st H.L.I. was established in Hamburg.

The 2nd Battalion The Highland Light Infantry were sent to Mersa Matruh, in the Western Desert, and experienced bitter action there in 1940. At the end of the year General Wavell switched the battalion to serve in Eritrea and Abyssinia. Operating with the 5th (Indian) Division, the 2nd H.L.I. was in the small force which tackled and hammered the Italians, who numbered about a quarter of a million, including native levies.

The battle for several weeks on the heights of Keren shattered the Italians, who considered their honeycombed system of defenceworks impregnable. Under heavy fire the H.L.I. men swung into the attack and winkled out scores of machine-guns after toiling up steep slopes, scrambling over jagged rocks, treading warily over crumbling ledges, and scaling precipices and 1,000 ft. crags which reminded old soldiers of operations on India's North-West Frontier.

At first the Italians had a merry time of it hurling down hand grenades and a variety of other missiles on the advancing Indian and South African divisions. But the Italians and their native levies, seeing the wink and glint of H.L.I. bayonets nearing their perches among the rocks and boulders, decided that discretion was the better part of valour, and, as the bullets began to ping and whine among them, up went their hands in surrender.

The Red Sea port of Massawa was captured. Addis Abbaba, the Abyssinian capital, was entered. From Massawa began the move towards Amba Alagi. where there was another mountain battle. Here the feat at Keren was repeated—crag by crag was cleared by artillery, mortars, machine-guns, then the final mop up with the bayonet.

The 2nd Battalion moved to Egypt and on to Iraq for garrison duties and rigorous training. The battalion also spent five months in Cyprus,

Presentation Silverware

SHIELDS, PLAQUES, BADGES, MEDALS, CUPS, ETC, in Silver or E.P.N.S.

The selection from stock is unrivalled in Scotland. Estimates for special designs prepared without obligation.

The sports trophy illustrated was designed, made and presented by us in 1892 for annual competition by amateur golfers.

EDWARD AND SONS. LTD.

9   BUCHANAN   STREET   ·   GLASGOW

jewellers and Silversmiths since 1838

the menu magnificent . . .

The famous menu and wine list at Rogano justly merits a cosmopolitan clientele. Sea food, sherry bar, and lounge are features of one of Scotland's Smartest Restaurants.

The smartest place in Town . . .

ROGANO

EXCHANGE PLACE (Off mid Buchanan Street) GLASGOW, C.2   CITy 6687   CEN 5677

and rejoined the 5th (Indian) Division in March, 1942, near Sollum, on the Western Desert. After severe fighting, including the Battle of Knightsbridge, the 2nd H.L.I. returned to Egypt and Palestine for special training which stood the battalion in good stead in the invasion of Sicily in June, 1943. Landing at Cassibile, the battalion moved forward to capture Syracuse in mid-July.

The 2nd Battalion took part in the Italian Campaign, operating in the northern area, until October, when it moved to Syria for training as a mountain battalion. It later served in Jugoslavia's Vis Islands, from May until September, 1944, after which it moved to Greece to perform garrison and security duties.

The far-travelled 2nd H.L.I. returned to Maryhill Barracks and Depot, Glasgow, in November, 1947, after serving in Palestine, Egypt, the Sudan, the Western Desert, Eritrea, Abyssinia, Libya, Cyrenaica, Iraq, Syria, Cyprus, Sicily, Italy, Albania, Jugosalvia and Greece.

In World War II there were 12 battalions of the regiment. The 5th and 6th Battalions and the 1st Glasgow Highlanders formed the 157th H.L.I. Brigade of the 52nd (Lowland) Division. This brigade experienced service in the short 1940 campaign in France until evacuated from Cherbourg in June. The 6th Battalion was in action at Nijmegen during the Arnhem operations. The 5th and Glasgow Highlanders assisted in clearing South Beveland and Walcheren, and were again joined by the 6th. Their operations resulted in the opening up of the port of Antwerp. The brigade served in Belgium, Holland and Germany, and ended the war in Bremen.

The 7th Battalion became a searchlight unit. The 10th Battalion and the 2nd Glasgow Highlanders landed in Normandy as part of the 15th (Scottish) Division, and took part in the assault crossing of the Rhine. During the campaign the two battalions served in France, Belgium, Holland and Germany.

The 11th Battalion was converted to a tank battalion and served in the U.K. It was disbanded in 1944. The 12th Battalion—later re-numbered the 30th Battalion—was employed on garrison duties in this country until disbanded in 1944. The 13th Battalion, formed from a holding battalion, became a motor battalion within the 42nd (Armoured) Division in the U.K., and was disbanded in 1944. The 14th Battalion was formed as a motor battalion

from miscellaneous units in North Africa in 1943, but was disbanded shortly afterwards. Gallantry awards made to officers and other ranks of the battalions for their services in the 1939-45 campaigns included a Victoria Cross and 210 other decorations.

Lying on the ground dying from wounds he received when he charged single-handed a Japanese machine-gun, an officer of The Highland Light Infantry cheered his men on to attack and carry the position. The enemy fled into the jungle. The officer—Captain Frank Gerald Blaker, M.C., attached 9th Gurkha Rifles—died as he was being carried away. A native of Taunton, Somerset, Captain Blaker was awarded a posthumous Victoria Cross for his gallantry in this action near Taungi, Burma, in early-July, 1944.

Forty-nine battle-honours were awarded to The Highland Light Infantry for service in the campaigns of 1939-45. These are:—Withdrawal to Cherbourg, Odon, Cheux, Esquay, Mont Pincon, Quarry Hill, Estry, Falaise, Seine, 1944, Aart, Nederrijn, Brest, Scheldt, Lower Maas, South Beveland, Walcheren Causeway, Asten, Roer, Ourthe, Rhineland, Reichswald, Goch, Moyland Wood, Weeze, Rhine, Ibbenburen, Dreierwalde, Aller, Uelzen, Bremen, Artlenberg, North-West Europe, 1940, 44-45, Jebel Shiban, Barentu, Keren, Massawa, Abyssinia, 1941, Gazala, Cauldron, Mersa Matruh, Fuka, North Africa, 1940-42, Landing in Sicily, Sicily, 1943, Italy, 1943-45, Athens, Greece, 1944-45, Adriatic, Middle East, 1944.

Six months after VE Day the 1st Battalion The Highland Light Infantry was moved by air from Germany to Cairo, and by the autumn of that eventful year it was serving in Jerusalem. The battalion was in Palestine until Britain gave up the Mandate and evacuated her forces.

The 1st H.L.I. was assigned the unenviable thankless task of maintaining order in the Old City of Jerusalem, a quarter notorious as a hide-out for thug gangs of the rival Jewish and Arab factions. The battalion performed dangerous police duties in trying to maintain law and order, and in doing so incurred over 80 casualties. The 1st H.L.I. was the last battalion to cross the municipal boundary of Jerusalem on May 14, 1948. The battalion returned to Glasgow in June, 1948.

In 1948 the 2nd Battalion The Highland Light Infantry—in common with all other second battalions of infantry regiments—was placed in suspended animation, after a cadre had amalgamated with the 1st Battalion. That year the regiment had re-adopted the kilt—its original dress.

The 1st H.L.I. was flown out to the Middle East in October, 1951, and after six months in Malta, the battalion arrived in the Canal Zone, Egypt, in September, 1952. It returned to the U.K. after three years' service abroad in November, 1954. Early in 1956 the 1st " trooped " again, this time for Cyprus, where it took part in anti-terrorist operations, in which a number of casualties were incurred, including three men killed. The battalion left " Trouble Island " for home early in January, 1957, and by the spring of that year the 1st H.L.I. was serving in Germany. It was while in Germany the battalion received news of the coming merger with The Royal Scots Fusiliers. The Highland Light Infantry Battalion was given a rousing welcome when it returned to Glasgow in mid-December, 1958.

The command " March Off ! " virtually brought to an end the military life of Maryhill Barracks, Glasgow, on September 26, 1958, on the square known to many thousands of infantrymen of several generations. The echo was drowned in the sound of marching feet at the final passing-out parade of Highland Light Infantry recruits. For the process of amalgamating The Royal Scots Fusiliers and The Highland Light Infantry had already begun at Churchill Barracks, Ayr—depot of The Royal Highland Fusiliers. The Royal Highland Fusiliers (Princess Margaret's Own Glasgow and Ayrshire Regiment) replaces The Royal Scots Fusiliers as the second senior regiment in the Lowland Brigade.

The walking-out dress of The Royal Highland Fusiliers incorporates the Glengarry of The Royal Scots Fusiliers and the Mackenzie tartan trews and white spats of The Highland Light Infantry—a smart and attractive uniform designed to please both regiments.

In the safe keeping of the Territorial Army battalions and the affiliated regiments in Canada, Australia and South Africa, are the fine traditions, fighting record, and " diehard " spirit of The Royal Scots Fusiliers and The Highland Light Infantry. The Territorial Army battalions are to retain their present titles and dress.

The first ceremonial parade of The Royal Highland Fusiliers was held at Old Anniesland, Glasgow, on May 12, 1959, when the regiment received new Colours from its Colonel-in-Chief, H.R.H. Princess Margaret. The old Colours of The Royal Scots Fusiliers and The Highland Light Infantry were marched away and the new Colours presented.

Princess Margaret, accompanied by the Colonel of the Regiment, Major-General R. A. Bramwell Davis, inspected the parade, then the old Colours were trooped. To the slow march " Auld Lang Syne " they were marched off parade for the last time. The regiment formed a hollow square and the new Colours were consecrated. The Princess presented first the Queen's Colour, then the Regimental Colour, to the kneeling ensigns, after which the parade marched past in slow time, then in quick time, and advanced in review order to give the Royal Salute.

Major-General R. A. Bramwell Davis presented Her Royal Highness with a brooch " as a memento of this historic occasion ". It consisted of the regimental cypher in gold with the flame of the fusil in rubies and the monogram of diamonds. The command " Remove Head-dress ! " rang out, to be followed by three rousing cheers for the Princess. The Royal Highland Fusiliers (Princess Margaret's Own Glasgow and Ayrshire Regiment) then marched off.

In George Square the Princess later received the Freedom of the City on behalf of The Royal Highland Fusiliers, and, on the following day, May 13, Her Royal Highness, on the Low Green, Ayr, accepted the Freedom of the Burgh on the regiment's behalf.

Seventy-five battle-honours are carried on the Queen's Colour and Regimental Colour. The Queen's Colour bears the battle-honours of the First and Second World Wars. The Regimental Colour is blue, befitting a Royal Regiment, and displays the regimental crest surrounded by the battle-honours before 1914 on a wreath of bay leaves. The corner badges are the Royal Cypher and Crown, originally granted to The Royal Scots Fusiliers in 1751, and the Castle and Key and the Assaye Elephant of The Highland Light Infantry.

On May 14 the old Colours of The Highland Light Infantry were laid up in Glasgow Cathedral. The colour-party and escort marched into Cathedral Square for inspection by Major-General Bramwell Davis. The Pipe Band, wearing the distinctive Erskine tartan, played " The 74th's Slow March ", and piped the Colours into the Cathedral to the stirring strains of " Scotland The Brave ".

The detachment marched in to the accompaniment of the Military Band, and, while a hymn was being sung, the colour-party approached the chancel steps where the Colonel of the Regiment presented the Queen's and

Regimental Colours in turn to the minister of the Cathedral. The colour-party then presented arms while the Colours lay on the communion table before being placed in a corner of the choir screen under the four Highland Light Infantry Memorial Windows.

The old Colours of The Royal Scots Fusiliers were deposited on May 15 in the Scottish National War Memorial at Edinburgh Castle. They were escorted into the Castle and to the forecourt of the Shrine by the pipes and drums of the regiment, and were handed over " for safe keeping in perpetuity within these walls." Within the Shrine the Colours were placed flanking the memorial to the fallen of The Royal Scots Fusiliers.

So ended for Glasgow, Ayrshire, and all associated with The Royal Highland Fusiliers four days of Royal favour, sunshine and colourful pageantry which only comes but once in a lifetime and then passes into the pages of history and the treasure trove of memories.

Sir David Baird discovering the body of Tippoo

From a print in " Pictures and Royal Portraits " by permission of Messrs. Blackie & Sons Ltd. Original picture by Sir David Wilkie

Photograph by courtesy of Camera Press Ltd.

H.R.H. THE DUCHESS OF GLOUCESTER

COLONEL-IN-CHIEF—THE KING'S OWN SCOTTISH BORDERERS

The King's Own Scottish Borderers

THE Scottish Capital was a sorely troubled city in the early spring of 1689. From Parliament House, Scotland declared in favour of William, Prince of Orange, as sovereign in place of King James VII, who had been deposed by the English Parliament. The city was packed with youths and men from all parts of the country, and tension quickly mounted.

Edinburgh Castle was held for the exiled King James by the Duke of Gordon—and there were many supporters of the House of Stewart within and without the capital. John Graham of Claverhouse—recently created Viscount Dundee—strode from Parliament House and rode off with 60 horsemen to rally the Highland clans to fight for King James. Scotland was on the eve of civil war.

On March 16 the Convention at Parliament House gave orders to blockade the approaches to the Castle, and nominated a committee to consider and report on the grave situation. On March 18 the Committee presented its report:—

"The Committee doe offer it as their opinion that for secureing the peace of the toune the meeting of the Estates may be pleased to grant warrant to the Earle of Levin, with all expedition to levie ane regiment of foot, consisting of eight hundred men, and to beat drummes to that effect; and that so soon as they are in readines he cause them to rendezvouze in the Abbey Close."

The Convention of Estates were discussing this report when information was brought that Viscount Dundee was holding parley with the Duke of Gordon over the Castle wall. The Estates acted quickly, and word went forth:—

"The meeting of the Estates of the kingdome of Scotland doe order and warrand the Earle of Levine to cause beat drumes and call together all persones who will assist him and joyne with the train bands to secure that no men be put into the Castle of Edinburgh and no persone be suffered to sallie forth thereof, and to dissipat any persones who may be together in armes without warrand of the Estates, and to secure the peace of the toune."

The Earl of Leven, an experienced soldier, at once implemented his warrant. The drums beat through the streets of Edinburgh, and in the record time of two hours he had his 800 men. In two more hours the number had risen to 1,000. Thus the origin of Leven's, or The Edinburgh Regiment—later to become The King's Own Scottish Borderers. For well over two and a half centuries the regiment has given faithful and distinguished service to the Crown.

The Earl of Leven's Regiment was set to dig trenches in several parts of the city. The Castle batteries thundered out, but in three months the Duke of Gordon and his men were forced to capitulate. On being relieved by General Hugh Mackay's small army consisting mainly of Scots troops in the Dutch service, the new regiment of foot was sent to Fife, where it was strengthened by numbers of enthusiastic recruits.

The regiment's baptism of fire came in the Pass of Killiecrankie, near Pitlochry, Perthshire, on July 27, 1689. The Jacobites waited as the Royalist troops toiled up through the wild forest. Then, in the gloaming, the Highlanders stole down from the hills and through the gloom of the pinewoods. The Highland charge was launched, the battle-cries of the clans resounding through the thin clear air of the pass. Lochaber axe, broadsword and claymore quickly made the Royalist ranks a shambles.

General Mackay's cavalry turned and galloped in panic from the field. His infantry had been armed with bayonets—then an innovation—and as they were screwing them into the muzzles of their guns and could not fire the Highlanders burst upon them. The infantry broke up in disorder and the Royalist rout was complete. But the Earl of Leven's Regiment stood firm.

"Bonnie Dundee" had won a brilliant victory, but he did not live to profit by it for he was mortally wounded at the commencement of the battle. After plundering the deserted Royalist camp the Highlanders disappeared into the hills laden with booty.

General Mackay was only able to save part of his force, and retreated to Stirling. He wrote in a despatch that "There was no regiment or troop with me but behaved like the vilest cowards in nature, excepting Hastings' and Lord Leven's."

After the Battle of Killiecrankie the formation was named Leven's, or The Edinburgh Regiment. The Scottish Capital honoured the regiment by granting it the unique privilege of recruiting in the city by beat of drum on any day, except Sunday, without securing permission.

The Edinburgh Regiment was sent to Ireland to take part in operations against the supporters of King James, who had considerable French assistance. With General Mackay's forces the regiment had a prominent role in crushing the Irish Rebellion.

In the summer of 1691 the regiment advanced on Ballymore, which surrendered. Athlone was besieged, and after its capture the regiment took part in the Battle of Aughrim, in July. Here the Irish were routed. Then followed the siege and capitulation of Galway, and the siege of Limerick, where The Edinburgh Regiment sustained heavy casualties.

In the War of the League of Augsburg, The Edinburgh Regiment was engaged in the bloody indecisive fighting at Steenkirk, in 1692, and at Landen, in 1693. At the siege of Namur, in 1695, the shattered regiment gained its first battle-honour. While the regiment was assaulting the demi-bastion of St. Roch an enemy mine exploded killing over 500 officers and other ranks.

At Namur, for the first time, the French used a new type of bayonet. This bayonet did not screw or plug into the musket, and allowed the gun to be fired with the bayonet fixed. As The Edinburgh Regiment braced to meet the expected enemy bayonet charge, it received a crashing volley of fire which temporarily threw its ranks into disorder, but rallying, the angry Scots flew at the French and hurled them back with heavy loss.

On its return from the Continent the regiment was dispatched to Fort George and Fort William to keep a watch on the turbulent Highlands. In November, 1715, at the Battle of Sheriffmuir, The Edinburgh Regiment clashed with the Earl of Mar's Jacobites. Rob Roy with his MacGregors and Mac-Phersons stayed out of the fray. They watched and waited nearby, ready to join in and support the winning party. But their leader could not judge the trend of the inconclusive battle and the clansmen dispersed.

In 1718 the regiment was in Ireland again, and in 1732 successfully defended Gibraltar for several months against the Spanish attacks. In 1736 all private soldiers in the regiment were drafted into Oglethorpe's Regiment from Gibraltar and sent to Georgia. The officers and N.C.O.s of The Edinburgh Regiment raised the formation afresh to a strength of 10 companies in Ireland.

In 1739 the regiment went out to the West Indies. It returned to Flanders in 1743, during the War of the Austrian Succession. The Edinburgh Regiment fought well at Fontenoy, in 1745, and later that year arrived in Scotland to oppose its old enemies, the Jacobite Highlanders, at Culloden, in April, 1746.

The Highlanders broke under the concentrated hail of cannon and rifle fire of the Royalist forces, but their wild charge threw the troops on the left of the Duke of Cumberland's line into confusion. At this crisis The Edinburgh Regiment joined battle, checked the inroads of the clansmen, and forced them back with considerable loss. The Highland charge lacked the impetuosity of the onslaught at Killiecrankie. After the long fighting retreat from Derby, the clansmen were exhausted, half-starved, ill-clad, and lacking in cannon and fire power.

Ordered to Flanders later in the year, The Edinburgh Regiment covered the Allied retreat from Raucoux, and in 1747 it was engaged in the desperate fighting at Val and Bergen-op-Zoom, suffering heavy casualties. Laffeldt was another day of glory for the regiment.

At the close of the War of the Austrian Succession, The Edinburgh Regiment was despatched to Ireland. It embarked at Williamstadt, in the Netherlands, in November, 1748, but, owing to contrary winds, the transports did not reach Harwich until December. In mid-January, 1749, they sailed from Harwich and made the Downs a day later, but were forced to remain there for almost two weeks because of head winds.

The ships sailed again at the end of the month, but were wrecked in a violent gale on the coast of Normandy. The men were saved, marched to Caen, and at Cherbourg embarked for the Isle of Wight. The regiment sailed from there after six weeks, but was driven into Falmouth where it remained for several weeks. The regiment did not reach Kinsale until the end of April.

The formation was styled the 25th, or The Edinburgh Regiment, in 1751. The 25th Foot was included in the force which raided the Isle of Aix in 1757, during the Seven Years'

War. It is one of that select company—The Minden Regiments.

At the Battle of Minden, in Germany, in 1759, The Edinburgh Regiment was one of six British regiments which stood fast under a murderous artillery cross-fire and with bullet and bayonet hurled back several furious charges by 60 French cavalry squadrons, and cut to pieces two enemy brigades of infantry.

While advancing into action the regiments passed through gardens ablaze with bloom, and many of the soldiers plucked roses and wore them in their head-dress throughout the fighting. Their successors cherish the privilege of wearing red roses on August 1 each year—Minden Day—to commemorate this British " tour de force."

There was more hard campaigning ahead for The Edinburgh Regiment, at Warburg and Campen, in 1760, at Vellinghausen, in 1761, and at Wilhelmstal, in 1762. After the Peace of Paris the 25th of Foot returned to the U.K. There followed brisk recruiting and a tour of duty lasting eight years in Minorca, after which the regiment returned to England.

The 25th of Foot was sent to reinforce the hard-pressed garrison at Gibraltar in 1782, and for the second time in its history the regiment helped to save " The Rock " from falling into the hands of French and Spanish forces.

The enemy was confident of success in the final assault, and the attack was witnessed by many of the fashionable people of Paris and Madrid, who arrived in coaches or on horseback, and took up " grandstand " positions on the surrounding hills.

Ten great floating batteries were moved up to bombard the garrison at close range preparatory to the launching of a general assault, after which there were to be victory celebrations. Every one of the batteries was set on fire and sunk by the hail of red-hot shot poured out by the British guns. The enemy abandoned the siege, and their " supporters " on the hills withdrew. The 25th of Foot remained on duty at Gibraltar for ten years, then entered the conflict against Revolutionary France.

In 1782 the formation became The Sussex Regiment, losing its Edinburgh identity until 1805. There are two possible explanations of this " mystery ". It may have been due to the influence of the Duke of Richmond, brother of the commanding officer, Lord George Lennox. The Duke's principal residence was at Goodwood, in Sussex. Or Lord Lennox

may have asked for the change of title himself in a " huff " at the behaviour of the Edinburgh magistrates, who, in contravention of the regiment's ancient privilege, vetoed recruiting in the Scottish capital by a party he had sent up from the South of England.

The regiment arrived at Plymouth in 1792, and in 1793 was required to furnish detachments to serve as Marines. Contingents in this role operated at the siege of Toulon with the St. George and the Egmont, of Admiral Lord Howe's squadron. On Toulon being evacuated, the regiment was included in the invading force which landed on Corsica. It took part in the storming of Convention Redoubt and in the operations round Bastia. The infantry manhandled heavy guns, ammunition and supplies up the steep cliffs, often under fire from the enemy.

The regiment was dispatched with a small expedition to Elba, where it experienced another series of sharp skirmishes with the enemy. In 1795 and 1796 the regiment was represented in naval engagements in the Gulf of Lyons and at the blockade of Toulon.

The detachment with the Egmont returned to Plymouth, but the contingent with the St. George remained until the autumn of 1797, taking part in the blockade of Cadiz, when Spain entered the war. This detachment later also rejoined the regiment.

Other detachments served in Lord Howe's squadron, in the Marlborough, Intrepid, and Gibraltar, and were involved in sharp action off Brest in June, 1794, which ended in the defeat of the French. A ship carrying £1,000,000 was captured, and officers and other ranks of the regiment serving with the Fleet as Marines shared considerable amounts of prize-money. Detachments also served in the North Sea and Mediterranean.

Headquarters at Plymouth had meantime been reinforced, and early in 1795 sailed for the West Indies, arriving at Grenada in April. It was attacked by brigands at Mount Pleasant, but the enemy was driven off with heavy loss. The regiment in turn incurred severe casualties in an assault on a brigand stronghold, but the enemy also suffered heavy losses, and was driven from Pilot Hill.

On February 25, 1795, a second battalion of the regiment was raised at Plymouth, formed in the main by detachments which had been serving as Marines in the Mediterranean, Channel and North Sea, in addition to a number of recruits. In September of the same year,

however, the new battalion was ordered to amalgamate with the 1st Battalion.

On the voyage out to the West Indies the transport conveying it was captured by a French corvette. A plan was laid by Lieutenant Johnstone, of The Sussex Regiment, for the seizing of the ship, but an informer betrayed it, and imprisonment followed on the island of St. Martin. In irons the men of the regiment were later put on board another ship. But their spirit had not been broken by captivity, and they overpowered the crew and ordered the master to navigate the vessel into Grenada, where they joined the regiment.

In 1796 the regiment was at Richmond Hill, Grenada, the only part of the island not in enemy hands. Reinforcements arrived from the Barbadoes and St. Lucia, and the enemy was attacked, suffering a heavy defeat which culminated in surrender. The regiment returned to England in July of that year, remaining on home service until 1799. In August, 1799, it took part in raids on the Dutch coast, distinguishing itself in operations at Egmont-op-Zee. The Sussex Regiment was one of 14 regiments which sent a contingent of picked men to form an experimental Rifle Corps, in 1800. This corps later became the 95th, now The Rifle Brigade.

In the early summer of 1801 The Sussex Regiment was sent out to take part in the siege of Alexandria, which capitulated in September, and Napoleon's forces evacuated Egypt. For its splendid service at Alexandria the regiment was rewarded with the Sphinx superscribed " Egypt " on the Colours.

The Sussex Regiment returned to England via Malta and Gibraltar, then went to Ireland, serving there until 1807. In 1805 the regiment was named The King's Own Borderers, but retained its old number as the 25th of Foot. In 1804 the 2nd Battalion was re-formed, and in 1807 sailed from Cork for the West Indies, where it experienced a tour of duty lasting ten years.

In this campaign against the French, The King's Own Borderers, participated in the capture of Martinique in 1809, and Guadeloupe in 1810. On its return, in 1816, the 2nd Battalion was disbanded. After the French defeat at Waterloo, The King's Own Borderers were engaged on garrison duties in Holland. While serving in South Africa the regiment took part in crushing a Boer rebellion in 1842—operations which led to the British annexing Natal.

After serving in India, The King's Own Borderers returned home in 1854, and a second battalion was again raised. It was formed at Preston, Lancs., in December, 1859. From 1870-75 the 1st Battalion was in Ireland. Back again in India in the Afghan War of 1878-80, the 1st was engaged among the scorched gorges and snows on " The Roof of the World ".

It was included in one of three columns which were sent into Afghanistan when the Amir, Shere Ali—influenced by the Russians—refused to have a British Mission in his capital.

One British column, with the 1st King's Own Borderers, entered the Khyber Pass, and took part in several punitive operations against the hill tribes, experiencing stiff fighting, particularly in the Bazar Valley. The King's Own Borderers secured the lines of communication in spite of the activities of the tribesmen. It was a hard exacting campaign this, against wild, tough hillmen, who fought to a finish and took no prisoners. These fanatics would rush on to the death-spitting British rifles and flashing bayonets believing that such an end would give them immediate entry into Paradise. They found The King's Own Borderers most accommodating.

In 1879 a favourable treaty was concluded with Shere Ali's son, under the terms of which the control of the frontier passes came into British hands. Advanced posts were established and the British troops commenced withdrawing from Afghanistan.

But later that year the British Envoy and his staff were murdered in Kabul, and military operations were at once resumed in answer to this treachery.

The King's Own Borderers advanced up the Khyber and again maintained the lines of communication in spite of sudden enemy raids and almost continual sniping by tribesmen perched on the rocks and crags above. A sharp echoing crack, a puff of smoke, and another man down. A quick rush up the steep slopes by the skirmishers, a fleeting glimpse of a white-clad figure as he escaped—and some hard swearing—then back to the toiling, marching column. A ragged volley from the heights, the whine of bullets, and more men staggering. So it went on high up in the passes . . .

A new and friendly Amir was established in 1880, and the campaign on " The Roof of the World " came to an end. The British columns wheeled and headed for base, leaving thankfully behind the eternal snows, the rushing mountain torrents, and the forbidding rearing masses of the Himalayas.

Then came the 1881 bombshell. In spite of the regiment's Scottish origin, character and traditions, a certain Secretary of State for War decided to re-name it as The York Regiment, King's Own Borderers, with the West York Militia affiliated, and the depot at York.

Scotland had other ideas. A deputation of protesting Scots met the War Secretary. The deputation was unanimous and emphatic, and the result was that the Scottish regiment was sent to Berwick-on-Tweed, but without a Militia battalion.

In 1887, however, a Militia battalion was transferred from The Scottish Borderers Militia (3rd Battalion The Royal Scots Fusiliers)— which drew recruits from the regimental district of the Borderers—and Volunteer Service formations were later added. And in 1887, too, the regiment received the romantic title of The King's Own Scottish Borderers. Another fight had been won !

At the close of 1898 authority was granted for the regiment to adopt the Leslie tartan for the trews in place of the Universal, or Government tartan, issued in 1882. The Earl of Leven had used his influence to secure the family tartan for the Borderers. The pipers wear kilts of the Royal Stewart tartan—their dress since 1805. There is an exception in the case of the 4th (Territorial Army) Battalion. Their pipers wear the " Shepherd's Plaid ".

The regiment had pipers since 1692. In fact, in 1691, the officers tried to detain the town piper of Musselburgh in order to have his services, but on his successful appeal to the Law Courts they had reluctantly to release him.

The privilege of recruiting without permission in Edinburgh was restored in 1888. And The King's Own Scottish Borderers have the additional privilege of marching through the streets of the Scottish Capital with bayonets fixed and colours flying.

In 1832 the old title, The Edinburgh Regiment, was revived and the regimental colour and appointments bore the arms of Edinburgh— the familiar three-turreted castle—and the city motto " Nisi Dominus Frustra ", and another motto, " In Veritate Religionis Confido ". Later that year the London Gazette noted that " In addition to the distinctions formerly granted to the 25th Foot, His Majesty has been pleased to permit the regiment to bear " the white horse " and motto " Nec Aspera Terrent " in the fourth corner of the regimental colour." The white horse was the White Horse of Hanover.

The 2nd Battalion was in Ireland in 1886 assisting the civil power during the eviction troubles. This battalion was in action in Egypt in 1888, distinguishing itself in the fierce fighting at Gemaizah against the fanatical Dervish hordes.

In 1889 the 1st Battalion arrived in Burma from India, and formed part of the punitive force sent against the troublesome Chins and Lushais. After seven months of hard campaigning and a number of clashes with the enemy, the 1st returned to England, its ranks considerably reduced by casualties and sickness.

The 2nd Battalion left Cairo bound for India. War-clouds had gathered again on the North West Frontier, and the battalion was included in the expedition which was rushed to the relief of the garrison at Chitral, besieged in 1895 by the hill tribes led by Umrah Khan. Two British columns pushed forward, and in three weeks the relief was effected. The King's Own Scottish Borderers advanced from Nowshera across the Malakand Pass into the Swat Valley, across the Swat and Panjkhora rivers, then over the Lowarai Pass to join battle at Munda, where the enemy was hammered and Umrah Khan captured.

The first enemy position, along the crest of the Malakand Pass, was very strong, the hillmen occupying a deep series of stone breastworks, each commanding the one below, and affording an excellent field of fire. The Borderers attacked from the valley, and fought their way up for several thousand feet into the mountains under a hail of fire and an avalanche of rocks from above.

Breastwork after breastwork, ledge after ledge, crest after crest was assaulted and carried. A brief pause, then a mad scrambling rush up and on again, the bayonets glinting, and, high over the valley, the enemy was hurled from the final ridge. The hectic pursuit of the fleeing tribesmen was only halted before the large walled village of Khor, on the Swat River, far beneath.

The fast-flowing Swat and Panjkhora rivers were crossed after more sharp fighting, and the hill tribes performed their familiar vanishing trick, disappearing without trace into the fastness of the mountains. The Chitral campaign was over. Silence returned to the passes.

The 2nd King's Own Scottish Borderers were again engaged on the North West Frontier in 1897, during the Tirah Campaign, which was touched off by raids by the hill tribes on British military posts. The route of the punitive expedition lay from Shinawari via the cleft in the Samana Range, at Chagru Kotal, down to the Khanki River, and then to the Sampagha Pass. This was the key to Orakzai Tirah.

A farther advance across the Arhanza Pass gave access to the Afridi Tirah and the rich valley around Maidan. The route then lay via Bagh and the Dwatoi defile to the Bera Valley, by which the column was to return to India before winter set in.

At each of the passes, and around Maidan, there was severe fighting, and a stiff rearguard action had to be fought before the expedition finally got clear of the enemy. In the 23 actions in the Tirah Campaign the Borderers enhanced their reputation for toughness in adversity as well as in success.

That final rearguard action was a triumph for the King's Own Scottish Borderers. The column had just settled down for the night when a howling mass of tribesmen came right at the troops from out of the scrub, firing as they charged. In the failing light the Borderers poured a withering fire into the oncoming horde. The survivors faded away into the gathering darkness, though prowling snipers continued to prove troublesome. The Borderers, in this sharp clash, inflicted the heaviest losses suffered by the tribesmen during the hard-fought campaign in the mountains.

After the Tirah expedition the 2nd Battalion remained in India until 1903, served in Burma until 1905, spent a year at Aden, and returned to Scotland in 1906. From 1898 until 1899 the 1st Battalion was occupied in Ireland. Early in 1900 it went out to South Africa, now in the throes of the Boer War.

The 1st King's Own Scottish Borderers were with the troops sent to establish themselves on Cronje's left flank and cut him off from Bloemfontein. Cronje was forced to retreat from his forward positions on the Modder River at Magersfontein back to Paardeberg, where he was eventually penned in. The battalion was part of the force detached to mop up the Boers in Jacobsdaal who threatened the British flank, and there was some sharp skirmishing before this danger was neutralised. The Borderers were in time to take a leading part in the fighting at Paardeberg early in February, 1900, as a result of which some 4,000 Boers surrendered. The Borderers then took part in the advance on Bloemfontein.

At Karee the Boers on hilly ground barred the way to Pretoria. Cavalry and mounted infantry moved out on each flank, the Borderers attacking in the centre. They came under a heavy well-directed fire and took cover until reinforced. Then, after several hours of stiff fighting the Boers retreated, and the march on Pretoria was resumed.

For the best part of two years the Borderers were engaged in the hard fighting and marching in the mobile guerilla war against the wily, elusive De Wet in the hills to the west of Pretoria. At the end of May, 1901, there was a sharp engagement at Vlakfontein. After operating on this barren terrain, a British column—including the Borderers—on its way back to camp, encountered a veldt fire. Suddenly, from out of the swirling smoke, charged several hundred Boer horsemen, supported by a hail of rifle fire from another strong force of the enemy.

In a few minutes two British guns were captured and turned on the column, and the rearguard was thrown into confusion. The Borderers dashed into the melee, re-capturing the guns and driving back the enemy. The Boers quickly retired, using the dense smoke to cover their escape. In this brisk action the Volunteer Service Company (later Territorials) shared the honours with the Regular battalion. A highlight of the Borderers' service in South Africa was the winning of the Victoria Cross at Lambrecht Fontein by Lieutenant Coulson, of the 1st Battalion.

In the campaign in South Africa companies from the 4th and 5th Volunteer Battalions, and the Militia (later Special Reserve) Battalion also served with distinction. The 1st King's Own Scottish Borderers served in Ireland from 1903 until 1905, and from 1910 to 1914 the 2nd Battalion served in that country. The 2nd Battalion in July 1914, was involved in the gun-running incident at Howth, and while returning to barracks the Borderers were compelled to fire on a hostile crowd near O'Connell Bridge, Dublin, causing a number of casualties.

Battle-honours granted to the regiment were: The Sphinx superscribed " Egypt ", Namur, 1695, Minden, Egmont-op-Zee, Martinique 1809, Afghanistan, 1878-80, Chitral, Tirah. For its services during the Boer War the honours Paardeberg, South Africa, 1900-02, were added.

From 1904 to 1913 the 1st Battalion was overseas, serving in Egypt and India. It went to Egypt to defend the Suez Canal in 1914, but returned to the U.K. early in 1915. Forming part of the 87th Brigade, 29th Division, the 1st Borderers landed on Gallipoli, at " Y " Beach, in April, 1915. The steep cliffs were quickly scaled, then all progress was halted by

a concentrated fire. Isolated, and without artillery support, the decimated battalion fought hard to maintain its position, but suffered such appalling casualties that it was ordered to withdraw at night.

The survivors disembarked a little to the south and joined in a further desperate battle to secure landing room for the remainder of the Mediterranean Expeditionary Force. There was more strenuous fighting around Gully Ravine, and the Borderers were among the last troops to leave that peninsula of privation, disease and death on the subsequent evacuation. The ill-fated 29th Division, with the gravely depleted 1st King's Own Scottish Borderers, was dispatched to France in March, 1916.

The battalion was soon engaged on the Somme, at Beaumont Hamel, Ancre, and Bapaume; it was involved in further grim fighting at Arras, and at the Third Battle of Ypres, and Cambrai, in 1917; then on the Lys, and at the last Battle of Ypres, in 1918.

The 2nd Battalion, with the British Expeditionary Force, reached Belgium in mid-August, 1914, and went into battle at Mons. There was stiff fighting at St. Ghislain, where the Borderers poured a withering fire into the advancing Germans. Another bitter clash followed at Wasmes, and the field-grey hordes were beaten back with heavy loss. The exhausted troops took up positions at Le Cateau on August 26, after fighting and marching for over a week. Here the 2nd Battalion, on the British right flank, took the full force of another powerful German attack.

The bearing of the Borderers at Le Cateau and Crepy helped to stem and turn the German tidal wave advance, and on September 6 the enemy was fought back from the Marne to the Aisne, the 2nd Borderers overcoming stubborn German resistance at St. Cyr. Soon the enemy was retiring on his final and strongest defence system, which became known as the Hindenburg Line.

The 2nd Battalion was heavily engaged at the First Battle of Ypres, at Messines Ridge and Hill 60, and in April, 1915, entered the Second Battle of Ypres. On the Somme, in July, 1916, the Borderers were in the thick of the fighting, suffering heavy casualties at High Wood and at Morval. Another Borderers' highlight was the capture of Vimy Ridge, in 1917.

The 2nd Battalion of the Borderers was sent to Italy in December, 1917, when Italian morale showed signs of cracking, but it returned to France in time to participate in the final battles of 1918, on the Lys, Bapaume, the Hindenburg Line, and Maubeuge.

Attacking in the long waves of the victorious Allied offensive, the Borderers saw the toils of vengeance close on the German Army, reducing it to a weary, starved, sleepless, dirty, unkempt rabble. Then came the inevitable collapse— and the Borderers were in at the " kill ".

In the war of 1914-18, twelve battalions of The King's Own Scottish Borderers answered duty's call. Seven served overseas, and 6,859 officers and other ranks gave their lives.

The 4th and 5th Territorial Battalions served with the 52nd (Lowland) Division in Gallipoli, Egypt, Palestine, and France. The 6th, 7th, and 8th—all Service battalions—also saw much active service. The 6th fought in the 9th (Scottish) Division on the Western Front, while the 7th and 8th were also in this theatre of war, with the 15th (Scottish) Division. The Reserve battalions of the regiment were in time to enter the final 1918 onslaught against the tottering German Colossus.

Four Borderers were awarded the Victoria Cross—Company Sergeant-Major J. Skinner, Company Quartermaster-Sergeant W. H. Grimbaldeston, Sergeant L. McGuffie, and Piper D. Laidlaw.

Company Sergeant-Major Skinner, of the 1st Battalion, who, in 1914, had been awarded the D.C.M. for gallantry at Neuve Chapelle, bombed three blockhouses and captured 60 prisoners, three machine-guns, and two trench-mortars at Wijdendrift, Belgium, in September, 1917. Sergeant-Major Skinner—who had been wounded on eight occasions—fell to a sniper's bullet in March, 1918. C.Q.M.S. Grimbaldeston's exploit was somewhat similar. With the aid of a private he bombed a blockhouse and took 36 prisoners, six machine-guns, and six trench-mortars. This was another epic of the bitter fighting at Wijdendrift.

Sergeant Lewis McGuffie, a Wigtown man serving with the 8th Battalion, earned his Victoria Cross at Wytschaete, Belgium. Leading a platoon, he captured several dugouts and over a dozen prisoners. His single-handed attack on a German escort guarding a party of British prisoners quickly effected their release. Sergeant McGuffie was killed in October, 1918, before the award for his heroism a few months previously was announced.

The outstanding courage and daring of Piper Daniel Laidlaw at Loos and Hill 70, in November, 1915, captures the imagination. In full view of the Germans, and under heavy

fire, he got up on the parapet of a trench to rally his battalion with the stirring notes of the Regimental March " Blue Bonnets O'er The Border ".

Dazed by gas and numbed by the tremendous enemy artillery barrage and the thunder of the British guns, the 7th Battalion had been slow to leave the trenches, but with the pipes skirling amid the din of battle, the Borderers scrambled over the top and rushed into a storm of shot and shell to get at the Huns.

Piper Laidlaw was hit, but in spite of his wound he limped forward with the charging battalion.

Two veterans of the Borderers who rejoined in 1914 were Pipe-Majors John Balloch and Robert Mackenzie, who were recruits 'way back in the eighties. Pipe-Major Balloch was the composer of several famous pipe tunes. Sixty-year old Pipe-Major Mackenzie fell at Loos after his name had been " put up " for the D.C.M. Such is the calibre of the Borderers . . .

Principal battle-honours awarded to the regiment for over four years' devoted service in the 1914-18 holocaust were:—Mons, Aisne, 1914, Ypres, 1914, '15, '17, '18, Loos, Somme, 1916, '18, Arras, 1917, '18, Soissons-Ourcq, Hindenburg Line, Gallipoli, 1915, '16, Gaza.

The 1st Battalion spent the winter of 1918-19 in Germany, and then went overseas, serving in India, Egypt, and Chanak. In 1923 it returned home for a spell, after which it arrived in Malta, and later served in Palestine. The 1st Battalion returned to the U.K. in 1936, and was at Portsmouth when war broke out in September, 1939.

The 2nd Battalion, after reorganisation at Dunfermline in 1919, left for a period of duty in Ireland. It left Devonport in 1923 for Egypt, and was off to Hong Kong in 1926. The battalion arrived in India in 1930, and was stationed in the Central Provinces at the outbreak of World War II.

Including the 1st and 2nd (Regular) Battalions, eight battalions of The King's Own Scottish Borderers served during World War II, six of them being committed to battle. The battalions, in addition to the Regular Army formations, were:—4th (Border) Battalion; 5th (Dumfries and Galloway) Battalion; 6th (Border) Battalion; 7th (Galloway) Battalion; 8th (Home Defence) Battalion; and the 9th Battalion. There were also, of course, several Home Guard battalions formed by the Territorial Army Association. The 9th, formed in 1940, was fully trained, but was stationed in the U.K.

On October 3, 1939, the 1st Battalion sailed from Southampton, disembarking at Cherbourg the following day. On the 16th the Borderers were in defensive positions at Fretin, near Lille, remaining in this area for over six months as part of the 9th Brigade, 3rd Division. This division was commanded by the redoubtable " Monty "—then Major-General B. L. Montgomery—who dubbed the 9th " The International Brigade ", as it contained Scottish, English and Irish regiments.

The Galloway and Dumfries men of the 5th (Territorial) Battalion, guarding points on the north and south shores of the Forth, near the bridge, " stole the show ", on October 16, 1939—the date on which the German Air Force launched its first raid on the U.K. The attack was directed at the cruisers Southampton and Edinburgh, anchored off South Queensferry. The Borderers quickly formed a " reception committee " and met the enemy raiders with a hail of fire. The Territorial fighting men of the Borderers serving in the 52nd (Lowland) Division, formed a light company which was included in the British force sent to Norway after the German invasion in April, 1940. The Borderers served creditably in the short Norwegian campaign, and had a foretaste of the desperate fighting yet to come.

When the Nazis invaded Holland and Belgium the 1st King's Own Scottish Borderers moved forward to the line of the River Dyle, near Louvain, taking over from units of the Belgian Army, but before fighting contact could be made with the enemy, came orders to withdraw from burning Louvain to an area west of Brussels. The bridges were blown behind them to impede the oncoming Germans.

The Borderers took up defensive positions along the banks of the River Dendre, near Alost. A few battered British tanks rumbled over the bridges, which were quickly blown, and after a clash with the German infantry which kept them from crossing the river, the Borderers retired to the River Escaut, near Oudenarde, with the roads almost blocked by a press of military traffic and thousands of refugees fleeing before the Germans. The Borderers on the west bank took up station south of Avelghem, then another retiral order came through which sent them back to Tourcoing.

Here the Borderers suffered severely from artillery fire. The fighting withdrawal continued, the depleted battalion moving through

Ypres to the River Yser, then falling back to the line of the Bergues-Furnes Canal under continuous shelling. By their unflinching series of costly stands against greater numbers and superior fire-power, the Borderers gained valuable time for other units of the shattered British Expeditionary Force, and French and Belgian formations to retire to the coast and be successfully evacuated.

The 1st Borderers marched and fought in unequal combat, practically without rest, from their first encounter with the Nazis, near Louvain, until the final clash on the Bergues-Furnes Canal, some three weeks later. From their last defensive perimeter at Bulscamp Bridge the battle-weary exhausted remnant of the 1st Battalion trooped on to the beaches at La Panne, and under artillery fire, trudged for some six miles across the soft sands to Bray-Dunes.

The night was dark, but the distant rumble of explosions and the lurid red glow in the sky over Dunkirk, ten miles away, guided them. The turn of the Borderers had come. They joined the long winding evacuation queues of the shattered British Expeditionary Force. Enemy aircraft zoomed in low to machine-gun the helpless troops straggling with their wounded and dying across the shell-pitted bomb-pocked beaches without any means to hit back.

But there were Borderers in France after Dunkirk. The 4th and 5th Battalions of the 155th Brigade, 52nd (Lowland) Division, crossed from Southampton to land at St. Malo on June 13. This move was made to hearten the French and retain a foothold for the operations of the 2nd British Expeditionary Force.

With tidings of disaster on every side, the 155th Brigade nevertheless pushed rapidly forward to the Seine, and reaching Domfort the Borderers heard the boom of guns and the crash of bombs and shells. Then, the military situation on the Continent being considered hopeless, the order was given on June 15 to retire on Cherbourg—over 160 miles away—for evacuation.

The 155th Brigade—with the 5th Borderers as rearguard—retired along roads cluttered up with a press of motor and horse-drawn traffic and thousands of refugees fleeing before the advance of the triumphant Wehrmacht. A series of hectic tussles developed, particularly at La Sensuriere and Carentan, and, with the co-operation of the French, a number of casualties was inflicted on the enemy.

The evacuation was successfully accomplished on June 18 while the town rocked with the extensive demolitions at the docks. Burning stores and equipment, and blazing abandoned vehicles added to the dense smoke pall which lay over Cherbourg. Then enemy planes came over to add to the scene of destruction.

The 52nd (Lowland) Division was the last organised British fighting force to leave French soil—and the men of the 5th King's Own Scottish Borderers were the last out. Two small parties of the battalion, with some wounded, who were cut off at Carentan by the German advance, "missed the boat" at Cherbourg. With French assistance, they succeeded in making their escape in two small craft, one of which was leaking. Both parties were picked up several hours later by ships bound for ports in the South of England, and the Borderers rejoined their battalion in East Anglia. Four years of rigorous hardening training with new weapons were to elapse before the Scots again crossed bayonets with the Germans.

From Razmak, Waziristan, on the North West Frontier, the 2nd Battalion The King's Own Scottish Borderers, brigaded with the 1st Battalion The Queen's Royal Regiment and the 1st Battalion The Somerset Light Infantry, took part in the relief of a beleagured garrison at Dhatta Khel in the summer of 1942. Over two weeks elapsed before the toiling column, averaging 15 miles a day, reached the hard-pressed garrison. The tribesmen on the heights harried the relieving force between Razmak and Gardai, but casualties were not heavy.

In November the 2nd Battalion, with the 4/8th Ghurka Rifles and the 7/6th Punjab Regiment, formed the 89th Brigade of the 7th Indian Division—the " Golden Arrow " Division. There was hard training in some of the roughest country on the Frontier, and later jungle-fighting techinque was perfected in the Central Provinces. In August, 1943, an advance party left for the Arakan Front, Burma.

With the 14th Army the Borderers fought hard and well in the severe campaigning through the scorched scrub, squelching paddy fields, steamy slimy swamps and rivers, dense jungles, and arid mountains of Burma from 1943 until 1945. Their dash in attack and tenacity in defence exploded the myth of the Japanese " super-men ". Properly trained and equipped, and acclimatised for operations in this theatre of war, the Borderers soon had the Japs in their gun-sights and did great execution among

Emperor Hirohito's troops, led by their fanatical sword-waving officers.

In October, 1943, the Borderers took over positions about 15 miles south of Bawli Bazaar, facing the Japanese-held Mayu Hills. First clash with the enemy came a few days later, near the village of Maungdaw. Here a small party of Borderers engaged a detachment of the Japanese Imperial Guard, inflicting a number of casualties before being separated. Several Borderers were killed in the fray, but the remainder made their way back to the battalion.

There were several skirmishes on Horseshoe Hill, where the Japanese announced their presence by planting their Rising Sun flag, but, fearing for its safety, the enemy soon removed it. In mid-January, 1944, the Borderers attacked the steep jungle-covered Able Hill at night. The battalion had a number of casualties, which were unfortunately added to when their supporting artillery mistook them for Japs and opened fire.

In February the battalion advanced towards Taung, meeting with stiff opposition. The Borderers were ordered to proceed to the assistance of an Indian artillery regiment which was threatened with isolation at Allwyn-bin. The battalion had to retrace its steps and risked annihilation by going through a bottle-necked defile held by the enemy. But stealing through the night mists the Borderers linked up with the Indian gunners.

The area was soon surrounded by the enemy, and all supplies had to be dropped from air-craft. At night the Japs, wearing masks, and many of them hooded, crept through the long grass, signalling to each other with animal calls. But, running into heavy fire, their attacks were quickly broken up. The Japanese overran positions near a dressing station, and vented their spleen by massacring the sick and wounded.

The situation improved in this sector, and breaking out of the Jap-surrounded " box " after 18 days of desperate fighting, the Borderers attacked Ngakyedauk Pass—" Okeydoke Pass " to the troops. Their last action on this front was the assault on Massive, a prominent hill feature, but on reaching the summit the Borderers discovered the enemy had fled. In April the Maungdaw-Buthidaung area was clear of the enemy. The Japanese grip on the Arakan was broken.

Early in May the 2nd Battalion flew into Imphal, and landed under fire from the enemy artillery, for the garrison here had been isolated for a month. The Borderers had been ordered

with their brigade to Kohima, but bad weather necessitated this change of destination. The 89th Brigade now came under command of the 5th Indian Division.

The Borderers were in the force which made the assault on Kanglatongbi Ridge, and with pipes skirling the battalion went storming into the attack through torrential rain. There was prolonged, stubborn, and indecisive fighting among well-constructed and strongly-held enemy positions, but the Scots pushed on uphill into a murderous fire. Then, after an all-out effort, they took the ridge. Kanglatongbi was in the safe keeping of the Borderers.

The battalion's fighting reputation was now well established, and the Borderers were given another hill feature to attack—The Hump, or Humpum. Casualties were again high, but the enemy had had enough and evacuated the position. The Japanese commenced their disastrous retreat to the east and south, and the Borderers took up the pursuit into the hills which became the graveyard of the Emperor's shattered disease-ridden army.

Early in July the 2nd Battalion moved eastwards to cross rugged mountainous terrain in torrential monsoon downpours. An attack was launched on Ukhrul Fort, and meeting determined resistance, the Borderers dug in behind Fort Hill, where they hurled back the enemy counter-blow with heavy loss. The enemy pulled out, evacuating Ukhrul, with the Borderers at their heels. There was brisk skirmishing on the way to Humpum and Finch's Corner, but the Japanese continued to withdraw eastwards to the Chindwin.

At the end of July the Borderers arrived at Nerhima, in the Kohima area. Here the exhausted depleted battalion was rested, re-inforced and reorganised for the decisive battles of 1945. Fighting fit again, the Borderers moved out in late December.

After marching about 170 miles, the Borderers engaged the enemy at Yozayat, within sight of the Irrawaddy, at the end of January, 1945. The battalion was now the southern spearhead of the 14th Army, and had made the first contacts with the Japanese. The Borderers cleared the Japs from the road to Pakokku early in February.

With the " Golden Arrow " 7th Indian Division, the 2nd Battalion took part in the assault crossing of the Irrawaddy at Nyaungu, an operation which succeeded in turning the Irrawaddy line. The Borderers were next in action in the attack on Nakyo-Aing, with tank support.

By another feat of marching in mid-April the Borderers surprised the Japs at Salin, and the enemy retired into the hills. The Japs were again thrown into confusion at Sagu, and there was a fierce local engagement at Padein, on the Prome road. Then news came through that Rangoon and Prome had fallen on May 2. About the middle of that month, during the monsoon deluge, there were spirited tussles at Nathe and Kama.

Towards the end of May the Borderers took up positions stretching for over three miles along the Prome road to plug an enemy escape route. Several hundred fleeing Japs were literally hosed with fire in this " killing ground ". The battalion fired its last shots in these encounters, and at the end of July the Borderers moved to Prome and then to Rangoon. Early in August the battalion sailed for Calcutta and later took over at Peshawar, at the entrance to the Khyber Pass.

From the initial assault on D-Day, June 6, 1944, until the cease fire order, on May 5, 1945, the 1st Battalion The King's Own Scottish Borderers was in the thick of the fighting. Under intense shelling the 1st Battalion, coming up from the Normandy beaches, dug in at the village of Le Mesnil. The Borderers attacked into Cambes Wood, and, surviving the ordeal of fire at Caen early in July, they advanced through concentrated shelling to Troarn, encountering stubborn opposition. Then on to the ruins of Vire, and another attack went in. The Borderers pushed the enemy before them across Normandy, fighting hard and suffering severely from the lashing German fire.

In August and September the 1st Battalion crossed a number of water barriers, advancing always towards the Rhine. The Borderers forded the Seine, then crossed the Albert Canal and Meuse-Escaut Canal, east of Gheel. The advance rolled on over the 1914-18 battlefields to Louvain, scene of the disastrous clashes of 1940, and from Achel, on the Belgian-Dutch border, the 1st Battalion entered Holland.

In October there was a stiff action to the west of Venraij, where the Borderers cleared the woods then went to hold a stretch of the damp sandy line at Smakt, near the River Maas. There was gruelling work for the 3rd Division at Overloon, and between the Mass and the Rhine several desperate clashes were fought out, particularly on the road to Weeze, at Winnekendonk and Bruch. So defeat came to the Germans on the west bank of the Rhine—and " Monty's " prophecy came true.

The 1st Battalion crossed the Rhine at Rees, on March 27, 1945, and pursued the enemy to Bocholt. There was a strenuous fight at Bramsche, near Lingen, and, at Wildeshausen Station, the Borderers encountered attacking formations from the 1st Parachute Army. There was much close fighting before the enemy finally gave way.

On April 24 the Scots, behind their pipers, marched on Brinkum, to enter the battalion's final action of the war—the assault and capture of Bremen. The 1st Battalion then served in the Middle East. With the 3rd Division in Palestine the Borderers operated in maintaining order during the racial and Mandate strife, which raged from 1945 until 1948. The Borderers later arrived in Hong Kong for a period of duty.

The 4th and 5th (Territorial) Battalions served with the 52nd (Lowland) Division throughout World War II. This division, though trained for a mountain warfare role, successfully assaulted low-lying Walcheren and freed the vital port of Antwerp. The 52nd hammered a way through Belgium and Holland, making assault crossings of the various river and canal obstacles to penetrate deep into the Reich. The Lowland Division ended its victorious advance by taking part in the capture of Bremen.

The 6th (Territorial) Battalion, with the 15th (Scottish) Division, landed on D-Day, and was soon committed to the fighting along the River Odon. The battalion later fought through the bocage of Normandy into Belgium and Holland, then attacked across the Rhine. The 6th Battalion's *piece de resistance* was its role in the dramatic capture of Bremen in the closing hours of the war. The 7th (Territorial) Battalion, in the 1st Airborne Division, put up a magnificent fight at Arnhem, where it sustained heavy casualties.

The following battle-honours were awarded to the regiment:—Dunkirk, 1940; Cambes, Odon, Cheux, Defence of Rauray, Caen, Esquay, Troarn, Mont Pincon, Estry, Aart, Nederijn, Arnhem, 1944; Best, Scheldt, Flushing, Venraij, Meijel, Venlo Pocket, Roer, Rhineland, Reichswald, Cleve, Goch, Rhine, Ibbenburen, Lingen, Dreirwalde, Uelzen, Bremen, Artlenberg; North West Europe, 1940 and 1944-45; North Arakan, Buthidaung, Ngakyedauk Pass, Imphal, Kanglatongbi, Ukhrul, Meiktila, Irrawaddy, Kama; Burma, 1943 and 1945.

The 1st Battalion was engaged in the Korean War, which began in June, 1950. The Borderers landed in Inchon, in April, 1951, and moved to a defensive position some 150 miles north-east of Seoul. The unit's arrival coincided with the opening of a big Communist offensive, and the next few days were spent in a withdrawal to conform with the general southward movement of the Eighth Army, over steep hills practically devoid of tracks.

On May 20th, it carried out an advance in heavy rain and low mist and soon encountered stiff resistance, but after heavy fighting captured a high precipitous feature which had been strongly defended. After four months of activity, with unexpected and ever-changing situations—during which time the battalion joined the 1st Commonwealth Division—active patrolling forced the enemy back some 10,000 yards north of the River Imjin, and in September a bridgehead was established and held.

On October 3 the battalion launched an attack on Long Hill and Point 355. The latter feature dominated the surrounding country of steep hills of rock and sandstone for the most part covered with dense pine forests rising from muddy paddy-fields. The enemy defence was fanatical and tenacious,

and there was ferocious hand-to-hand fighting. Eventually Point 355 was scaled, and the enemy hurled from it. A battalion of Australian infantry fought a very gallant action alongside the Borderers and captured Point 317.

There followed a month of great activity, and then, on November 4 at 4 a.m., the enemy's shelling increased in intensity on the positions held by the three forward companies of the battalion. By 4 p.m. the volume of the bombardment had reached some 6,000 shells an hour, and shortly afterwards the enemy attacked in greatly superior numbers. They came forward in waves in their hundreds regardless of the defensive fire and their own bombardment, and by 10 p.m., in spite of terrible losses and bitter hand-to-hand fighting, the enemy succeeded in over-running the three forward companies, who fought their way back to other positions.

One company commander ordered his men to take cover while he called on the artillery to bring down defensive fire on the position for twenty minutes to clear it of the milling masses of the enemy. By 2 a.m. on November 5 the attack had petered out, and dawn found the Borderers still firmly established.

EDINBURGH CASTLE—The Birthplace of the Edinburgh or Lord Leven's Regiment now known as the XXX, or The King's Own Scottish Borderers

It was in this desperate battle that "Big Bill" Speakman, a Black Watch giant of 6 ft. 7½ in., attached to the Borderers, won his Victoria Cross. Private Speakman flung back wave after wave of the enemy with showers of grenades. "Big Bill" was later transferred to the Borderers.

During the next four winter months there were no operations of importance in the battalion sector. Only one more attack was delivered on the unit in April, 1952, which was successfully repulsed, and the remainder of the battalion's time in Korea was comparatively uneventful. On August 1, 1952—Minden Day—the battalion took leave of the Commonwealth Division and embarked on August 12 for Hong Kong.

Battle-honours awarded to The King's Own Scottish Borderers for service in Korea were:—Kowang-San, Maryang-San, Korea, 1951-52. Kowang-San includes the desperate Point 355 action, and Maryang-San the bitter engagement for Point 317. Kowang-San and Korea, 1951-52 are emblazoned on the Colours.

At the close of 1955 the 1st Battalion arrived in Malaya to deal with the Communist terrorists. Three companies and a tactical H.Q. operated with a Ghurka brigade in South Johore mainly against the self-styled "4th Regiment of the Communist Malayan Races Liberation Army".

Two years later the battalion was reunited, and, with another Ghurka brigade, served in Central Johore. It was largely due to the efforts of the Borderers that the Yong Peng area in Johore was declared "white"—terrorist activity there having ceased.

Fresh from their successes in Malaya, the 1st Battalion sailed from Singapore to arrive in the U.K. in mid-October, 1958. After being inspected at Berwick-on-Tweed on February 7, 1959, by their Colonel-in-Chief, H.R.H. The Duchess of Gloucester—herself a Borderer and a "bold Buccleuch"—the 1st "trooped" again. The battalion left for Germany on another tour of duty.

In 1947 the War Office announced that all second battalions of Infantry of the Line—except those of the Guards—were to be disbanded. Thus the 1st Battalion became custodian of the many proud achievements and trophies of the 2nd Battalion. The glorious record of the 2nd Battalion The King's Own Scottish Borderers is in safe keeping.

Photograph by courtesy of Kemsley Picture Service

HIS MAJESTY KING GUSTAV OF SWEDEN

COLONEL-IN-CHIEF—THE CAMERONIANS (SCOTTISH RIFLES)

The Cameronians

(SCOTTISH RIFLES)

ONLY one regiment in the British Army has a religious foundation. It is The Cameronians—Scotland's only Rifle Regiment. The name " Cameronians " was given to the most militant of the Presbyterian sects, who upheld the principles of the National Covenant, signed in Greyfriars Churchyard, Edinburgh, on February 28, 1638—in the reign of Charles I. The Covenant sought to prevent any encroachment on the Presbyterian faith, and the Cameronians refused to compromise in any way with a Government bent on imposing the religion of its rulers on a people who claimed it as their inalienable right to worship as their conscience dictated.

The Cameronians—also known as the Mountain Men, the Hill Men, the United Societies, the " Wanderers ", and " The Phanaticks "—were devout Presbyterians, who at first protested their loyalty to the King, but they were regarded with suspicion and disfavour by the later Stewart monarchs. A grave situation arose on the accession of Charles II, in 1660. The Covenanters had to hold their religious meetings in secret, as the King virtually outlawed them in attempting to impose Episcopacy by force on the whole of Scotland. Covenanters and Cameronians met on hillsides, a Bible in one hand, and sword and musket lying nearby in case of attack by the " bluidy dragoons."

These hillside conventicles were harried and butchered by the King's troops. Supporters of the Covenant who took up arms were defeated at Rullion Green, in the Pentland Hills, in 1666. Many excesses were committed by the Royalists. A number of the prisoners were tortured before being hanged or executed.

On a Sunday morning in May, 1679, a conventicle assembled on Loudon Hill, near the borders of Ayrshire and Lanarkshire, was warned of the approach of the King's troops led by John Graham of Claverhouse, a ruthless oppressor of the Covenanters. Battle was given at Drumclog, and the Royalists were routed. But later that year, at Bothwell Brig, near Hamilton, the Covenanters again knew the bitterness of defeat. Here they clashed with a force led by the Duke of Monmouth, a son of the King. And once more atrocities were committed against the helpless prisoners and wounded.

Driven to desperation by the expulsion of their ministers from church and home, the Cameronians approved the act of two of their leaders—Richard Cameron, a licensed preacher, of Falkland, Fife, and Donald Cargill—who, with a small body of men, entered Sanquhar, Dumfriesshire, in 1680, and affixed a document to the town cross. This disowned Charles II as King, and declared war on him because he had broken the Covenant. Persecution of the Covenanters increased, and many of them became hunted men with a price on their heads.

In July, 1680, a few weeks after the Sanquhar Declaration, a band of Covenanters met at Auchinleck, Ayrshire. Troops were sighted approaching, and the Covenanters, though outnumbered, engaged the much better-equipped Royalists. In this battle at Aird's Moss Richard Cameron was slain. His head and hands were cut off and taken to Edinburgh for display in public places.

Thousands of Covenanters were killed in battle or massacre, on the gallows, under the executioner's axe, or in torture chambers. Close on 2,000 were transported overseas to work as plantation slaves, and as many more were flung into prison without trial. The martyring of Richard Cameron, and scores of others, did not quench the fierce flame of revolt in Scotland. Defenders of the Protestant faith arose ready to fight to the death for their religious beliefs. They sprang from the blood and inspiration of Richard Cameron, Lion of the Covenant, and his fellow martyrs. These men rejoiced in the name " Cameronians ".

Their day came when the Protestant William, Prince of Orange, was welcomed to the throne in November, 1688. James VII fled the country, and Presbyterianism was confirmed as the national religion of Scotland. The Convention of Estates met in Edinburgh on March 14, 1689. The Cameronians sent a delegation, and with it went 500 armed men, mainly from the Covenanting counties of the West and South-West.

While the Estates deliberated, the Cameronians blockaded the approaches to Edinburgh Castle, then held by the Duke of Gordon, and they also immobilised John Graham of Claverhouse—Viscount Dundee—who wished to join forces with the Duke in support of the deposed King James VII. A week later the Convention of Estates dispensed with the services of the Cameronians, as they considered the crisis was past. The Cameronians returned to their homes, refusing any reward. But many of the Covenanter and Cameronian veterans had other views about the danger being over.

Later that year it was proposed to enlist Covenanters to serve the new King, and the Estates gave this its blessing. The Covenanters assembled in Douglas Parish Kirk, Douglas, Lanarkshire—the heart of the Covenanting country. At first there was considerable disagreement, but impassioned speeches by Alexander Shields, a famous hillside preacher, and William Cleland, who had fought at Drumclog and Bothwell Brig, brought unity, and it was decided " in this juncture of affairs when religion, liberty, country, and all were in danger " to raise a regiment.

On May 16, 1689, The Cameronian Regiment, with a strength of 1,200 men, forming 20 companies, and organised in two battalions, was raised at Douglas Dale " in one day on the instant without beat of drums and without levy money ". A declaration was read out and explained to the muster.

" All shall be well affected, of approved fidelity and of a sober conversation. The cause they are called to appear for is, the service of the King's Majesty in the defence of the nation, recovery and preservation of the Protestant religion; and in particular the work of reformation in Scotland in opposition to Popery, prelacy, and arbitrary power in all its branches and steps, until the government of Church and State be brought back to that lustre and integrity which it had in the best times."

Thus there came into being a regiment that was as much a congregation as a military force. Each company had its elder, and every man carried a Bible. The first Colonel was the 18-year old James, Earl of Angus, son of the Marquis of Douglas. Tenants on his father's estates were prominent at the original muster of the regiment. The Lieutenant-Colonel was William Cleland, then under 30, who, as a youth had clashed with the hated redcoats.

Later the regiment was numbered the 26th. The new formation was for a time also known as The Lord Angus Regiment. The links with the Covenanters, Lanarkshire, and the Douglas family have never been broken. The Black Hackle and black buttons suggest Puritan origin. In the depot at Lanark there is a Cameronians' Kirk. The connection with the Douglases is maintained in the centrepiece of the thistle-fringed badge, which shows the mullet, or spur-rowel device of this family surmounting the bugle emblem of the 90th Regiment, or The Perthshire Volunteers (Light Infantry), which became the 2nd Battalion The Cameronians in 1881. And The Cameronians wear trews of the Douglas tartan—the tartan of the Earl of Angus.

The Cameronians still post sentinels at church parades. The sermon does not commence until an officer notifies the minister " All Clear ! ". So the regiment remembers days when the Covenanters dared the wrath of their persecutors by attending the forbidden hillside conventicles and posted sentries at vantage points to give warning of the Dragoons.

The Cameronians marched to Stirling, where they were armed and equipped. Then they were ordered to move on Dunkeld. Here three troops of Dragoons had mutinied and abandoned their positions. At Dunkeld the 1,200 Cameronians were attacked by 5,000 of General Cannon's Highlanders, who supported the exiled James VII. There was bitter house-to-house fighting as the Highlanders swept into the small town, and Lieutenant-Colonel Cleland was killed.

The Cameronians had to retire to the Cathedral and the adjoining residence of the Marquis of Atholl. At a critical stage in the battle they ran out of bullets. The fight went on while a party of Cameronians stripped lead from the roofs of the Cathedral and the mansion house, melted it down, and ran it into moulds on the ground to make ammunition for their muskets.

The Jacobites got into a number of houses, and, firing from the windows, caused heavy losses among The Cameronians. With burning faggots at the end of their pikes, The Cameronians rushed at these enemy-occupied houses, set fire to them, and locked the doors. The fighting went on for over four hours. The defenders were now sadly depleted and their powder was running low, but the survivors quoted the Scriptures and battled on against superior numbers and inflicted severe casualties on the Jacobites.

The Cameronians were preparing to make a last desperate stand when the Highlanders gave up and withdrew into the hills. As they saw their enemies retire, the exhausted Cameronians

UNIFORMS

of the

Scottish Regiments

THE SCOTS GUARDS, 1792

*From a contemporary print from drawings
by E. Dayes, draughtsman to the Duke of York.*

The 3rd Regiment of Foot Guards was
raised first in 1642 and was later to be the nucleus
of the Foot Guards of Charles II at his restoration.
The uniform of the guardsmen has never been
Scottish in character but is basically that of the
other regiments of Guards with regimental
differences. The Scots Guards pipers however
wear the highland dress.

Above

25th REGIMENT (K.O.S.B.) c. 1843

From a contemporary print of a drawing by M. A. Hayes. Raised in Edinburgh in 1689, the 25th wore the same uniform as other regiments of the line until after the 1881 reorganisations. In this picture the Grenadier Company are shown wearing bearskin caps.

42nd, 79th and 92nd HIGHLANDERS, 1815

This illustration of Black Watch, Cameron and Gordon Highlanders is from a series of prints produced by French artists during the occupation of Paris after Waterloo, which are among the most valuable costume documents of the period.

ROYAL SCOTS FUSILIERS

THE ROYAL SCOTS GREYS, 1813

From a contemporary print.

Scotland's only regular cavalry regiment were known at this time as the Royal North British Dragoons, and were dressed and equipped as other British Cavalry, except for the distinction of being the only cavalry regiment to wear a bearskin cap. The larger figure is in review order, the smaller is in marching order.

92nd HIGHLANDERS, Viceregal Guard, Dublin, 1847

ROYAL SCOTS (Royal Regiment)
From print in Historical Records of the British Army.

THE 74th HIGHLANDERS

Reproduced from Ackermann's Costume of the British Army, 1853.

This Regiment which was to become the 2nd Battalion of the H.L.I. had been raised as a kilted unit in 1787. The Highland dress was discontinued for a period but was authorised again in the above form in 1845. The tartan is a regimental pattern worn until the amalgamation with the 71st in 1881.

THE DUCHESS OF GORDON RAISES THE GORDON HIGHLANDERS.

"RAISING OF THE GORDONS"

from the picture by W. Skeoch Cummins.

ARGYLL AND SUTHERLAND HIGHLANDERS, c. 1890

The uniform as worn by the regiment formed from the 91st Argyllshire and 93rd Sutherland Highlanders. The tartan worn by the new regiment was that of the 93rd, sometimes called Sutherland tartan, although that officially laid down by regulations for the 93rd was Black Watch. The rifle shown in the illustration is the Le Metford magazine rifle, which the regiment received in 1890 in place of the Martini Henry.

THE 78th HIGHLANDERS

Reproduced from Ackermann's Costume of the British Army, 1846.

This Regiment which was to become the 2nd Battalion of the Seaforth Highlanders, was raised in 1793 by Francis Humberstone Mackenzie of Seaforth. When joined to the 72nd Highlanders in 1881, the uniform of the new regiment was basically that of the 78th, including the Mackenzie tartan.

CHRISTIAN DAVIES

The Woman Trooper of the Scots Greys, 1706

After dressing as a man and following her husband into the army, she became so fond of army life that she joined the Greys. Her sex was discovered after being wounded at the battle of Ramiliers.

She died in 1739 and was buried with military honours in the Chelsea Hospital cemetery.

THE ROYAL SCOTS, 1742

The oldest Regiment in the British Army, the 1st Foot were raised in 1633. The uniform shown is from the 1842 Clothing Book, and gives a contemporary illustration of an infantry soldier of the period. Until considerably later, when a more Scottish character appeared in the uniform the Royal Scots were dressed as other line infantry.

BLACK WATCH, 1843

This is from a series of valuable contemporary prints of the Black Watch mutineers shot in the Tower. This one depicts Corporal Malcolm McPherson. The illustration shows the uniform of the oldest Highland Regiment as it was shortly after the formation.

ROYAL SCOTS FUSILIERS, 1890

THE CAMERONIANS, 1882

From a drawing by Simpkin.

The 26th Foot were raised in 1689, and on amalgamation with the 90th Light Infantry in 1881 became 1st Battalion Cameronians. The new formation being a rifle regiment adopted a green uniform. The illustration shows the Regiment in the original dress with Government tartan trews (changed in 1896 to Douglas). The helmet was replaced by a shako in 1892.

79th HIGHLANDERS, 1799

A private in Field Dress uniform.

From the Water Colour by Major J. W. Van Oorschot, 1926.

THE PRINCESS LOUISE SCOTTISH HOSPITAL at ERSKINE

. . . . Do you remember, not so long ago really, in the darkest days of the war, that feeling experienced by most of us, that dread thought banished quickly from our minds ? Yes, it would have been much harder for us all but for the agony, the fear, cold, hunger and exhaustion endured by such as those men of the Forces and Merchant Navy who have been, are still being, helped at The Princess Louise Scottish Hospital at Erskine. There, more than twenty thousand war-ravaged bodies have been mended. Almost countless numbers of men have been restored to useful civilian life. Many others, some since the first World War, enjoy companionship and a permanent home at Erskine, in some cases re-united with their families in cottages on the Hospital's beautiful grounds. More, after training, live out but have found regular employment in the Workshops. Please remember these men of Erskine who, in helping you, now need your help.

The Hospital is NOT " NATIONALISED," nor does it canvass in any way, but there is *so* much to do. Any donations will be acknowledged gratefully by Colonel T. A. Harvie Anderson, C.B., 201 West George Street, Glasgow, C.2.

raised their voices in a psalm of triumph. After this defeat at Dunkeld the Highlanders did not rise again during the reign of William II, so it could be claimed that in their first battle the heroic stand of The Cameronians had saved the dynasty—and their faith.

In 1692, at Steenkirk, in the Low Countries, The Cameronian Regiment experienced its first battle on the Continent. In this indecisive encounter with the French, the regiment lost its young Commanding Officer, the Earl of Angus. The Cameronians saw further service in this campaign at Landen, in 1693, which was another inconclusive battle, and at the assault on Namur, in 1695, where the Grenadiers of the regiment led the attack and broke into the town.

There was a brief respite under the Treaty of Ryswick, after which the regiment again took the field against the French with the army of John Churchill, Duke of Marlborough. In this War of the Spanish Succession The Cameronians fought at Schellenberg and Blenheim (1704), at Ramillies (1706), Oudenarde (1708), and Malplaquet (1709). The Treaty of Utrecht, in 1713, terminated the strife.

Coming over from Ireland, The Cameronians successfully operated against the Jacobites at Preston in 1715, being the only infantry force engaged. In 1727 the regiment defended Gibraltar against the besieging French and Spaniards, remaining on " The Rock " until 1738. During the Seven Years War, The Cameronians served in the West Indies during the campaign to oust the French and establish naval bases for the better control of the Atlantic. Guadaloupe (1759), Dominica (1761), and Martinique and Havana (1762) fell, but yellow fever proved a more deadly foe than the French, and hundreds of troops succumbed to this and other tropical diseases.

In 1767 The Cameronians arrived in Canada. During the American War of Independence the regiment fought in the defence of Quebec, and at the capture of Fort Montgomery and Fort Clinton. Though the war was lost, The Cameronian Regiment came out of it with its honour untarnished.

The regiment was with General Sir Ralph Abercromby's force which landed at Aboukir in March, 1801, and defeated the French before Alexandria. This battle, and the later French surrender, doomed Napoleon's hopes of success in Egypt. The Cameronians were in General Sir John Moore's force which escaped annihilation by several strong converging French columns at Salamanca towards the close of 1808.

The regiment took part in the ensuing retreat through the Cantabrian Mountains in the dead of winter to Corunna. And at Corunna, in mid-January, 1809, the starving, ragged, exhausted British troops turned and hammered back the French, who retired to a safe distance and watched them embark.

On returning from Spain, the regiment was included in the expedition dispatched to low-lying Walcheren, on the Dutch coast. Fever so thinned out the ranks that The Cameronians were unable to re-enter the Peninsular War after the withdrawal from Walcheren.

In 1840 the regiment left India for China, where the authorities had permitted a number of outrages against British subjects and failed to give redress or any promise of future protection. Placing their faith in vastly superior numbers, the Chinese leaders decided to fight, but they were soon brought to a more reasonable state of mind when several important cities changed hands. In this campaign The Cameronians suffered severely from disease, but men of the regiment were the first to mount the walls at the capture of Amoy. On peace being signed Hong Kong was ceded to Britain.

In Abyssinia, in 1868, The Cameronians operated against the warriors of King Theodore, who had imprisoned British missionaries. With General Sir Robert Napier's force the regiment fought several actions in the hills. King Theodore was found dead when his fortress stronghold at Magdala was assaulted and taken.

Under the Army reorganisation of 1881, the 26th, or The Cameronian Regiment became the 1st Battalion The Cameronians (Scottish Rifles), and the 90th Regiment, or The Perthshire Volunteers (Light Infantry) entered the regiment as its 2nd Battalion. The founder and first Colonel of the Perthshire formation was Thomas Graham of Balgowan—later General Lord Lynedoch.

This Scottish laird was married to the beautiful Catherine, second daughter of Lord Cathcart. Her portrait by Gainsborough hangs in the National Gallery, Edinburgh. Mrs. Graham suffered from tuberculosis and spent much time abroad. When she died on the Mediterranean coast of France her husband had her body placed in a coffin intending to bury her in Scotland.

At Toulouse the revolutionaries suspected he was smuggling arms to the aristocrats—or possibly that an " aristo " was cheating the guillotine. In spite of Thomas Graham's vehement protests they burst open the coffin

F

EUCLID *moves the earth*

. . . All over the world. Whenever there is a big job to be done. Whether it be dams for power and irrigation, roads, railways, canals, and airfields for better communication or quarries and opencast coalmines for minerals . . .

EUCLIDS ARE THE BEST INVESTMENT

EUCLID (Great Britain) LIMITED
NEWHOUSE · LANARKSHIRE · SCOTLAND

o examine the contents. He was so incensed that he vowed to devote the rest of his life to fighting the French.

Arriving at Gibraltar, he later served as a volunteer in the force dispatched against Toulon. This experience gave him confidence in his ability as a soldier and to command men, and, on his return to Scotland, he sought permission to raise a regiment for service against the French Revolutionaries—his sworn enemies. Authority forthcoming from King George III, on May 13, 1794, this civilian mustered at Perth, at his own expense—£10,000—a regiment of 746 men—The 90th or The Perthshire Volunteers. The formation consisted of 430 Lowlanders, 165 Englishmen, 95 Highlanders, and 56 Irishmen. Two years later Thomas Graham raised a second battalion, but this became a force of Marines.

Professional soldiers soon became jealous of this " amateur ", whom they regarded as a gate-crasher. At first he was denied a commission as Colonel, but, on the insistent requests of General Sir John Moore—to whom Thomas Graham was aide-de-camp—he was granted the rank of Major-General. He was second-in-command to the Duke of Wellington during the Peninsular War, and was with General Sir John Moore when he was mortally wounded at Corunna.

The 90th—frequently referred to in its early days as the Perthshire " Greybreeks " because of the colour of the pantaloons worn—had its baptism of fire in March, 1801. With General Sir Ralph Abercromby's expedition to Egypt the regiment landed at Aboukir, and at Mandora stood firm when charged by the French cavalry. The collapse of enemy resistance at Alexandria brought this short campaign to a close.

The regiment was sent out to the West Indies and took part in the capture of Martinique (1809) and Guadeloupe (1810). In the fighting at Guadeloupe the men of the 90th seized the Eagle standard of the 80th French Regiment. The first British regiment to be equipped and armed as light infantry, the 90th was designated The Perthshire Volunteers (Light Infantry), During the American War, 1812-14, it served at Montreal, where it arrived at the close of the campaign.

Arriving in the Crimea, the 90th distinguished itself in the fierce fighting, particularly before the great Russian stronghold of Sevastopol, and, when the Victoria Cross was instituted by Queen Victoria in 1856, several men of the regiment were awarded this coveted decoration for heroism. The 90th endured all the privations and horrors of this ghastly campaign—concentrated bombardments by the massed Russian cannon, attacks by dense columns of infantry and hordes of cavalry, frequent raiding, and incessant sniping—and incompetence in high places made the troops wonder whether the General Staff was on the side of Britain or Russia !

The troops in the Crimea were frequently short of vital supplies, and food too was scarce. The Army was ravaged by cholera and dysentry, and only the common soldier emerged from the battle-smoke with any credit in this campaign of misery, chaos, blunder and muddle.

In 1857 the regiment was bound for India, then in the throes of the Sepoy Mutiny. The voyage was interrupted by shipwreck, and part of the regiment, arriving at Calcutta, was in General Sir Henry Havelock's column which broke through the mutineers and marched to the relief of Lucknow. Here, in the Residency, a small garrison—including a number of loyal Indian troops—was holding thousands of sepoys at bay. On reaching Lucknow, however, the relief force was itself hemmed in by the rebels and joined the defenders.

The other wing of the regiment arrived later and marched with General Sir Colin Campbell in the successful relief operation. The troops in the besieged Residency fought their way out to meet the relieving force, and, after desperate fighting, the two halves of the 90th met on the square in front of the Motee Mahal.

Fighting raged over an area stretching from Calcutta along the entire length of the Ganges Valley, and, when organised resistance broke before the onslaughts of the British troops and loyal sepoys and sowars, the 90th was engaged in mobile columns rounding up roving plundering bands of mutineers, and in pacification duties. Six Victoria Crosses were awarded to men of the regiment for heroism in a series of fiercely-fought engagements on the heat-laden plains of India.

In the late seventies the 90th operated in South Africa against the murdering, thieving Gaikas and Galekas. Campaigning against the warriors of truculent Chief Cetewayo, the 90th formed part of the British square at Ulundi. Here the massed Zulu attack withered away before the crashing fire from the long lines of death-spitting rifles. Further awards of the Victoria Cross were made to men of the 90th during the Zulu War.

The 1st and 2nd Battalions The Cameronians (Scottish Rifles)—formerly the 26th and 90th Regiments respectively—fought in the South

African War of 1899-1902. The affiliated Militia formations, and men from the Volunteer Force battalions also saw active service against the Boers.

Principal action for The Cameronians was the fighting advance on Ladysmith, which was relieved after much hardship and bloodshed on the hard sun-baked rolling veldt and scrub-covered hills. The 2nd Battalion was engaged in the dour fighting on the Modder River, and formed the rearguard during the retiral from Spion Kop, where heavy losses had been incurred in trying to clear the Boers from the hill. Finally a precarious hold had to be abandoned under heavy enemy fire.

Battle-honours of the regiment to date were:— Blenheim, Ramillies, Oudenarde, Malplaquet, Mandora, Corunna, Martinique, 1809, Guadaloupe, 1810, South Africa, 1846-47, Sevastopol, Lucknow, Abyssinia, South Africa, 1877-8-9, Relief of Ladysmith, South Africa, 1899-1902.

The 1st Battalion The Cameronians (Scottish Rifles) left Maryhill Barracks, Glasgow, and arrived in France with the British Expeditionary Force in mid-August, 1914. Within a few days it was the left flank battalion facing the Germans on the Mons-Conde line. The B.E.F. retired, fighting off the attacking masses of German infantry, and subjected to heavy artillery bombardments. Arriving in the Cambrai-Le Cateau area, a grim stand was made against overwhelming odds. This bought time with blood for the orderly retreat to continue, and, escaping encirclement, the B.E.F. came to the Marne. Here a strong attack was launched, which drove the enemy back, and the exhausted sadly-depleted B.E.F. advanced to the Aisne.

The 2nd Battalion, coming from Malta, entered the line early in November, and soon experienced the bombardments, raids, alarms, sniping, machine-gunning, close combat, attack and counter-attack, and all the other horrors of trench warfare in appalling weather. Snow, rain and sleet made rivers and quagmires of the trenches. Rest was out of the question, and hot meals impossible; relief often arrived late— sometimes too late. In this cheerless desolation even the wounded and the dying fought till they dropped, and when they went down in the bloodstained mud they died quietly, causing no let up in the fight of their comrades as the attacking waves of the enemy came over. Stretcher-bearers, padres and burial-parties were busy. And when the frost came the living and the dead froze together. The whine of bullets,

the rattle of machine-guns, and the booming roar of the artillery was their requiem.

The first Cameronian V.C. of the 1914-18 war was won by Rifleman Henry May, who gained this award at La Boutillerie in October, 1914. In the same month Lieutenant-Colonel C. B. Vandeleur, D.S.O.—who had joined the regiment in the eighties—was the first British prisoner to escape from the Germans. He was back in England before Christmas, and took over command of the 2nd Battalion soon afterwards. Sergeant J. Erskine earned the Victoria Cross at Givenchy, and Rifleman J. Towers at Mericourt.

At Neuve Chapelle the 2nd Cameronians advanced against uncut barbed wire and suffered very heavy losses. But the survivors fought on and carried their objective. When relieved a young subaltern and 150 men were all that remained of the 900-strong battalion which went into the attack.

The Cameronian fighting men of the two Regular battalions fought in all the major engagements of the Western Front until the Armistice. They were at Mons, Le Cateau, the Marne, at Neuve Chapelle and Rosieres, at Arras and Epehy, at the breaking of the Drocourt-Queant line, at the storming of the Canal du Nord, and in the final victorious advance of the Allies. Twenty-seven battalions— Regular, Service, and Territorial—served during World War I, in France, Belgium, Germany, Gallipoli, Egypt, and Macedonia. A total of 7,074 officers and other ranks gave their lives.

The principal battle-honours awarded to the regiment for its outstanding contribution to victory in the campaigns of 1914-18 were:— Mons, Marne, 1914, '18, Neuve Chapelle, Loos, Somme, 1916, '18, Ypres, 1917, '18, Hindenburg Line, Macedonia 1915, '18, Gallipoli, 1915-16, Palestine, 1917-19. As the regiment is a rifle corps, no colours are carried, and battle-honours are borne on the appointments only.

Between the two World Wars the 1st Battalion served in Ireland, China and India, and the 2nd in Iraq and Palestine. Both battalions experienced the rigours and alarms of India's North West Frontier. The 2nd, with the 1st Division, was engaged in maintaining order under the British Mandate during a troubled period in the Holy Land, and the Cameronians acquitted themselves creditably in a number of tense situations fraught with difficulty and danger. While stationed at Lucknow, in 1933, similar firmness and tact was exercised by the 1st during communal disturbances.

When war broke out in September, 1939, the 2nd Battalion The Cameronians was at Catterick. It sailed from Southampton and arrived at Cherbourg on the 12th, and, as part of the 13th Brigade, 5th Division, British Expeditionary Force, the battalion was soon engaged in defence construction along the Ypres-Comines Canal, on the Franco-Belgian border.

When the Germans invaded Belgium early in May, 1940, the 2nd Cameronians moved up to the line of the Brussels-Charleroi Canal. Digging-in commenced, and all bridges were blown. German aircraft dropped bombs, and D Company claimed to have downed one plane. On May 17 the enemy was contacted, and the Cameronians engaged the Germans at Lembecq, but were ordered to withdraw. There was another clash with the enemy on the railway between Rouex and Biache.

An assault boat crossing of the River Scarpe by a Cameronian patrol drew heavy enemy fire, but much valuable information was brought back concerning German strength and dispositions in this area. Refugees crowded the roads and seriously impeded the flow of military traffic, and air raids now became heavier and more frequent.

At Vimy the Cameronians were machine-gunned by low-flying aircraft. There was a spirited exchange of fire with the advancing Germans near Wytchaete. The position held by the battalion on the long forward slope of the Ypres-Comines Canal was in full view of the enemy, who subjected the series of defence posts to heavy machine-gun fire, mortaring and shelling. Owing to lack of rain, the canal was low, and strong enemy groups succeeded in crossing and the situation quickly deteriorated in spite of local counter-attacks.

A withdrawal of about 1,500 yards was made to a ridge covering the Ypres road, but before the Cameronians had settled in the Germans brought their machine-guns and mortars into action, and the position again took a critical turn. Lieutenant-Colonel G. H. Gilmore, D.S.O., organised and led a counter-attack with artillery support. This furious sally surprised and shook the success-flushed Germans, who sustained severe casualties. The Cameronians went at them with the bayonet. Lieutenant-Colonel Gilmore received a bar to the D.S.O. he had been awarded in World War I.

The 13th Brigade moved across a mile of the enemy front to take up a new position, and at the end of May was covering Wytchaete, east of the village. Sniping, mortaring and shelling caused further losses among the Cameronians, and it was learned that the Germans had received strong reinforcements. The enemy was seen massing for an attack. Every Cameronian rifle and machine-gun fired into them, and this move was shattered at its outset, the Germans running and diving for cover under a hail of bullets.

At the end of May, the decision to evacuate the British Expeditionary Force became known, The Cameronians abandoned Wytchaete and moved back through Furnes and Moeurs to enter the Dunkirk defence perimeter. The dock area was ablaze and under continuous air attack and artillery bombardment, and the town was congested with British, French and Belgian troops.

The fighting ships of the Royal Navy, the ships of the merchant fleet, graceful motor yachts, and little craft which conveyed holiday-makers " round the bay for a bob ", saved the day. They braved the bombs and shells to snatch the survivors of the shattered British Expeditionary Force and the soldiers of our French and Belgian allies from the maws of destruction and death on the mole and beaches of Dunkirk.

The bombs whistled down, the shells whined and crashed, and low-flying aircraft machine-gunned the long winding lines of men waiting to embark. Many of the rescue ships were hit and sank. Others took their place, filled up with troops, and departed to run the gauntlet of German bombers and fighters across the Channel. Long marches, desperate close fighting and heavy losses against a numerically superior and better equipped enemy, lack of rest and food, and defeat failed to break the discipline of the British Expeditionary Force, and the lines of soldiers stood firm with shells and bombs bursting all round them and among them.

The last of the 2nd Battalion had embarked by the evening of June 1. The sky over Dunkirk glowed red—and there was a red glow too in the hearts of the Cameronians, who had lost 360 of their comrades in casualties. Arriving at Dover, the survivors were re-organised, rested, re-equipped and reinforced. Then they trained hard for another day when they would meet the Wehrmacht in battle on equal terms.

The 1st Battalion left Secunderabad, India, in mid-February, 1942, and embarked at Madras for Rangoon. Moving out from Pegu, patrols

of The Cameronians collected and escorted back to safety several thousand refugees and exhausted parties of British and Indian troops and their wounded during the 17th Division's retiral from the Sittang River Line. During these operations many snipers were accounted for by the riflemen of the 1st.

There were several sharp clashes with the Japanese at Waw, Payagyi, Thanatpin, Pyinbon, Naungpattaya, Shandywagyi, Payagale and Kyakhla, and during the fighting withdrawal to Prome, which was reached at the end of March. In the Prome area there were bitter engagements to clear road blocks at Ywahla and Shwedaung, where tanks and artillery were also in action.

As the Japanese were thrusting north and west of the Irrawaddy, a further withdrawal had to be made, and there was heavy enemy bombing during the move to Allanmyo. The oilfield installations in the area were demolished, and the 1st Cameronians passed through blazing Magwe to go into fierce action at several road blocks before arriving at Mount Popa. In mid-April the battalion marched to Sammeikon and crossed the Irrawaddy. There was a brush with the enemy at Monywa.

With the enemy now across the river in force, the decision was taken early in May to withdraw the Burma Army to India, and the move back to the Chindwin commenced. It was a race against the monsoon rains, which would make the roads impassable. It was a race too with starvation and a fast-moving enemy.

The 1st Cameronians covered the canal crossing at Meo, then marched to Kaduma and Pingaying. Coming out of dense jungle at Shwegyin, the battalion was ferried across the Chindwin and disembarked at Kalewa to take up position along the Myittha River. The following day the Cameronians marched to Onbaung, and on May 10 arrived at Moreh, west of Tamu.

On the same day the Japanese attacked the ferry point at Shwegyin. As there was now no need to conserve " ammo ", the gunners and tank-crews hurled all they had at the enemy in this final battle of the first Burma Campaign. Battered and shaken by the concentrated barrage, the Japanese retired under cover of darkness. A few days later the rains came— but the Burma Army was safe across the broad Chindwin to reorganise and train for the next and conclusive round.

In mid-March, 1942, the 2nd Battalion The Cameronians embarked with the 13th Brigade,

5th Division, at Glasgow. Arriving at Durban, the battalion later sailed for Madagascar, and, on May 6, landed on this French island, forestalling the Japanese. The 13th Brigade went ashore south of Antisarani. It had a reserve role, but there was some skirmishing with snipers before the bivouac area was reached near Concession Grignon.

As the Madagascar operations were proceeding favourably, the voyage to India was resumed, and the 2nd Cameronians disembarked at Bombay at the close of May. The 5th Division was ordered to Persia early in August, and arrived at Basra about the middle of the month. The 2nd Cameronians moved to Kermanshah, and later, to Qum, 70 miles south of Teheran.

The German defeat at Stalingrad, and the reverses suffered by the Wehrmacht during the winter of 1942-3 in Russia, ended the threat to the oilfields of Iraq and Persia, and removed the danger to India, Egypt and Palestine. The 5th Division left " Pai-Force " in mid-February, 1943, and arrived at Damascus, via Baghdad and the Transjordan. Early in June the 2nd Cameronians reached El Shatt, east of Suez, and embarking at Port Tewfik on July 1, sailed with the Eighth Army—destination Sicily.

On July 10 the invasion fleet was off the island. The darkness was punctuated with gun-flashes and the fires which flared up on shore and well inland under the rain of shells. The 2nd Cameronians went ashore on George Beach, south-west of Syracuse, and advanced through Cassibile.

Contact with the enemy was made near Floridia, and there was sharp fighting before this objective was carried on July 11. There was stubborn resistance by the Germans, but the Italians were battle-shy and many of them surrendered. The division pushed northward, and Priolo and Villasmundo were occupied. The advance came under occasional air attack, but there was heavy shelling.

Passing through the shattered village of Sferro early in August, the division crossed the River Simeto. There was a spirited engagement to clear the hill feature of Poggio la Guardia, and the Cameronians battled forward to straddle the main Paterno-Catania road. The rubble that was now Paterno was entered, and the battalion took Monte Gervasi and Monte Arso. Over the lava rocks and hills they skirmished to Fleri, and here the 2nd Cameronians fired their last shots in Sicily.

On September 3 the 2nd Battalion embarked at Galati to invade the " toe " of Italy across

the Straits of Messina. Apart from mortar fire, the Cameronians were unopposed when they went ashore, but soon the build-up on the beaches came under heavy air attack, and shelling commenced. The battalion concentrated at Catona, on the coastal road, then moved to San Giovanni. As a result of enemy demolitions and the congested state of the roads, the 13th Brigade was taken in assault craft to a beach near Gioia, some twelve miles up the coast.

The 2nd Cameronians pushed ahead on September 7 to capture Rosarno in the face of stiff opposition from the Germans, but a foothold in the village was soon extended. The Germans began a retiral, and the Cameronians advanced to and crossed the River Mesima. The battalion was relieved and ordered to Pezzo, and during the march news came in that Italy had surrendered. The destination was changed to Vibo Valentia. On September 14 the Cameronian battalion moved 100 miles north by sea, and from Scalea, moved to Sapri.

The 13th Brigade was ordered to capture Sansa in mid-September. The enemy was holding up another brigade at Lagonegro, and the 13th cut in behind the Germans. This operation was led by the 2nd Cameronians, who entered Sansa unopposed and occupied it, the German defenders having withdrawn during the night. The battalion moved to Auletta later in the month, and, early in October, arrived at Pietragalla. Since landing on September 3, the 2nd Battalion had advanced about 260 miles from the " toe " up the long " leg " of Italy. The 13th Brigade concentrated near Foggia, and in this area the Cameronians trained hard for their important role in the winter campaign.

In late October the battalion took over a section of the line at Bojano, and early the following month, as brigade reserve, advanced several miles to high ground overlooking the River Vandra, where there was active patrolling. After a heavy bombardment on November 20, the Cameronians moved from Cerro without opposition to secure ground calculated to open the way for the capture of Alfedena.

There was patrol skirmishing around Cerro, and in mid-December the battalion arrived at Castiglione. There were further patrol clashes in the Lanciano-Mozzagrogna sector in appalling weather conditions, which bogged down other movement. Early in January, 1944, the 5th Division left the Eighth Army and came under command of the Fifth Army, on the west coast. The 2nd Cameronians were then stationed at Mondragone.

The battalion crossed the Garigliano unscathed, but had severe casualties in the attack on Tufo. At Point 201 D Company had good shooting among the German machine-gunners and recaptured this feature. Tufo was entered at the end of January. In the middle of February the Cameronians took over positions around Damiano, where activity was limited to aggressive patrolling. Later in the month the battalion was located at Minturno, and, early in March, re-crossed the Garigliano to concentrate at Casaluce.

Reinforcements being urgently required in the Anzio beachhead, the 5th Division was ordered into the desperate fighting. The division arrived on March 12, and the 2nd Cameronians took over a key position known as " The Fortress ". on the north of the beachhead perimeter, near the highway to Rome. The Germans launched a determined onslaught, and a local counterattack was made, which restored a dangerous situation. The Cameronians made a series of raids on the enemy, and there was fierce fighting, losses being high on both sides.

The 2nd Battalion area came in for heavy mortaring, and casualties began to mount. The Cameronians took over the " Lobster Claw " position, on the right of " The Fortress ", at the beginning of April. At the end of the month the battalion carried out an operation to assist the occupation of Ardea before relieving the exhausted defenders of " The Fortress ". About a week later the hard-fighting riflemen were again holding the " Lobster Claw ".

In the south of the beachhead there was a link-up with forward troops of the Fifth Army, and, on the night of May 27, the Cameronians found that the enemy had withdrawn from " The Fortress " area and other positions. On June 5 the 2nd Cameronians led the 13th Brigade's advance on Rome, and the riflemen fought forward to occupy Castel Porziano. Twelve more miles to Rome !

The Cameronians of the 2nd Battalion were the first British troops to reach the Tiber, and, a few days later, their pipers were marching through the Italian capital. The battalion moved to Zuni, some 30 miles north of Naples, on June 17. On the 29th the 2nd Cameronians arrived at Taranto, and, on July 4, sailed for Port Said, arriving there on the 8th.

After a short stay near Alexandria, the battalion left Egypt for Beit Lid, Palestine.

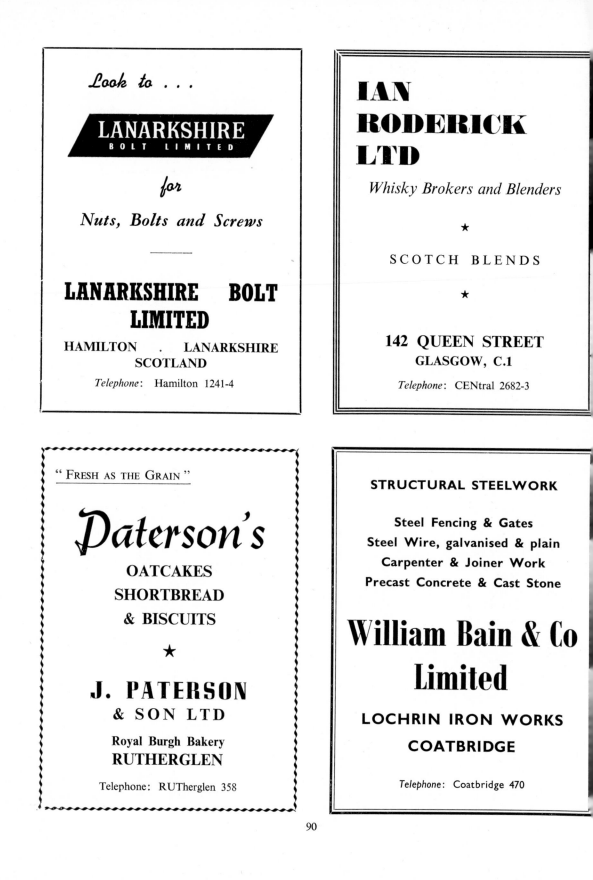

A further move took the Cameronians to Jebel Mozar, north of Damascus, Syria, in September. In October the battalion was back in Palestine, being located near Tel Aviv.

In February, 1945, while stationed at Beit Jirja, Palestine, orders were received which sent the 2nd Battalion back to Italy, over the Mediterranean to France, and across the Continent to North West Europe. In mid-April the Cameronians crossed the Rhine and went into action on the 21st. Supported by tanks, they ran into some sniping near Breetze, and at Bleckede encountered stiff opposition and heavy shell-fire. The attack was renewed the following morning, resistance quickly crumbled, and many prisoners were taken.

On May 1 the battalion crossed the Elbe, where the Cameronians experienced their last German air raid. The battalion pushed on to Molln. In this area an entire German regiment surrendered, and thousands of prisoners were herded back. On the 3rd the riflemen entered Lübeck, where Battalion H.Q. took the surrender of the staff of the 27th Corps. On the evening of the 6th the German Armies capitulated, and next day the battalion moved to Sprenge. The 2nd Cameronians had been in at the " kill ".

When the 1st Battalion The Cameronians came out of the 1942 Burma Campaign it was reduced to three platoons. The survivors of this fine battalion moved down into the Kaban Valley, where malaria took further toll, but, a few weeks later, a number of men who had been sick or wounded, rejoined the unit, which then moved south.

The battalion was included in one of the three brigades of Brigadier (later Major-General) Orde Wingate's Chindit force, whose object was disruptive action to harass, destroy or dislocate Japanese communications, troop movements and dumps—and kill the enemy. The Chindits were, in fact, highly organised guerilla fighters, lightly equipped, extremely mobile, with all their requirements met by air-drops.

The 1st Cameronians joined 111 Brigade in March, 1943, and, in August, became part of " Special Force ". From then until the early spring of 1944 arduous training for this new role was carried out in India's Central Provinces. Arriving at Silchar, the Cameronians marched 100 miles over the Naga Hills to reach the camping site on the Imphal-Tiddim road. In this area hard training was commenced in the loading and unloading of gliders with men, mules and equipment.

The battalion entered Burma on the night of March 10, 1944, landing on a hastily-prepared airstrip about 60 miles east of Mawlu. Orders were to concentrate at Dayu, south of Banmauk, in the Indaw-Mansi road, by the 19th—necessitating another march of 100 miles. The Cameronian battalion was organised in two completely self-contained columns—the 26th and the 90th—significant numerals in the history of the regiment.

In mid-March the two columns, acting independently, crossed the railway between Myitkyina and Indaw. The 26th forded the Meza River and went over the main Banmauk-Indaw road. The 90th, however, encountered stiff opposition, but a second attempt to cross the river succeeded. Severe casualties were inflicted on the Japanese, those of the Cameronians being light.

The columns met, and, at the end of the month, arrangements were well under way for the projected road-block, when orders were changed. The serious enemy threat to Imphal made it imperative that a more offensive role should be adopted. The Cameronians were assigned the task of harassing the enemy on his main Indaw-Tamu communication line. So, for several weeks the riflemen were engaged in destroying dumps and ambushing troops.

As a result the Japanese Command resorted to dispatching formations several hundred strong escorted by tanks and guns—thus stretching enemy resources elsewhere. But this did not save the Japanese from sudden ambush and heavy losses at the hands of the will o' the wisp Cameronian Chindits, who disappeared into the jungle as quickly as they had appeared.

After a brief respite, the brigade, early in May, moved north to form a road block on the main road and railway in the Hopin area, about 30 miles south-west of Mogaung and Kamaing. The intention was to ambush, raid, patrol and disrupt, and prevent Jap reinforcements from reaching the Mogaung-Kemaing region. The monsoon downpour came earlier than expected, causing delay and impeding the fly-in of supplies. The Chindit force was located in a jungle clearing on a hill near Namkwin, a village situated on the railway.

Unfortunately there was a sharp rise in sickness, considerably reducing activity, and, within three days of its arrival, the enemy located the Chindits, and shelling commenced. The Japanese made several determined attacks, which were beaten back with heavy loss to the enemy, but it was soon evident that the enemy was building up for an all-out onslaught. Mortaring and artillery fire increased, and the appearance of " ack ack " guns interfered with air-drops.

The Japanese captured the airstrip, and the defenders had to retire into the perimeter. Ammunition was running low, and only a trickle of the air-dropped supplies could be gathered because of the constant shelling. Then, by sheer weight of numbers, the enemy penetrated the defences, but was driven out by a desperate bayonet charge. Later the Japs returned to the attack and again established themselves in the perimeter. The position was now critical, and a withdrawal was decided upon.

The survivors, still fighting back, withdrew along a route held by the Cameronians, who maintained their position on the last covering ridge. The Chindits entered the dense jungle with the Cameronian riflemen acting as rearguard, and under heavy artillery and machine-gun fire.

The Japanese were estimated to have sustained over 2,000 casualties in killed and wounded and were so weak that they made no attempt to follow up the retiring Chindits. Wireless sets were out of action, and there was no contact with base. On reduced rations the Chindits, with their numerous sick and wounded, snaked through the jungle and toiled over 3,000 ft. high hills, in torrential rain, and, after an exhausting five-day march, reached the shores of Lake Indawgyi. The sick and wounded were flown to India, and, owing to reduced numbers, the battalion was formed into one column.

In mid-June the Cameronian Chindits commenced an advance on Mogaung. Leeches, myriads of mosquitoes and other insects, winged and crawling, added to the torment of the jungle fighters. Sawnching, in the western foothills of the Mogaung Valley, was occupied by the Cameronians, who were joined in this area by a column of Gurkhas. The Cameronians and Gurkhas patrolled the hills, and a patrol of Cameronians succeeded in penetrating into the enemy-held Mogaung Valley.

In July the Cameronian battalion—now reduced to a mere cadre—was withdrawn and employed on lines of communication duties. Most of them were completely exhausted by their recent strenuous exertions and hard fighting. All were suffering from general debility, and sickness was rife. At the end of the month the gallant little band of Cameronians was flown to India.

As Chindits they had been operating in the heart of enemy-occupied territory in Burma for five eventful months. They had fought courageously and skilfully, enduring privations in the steaming jungles and monsoon-sodden hills, causing heavy losses among ambushed Japanese troops, destroying vital supplies, cutting important communication lines, and creating panic and confusion among the enemy. Thus the Cameronians' contribution to victory over the Japanese. And they had avenged their fallen in the 1942 campaign.

The 6th and 7th (T.A.) Battalions were in the 156th (West of Scotland) Infantry Brigade of the 52nd (Lowland) Division, serving with the Second British Expeditionary Force in France in 1940, until evacuated from Cherbourg. In 1944 this division fought from the Dutch coast deep into Germany, with the 7th Battalion transferred to the 157th Brigade.

The 9th and 10th Territorial Battalions were revived in the spring of 1939, and were in the 15th (Scottish) Division, both being in the 45th Infantry Brigade. In 1942 the 10th Battalion left the division to become a training unit, and the 9th Battalion was switched to the 46th (Highland) Infantry Brigade of the 15th Division. Landing in Normandy in 1944, the 15th battled across the Continent and over the Rhine to final victory.

The 12th Battalion was formed at Lanark in May, 1940. In Caithness it joined the 227th Independent Infantry Brigade, responsible for the defence of the Orkney and Shetland Islands. Leaving this brigade in May, 1942, the 12th Battalion went to the Faroes, but was disbanded in the spring of the following year.

After the Munich Crisis, in the autumn of 1938, it was decided that the 5/8th Battalion should have a change of role. In November of that year the 5/8th ceased to be an infantry battalion, and it became the 56th Searchlight Regiment, R.A.

Following the German surrender, the 2nd Battalion The Cameronians (Scottish Rifles) was engaged in occupation duties. Early in 1947 the battalion proceeded to Gibraltar.

On returning to India after the Chindit operations in Burma, the 1st Battalion was stationed at Dehra Dun, and in May, 1945, joined the 36th Division at Poona. Early in November the 1st Battalion left Bombay for Singapore, and from there moved to Kluang.

On December 15, 1945, the 1st Battalion The Cameronians featured in an historic ceremony.

Lieutenant-General Senechi Tazaka, commanding the Singapore defences, and several other Japanese generals, formally handed over their swords on surrendering to Lieutenant-Colonel W. B. Thomas, C.B.E., D.S.O., commanding officer of the battalion.

At the close of 1946 the 1st Battalion was informed that it was being placed in "suspended animation" owing to the post-war reorganisation of the Army, and parties of Cameronians, joined other regiments. The 2nd Battalion was re-numbered the 1st, and, at the close of 1948, it moved from Gibraltar and arrived in Trieste. The riflemen patrolled the Jugoslav frontier for a year while engaged on international police duties. In December, 1949, the 1st Battalion went to Hong Kong. In March, 1950, the Cameronians were ordered to Malaya.

At the end of three years of operations in the steaming green hell of the jungle, foul treacherous swamps, scrub-tangled hills and sun-scorched rocks, the Cameronians had killed 125 terrorists and captured 24 for the loss of two officers and six other ranks. Later a number of awards for gallantry in Malaya was announced. The battalion returned home in May, 1953, and departed for Germany in July, 1954. The Cameronian battalion came back to the U.K. in September, 1956.

Action came again in the summer of 1957, when the riflemen were flown to Bahrein, on the Persian Gulf. They went to the assistance of the Sultan in suppressing a tribal revolt in this important oil-producing country. The Cameronians moved to Sharjah, and, co-operating with loyal tribesmen, drove across the desert towards the rebel-held fort at Nizwa.

In a temperature of 168 degrees, a sharp action was fought with the insurgents, and the Cameronians seized an important hill feature dominating Firq, which opened the way for the capture of the Nizwa stronghold. The riflemen were later employed on patrol and escort duties, and had several skirmishes with the rebels, in which casualties were inflicted. When peace was restored in the Sultanate, contingents of Cameronians returned to Nairobi, Kenya, in May, 1958.

Early in August that year the Cameronians were rushed by aircraft-carrier through the Red Sea and Gulf of Akaba to Jordan. Arriving at Akaba, the riflemen were flown to Amman, the capital, to secure important communication lines and strengthen the force of over 2,000 British troops stationed in Jordan at the urgent request of King Hussein. In mid-October, the emergency over, the Cameronians began the fly-out. While located on the outskirts of Nairobi, the battalion received a visit from Queen Elizabeth The Queen Mother, in January, 1959.

In the Regimental Museum at Lanark two relics span over two and a half centuries of Cameronian history. One is the Andrea Ferrara blade with which William Cleland defended the faith at the Battle of Bothwell Brig. The other is the Samurai sword surrendered to the Commanding Officer of the 1st Battalion when the Japanese capitulated at Singapore.

Photograph by courtesy Associated Press

HER MAJESTY QUEEN ELIZABETH THE QUEEN MOTHER

COLONEL-IN-CHIEF—THE BLACK WATCH

The Black Watch

(ROYAL HIGHLAND REGIMENT)

" THE AULD FORTY-TWA "—The Black Watch —was formed when a number of Independent Companies of Highlanders were regimented, 1,000 strong, the first muster taking place in May, 1740, on the banks of the Tay, near Aberfeldy, Perthshire. A cairn still marks the spot, and, in 1885, a monument was erected portraying a soldier of " The Watch " in the uniform of 1740.

Six Independent Companies were raised in 1725. These units were responsible for policing the turbulent Highlands. The three larger companies, with a strength of about 100 men each, were commanded by Lord Lovat, Sir Duncan Campbell of Lochnell, and Colonel Grant of Ballindalloch. The other three of, about 75 men each, were led by Colonel Alexander Campbell of Finab, John Campbell of Carrick, and George Munro of Culcairn. Four more companies were raised in 1729.

The Disarming Act of 1725 forbade the carrying of arms by private individuals, with severe penalties for those who broke the law. That year, however, certain Highland chieftains were commissioned to form bodies of clansmen to maintain order in their respective areas. This idea was by no means new, as, in 1667, in the reign of Charles II, several Independent Companies existed, but they were disbanded in 1717.

The Highlanders did not take kindly to the Disarming Act, so, when recruits were required for the Independent Companies, there was an immediate and hearty response, for the Highlander, bereft of his good broadsword, dirk, pistols and targe, was a very dispirited and downcast man. Several of the companies wore dark-coloured tartans, and the force became known as Am Freiceadan Dubh—The Black Watch—in contrast to Saighdearan Dearg—the " Redcoats " of the Regular Army.

From 1725 until 1739 the Independent Companies of The Watch, or The Black Watch, patrolled and policed the Highlands, maintaining order, and preventing clan clashes and cattle-raiding. In September, 1739, King George II issued a warrant, or Letter of Service, forming the companies into a Highland regiment, and giving it the number " 43 ". In order that no feeling should be aroused by choosing a commanding officer from a particular clan, the command of the new Highland regiment was given to a Lowlander—John, 20th Earl of Crawford.

The Black Watch was the first British regiment to wear Highland uniform as Regular soldiers, and is Scotland's senior Highland regiment. The original uniform of the 43rd, or Highland Regiment of Foot, was similar to that worn by the former Independent Companies—the short red jacket faced with buff and white lace, red waistcoat, plaid, black leather belt to hold the kilt in position, red and white hose, buckled shoes, and blue bonnet with a tuft of feathers or piece of bearskin on the left side. Sporrans were of badger skin.

The tartan worn has been the subject of much controversy, but it has now been established as the Government tartan, which was available to all Scottish regiments. In slightly modified form—with coloured over-stripes, etc.—it became the basis for several regimental and clan tartans. The tartan worn by The Black Watch ere long also became known as the " 42nd ", but has no clan connection.

Whereas the kilts of the other Highland regiments have flat pleats, the kilts of The Black Watch have piped pleats. The spats— first introduced for Highland regiments in 1801—are cut square, while those of the other Highland regiments are rounded. Their bonnet has four fox-tails, while the others have five, and, in one case, six. Pipers wear the feathered bonnet, though the other Highland corps ceased to wear this headgear late in last century. Pipers are dressed in the Royal Stewart tartan. And, of course, the distinctive Red Hackle at once identifies the wearer as belonging to this grand old regiment.

The Government provided each man with a musket, bayonet and broadsword, but many of the Highlanders supplemented this with a brace of pistols, dirk, and targe, or shield. Sergeants carried the Lochaber axe. After the original muster near Aberfeldy, the 43rd, or

95

Highland Regiment of Foot, was employed for three years in detachments in the Highlands. In March, 1743, it assembled at Perth and marched to London to embark for Flanders.

While encamped at Finchley, near London, an unfortunate mutiny broke out, which led to large-scale desertion. The men were under the impression that, under the terms of enlistment, they would not be required to serve abroad, and paid agitators spread rumours that the regiment was to be sent to the disease-ridden West Indies.

A number of Highlanders gathered on Highgate Common and marched north for Scotland. They were overtaken by cavalry and infantry at Oundle, Northamptonshire, and brought back to London under heavy guard to be court-martialled. The three ringleaders were shot, and 200 men were drafted to other regiments serving overseas. The remainder of the regiment, numbering over 900, then embarked for war service.

For the next two years the 43rd served in various parts of Flanders, and the stain of mutiny was speedily offset by the gallantry of the Highlanders at the Battle of Fontenoy, in May, 1745, during the War of the Austrian Succession. Though the French were the victors, the 43rd fought valiantly, and rushed the enemy to cover the British retiral, thus preventing defeat from becoming a rout.

In October of that year the regiment returned to England, and in June, 1746, it sailed for America. The ships were driven back three times by adverse winds, and the 43rd arrived in Ireland, being stationed in Limerick for several months. It was in 1746 that the 43rd landed at Quiberon and captured a fort and a number of guns. The regiment proceeded to Flanders in 1747, returning towards the close of 1748. While serving in Ireland in 1751, the regiment was re-numbered the 42nd. The Highlanders were in Ireland until May, 1756, when they sailed for America to operate against the French and their Indian allies.

Arriving at New York, the 42nd went on to Albany, where the Highlanders were trained in Indian warfare, and returned to New York in August, 1757. The 42nd was included in the force which General Abercromby led in June, 1758, against Ticonderoga, a strongly fortified French position situated between Lake George and Lake Champlain.

In July, without artillery support, an assault was launched, which was hurled back with heavy loss. The 42nd, in reserve, witnessed the terrible execution wrought by the French guns and, without waiting for orders, the Highlanders charged to avenge their comrades. They succeeded in reaching and mounting the fortifications, and a number hacked their way inside only to fall under the murderous fire. Three times they were ordered to retire from the carnage before they obeyed. In five hours of ghastly fighting the regiment lost 647 men out of a total of 1,100.

While still serving in America, a Royal Warrant in July, 1758, conferred on the regiment the title of " Royal ", and the uniform facings were changed to blue. In the same month authority was received for the raising of a second battalion. This was completed in Perth by October, 840 Highlanders responding.

The 2nd Battalion was at once dispatched to the West Indies, and in 1759 formed part of the force which made an unsuccessful attack on Martinique, after which the battalion participated in the expedition against Guadaloupe. The 2nd Battalion later arrived in North America, and, with the 1st, took part in the second assault on Ticonderoga. On this occasion Ticonderoga fell after a sharp action lasting half an hour. Both battalions were present at the capture of Montreal, in August, 1760, as a result of which all Canada came under British control on the surrender of the French.

In 1761 the two battalions of The Royal Highland Regiment were in the force which was sent to the West Indies and captured the Windward Islands. Early the following year the 1st and 2nd took Martinique and Havanah. Men of the 2nd Battalion were drafted into the 1st when the 2nd was disbanded in 1763.

After four years of operations against the Indians, the 42nd embarked at Philadelphia in July, 1767, and arrived at Cork in October. From 1767 until 1775 the regiment served in various parts of Ireland during a period of religious and political unrest. In May, 1776, The Royal Highland Regiment embarked at Greenock to serve against the American Colonists, who had declared their independence.

A gale separated the transports, and one ship was captured by an American privateer craft. A prize crew was sent on board, but a few days later the 42nd men overpowered their captors. They brought the ship safely into port to be again captured by the Americans, who vainly tried to enlist the Highlanders to fight for their cause. Two years later the Highlanders were exchanged for American prisoners and rejoined the regiment.

The other transports landed the regiment at Staten Island in August, 1776. The Highlanders fought well at Brooklyn, Bloomingdale, Fort Washington, White Plains, Brandywine, Germantown, Monmouth and Pisquatua, and at the siege of Charlestown, and at Yorktown. When peace came in October, 1783, the 42nd moved to Halifax, Nova Scotia, and in 1786 proceeded to Cape Breton.

In 1779, another second battalion was embodied, on this occasion at Perth. It was placed under the command of Lieutenant-Colonel Norman McLeod of McLeod, who had been transferred with several other officers from the 1st Battalion. In 1782, the new formation was ordered to India to operate against Hyder Ali and his French supporters.

In 1783 the 2nd Battalion took part in the capture of Mangalore, and then held it under siege. The small garrison of 400 British troops and 1,500 sepoys was attacked by a large army of Indians and French, but held out for nine months. Reduced by disease, famine and casualties the garrison was forced to surrender at the end of January, 1784. Tippoo allowed the survivors to march out with all the honours of war. In 1786 the 2nd Battalion became a separate corps—The 73rd Highland Regiment.

The 42nd returned to Britain from Canada in October, 1789. In 1793 the regiment was campaigning again in Flanders. At Geldermalsen, in January, 1795, two companies attacked the French cavalry and re-captured two guns which had been taken in the enemy's charge. Without horses, the Highlanders hauled back the heavy guns, fighting off the enemy all the way, and suffering considerable casualties.

For the Highlanders this was the one bright spot during a campaign in which the British troops were very short of supplies, the ground deep in snow, and the cold intense. The 42nd men were without greatcoats, and in spite of the appalling conditions the regiment had comparatively light losses due to the natural hardiness of the Highlanders and their firm discipline. The regiment returned to England in the spring of 1795, and it was in the summer of that year The Royal Highland Regiment adopted the Red Hackle.

In October, 1795, the 42nd embarked for the West Indies, but the ships were dispersed by gales. Five companies reached Barbados, but H.Q. and the other five companies were driven back to Portsmouth, and were then ordered to Gibraltar. The companies in the West Indies were at the capture of St. Lucia and St. Vincent, in 1797, after which they returned to Portsmouth.

Reunited at Gibraltar, the regiment proceeded to Minorca, which they captured in 1798. The 42nd was also engaged in the expeditions launched against Genoa and Cadiz. With General Abercromby's force, the 42nd arrived off Alexandria on March 1, 1801. A week later the Highlanders led the landing, and were heavily engaged with the French cavalry and infantry at the Battle of Aboukir. The assault landing and battle ended with Napoleon's troops retiring on Alexandria hotly pursued by the British.

At Alexandria the 42nd fought one of its hardest engagements. Major Stirling captured the standard of Napoleon's "Invincible Legion", and a Highlander saved Sir Ralph Abercromby from being cut down by French cavalrymen. After the enemy retiral commenced the 42nd pursued the French infantry into the ruins of Cleopatra's Palace. The French surrender of the town followed the Battle of Alexandria, ending this campaign in Egypt, and the regiment returned to the U.K. In 1802 a second battalion was again raised. This formation was sent to Ireland in 1805.

The 1st Battalion proceeded to Gibraltar in November, 1805, and left "The Rock" in July, 1808, to join the British Army at Lisbon and take part in the Peninsular War, which raged across Spain and Portugal. When General Sir John Moore learned that several strong French columns were converging on him at Salamanca, he ordered a retreat to the coast for evacuation.

In the severe winter of 1808-9 the ill-clad, famished exhausted British troops marched over the Cantabrian Mountains, through snow, sleet, icy drizzle, freezing rain and deep mud. The 42nd was ordered to hold the pursuing French at bay as rearguard. Before getting at the main column the French had to cut through the 42nd. They did not succeed. There were several fierce rearguard actions, but the Highlanders hurled back the numerically superior enemy with rifle and bayonet, and, on reaching Corunna—after retreating and fighting for over 200 miles—the 42nd once more joined battle with the French, thus gaining time for the transports to arrive.

Decisively beaten by the ragged, starving exhausted British force, the French retired to a safe distance and were spectators of the embarkation of the British troops—many of whom were soon to wreak a terrible revenge

on Napoleon's colourful regiments. But General Sir John Moore was killed in this last battle of the historic Retreat to Corunna.

In July, 1809, the 1st Battalion formed part of the unfortunate expedition dispatched against Walcheren. The force was soon ravaged by sickness and was withdrawn from the Dutch coast the following September. In the spring of 1812 the battalion embarked at Portsmouth for Portugal. The 2nd Battalion, which had been stationed in Ireland since 1805, was ordered to Portugal early in 1809.

In September, 1810, the 2nd Battalion was at the Battle of Busaco, and in May, 1811, fought at Fuentes d'Onor. In January, 1812, this battalion was at the siege of Ciudad Rodrigo. In April of the same year the 1st Battalion was brought up to strength by receiving into it all the men of the 2nd Battalion.

The 42nd joined battle with the French in July, 1812, at Salamanca, and operated at the siege of Burgos in September and October. During 1813 the regiment was in numerous actions in the Pyrenees. It fought at the battles of Nivelle and Pampeluna in October, made an assault crossing of the Nive in December, fought at Orthes in February, 1814, and advanced into battle at Toulouse in April. Here the enemy made his last stand, after which the victorious army of the " Iron Duke " (Wellington) marched into France and Napoleon abdicated.

In June, 1814, the 42nd Highlanders arrived in Ireland. In October of that year the 2nd Battalion was disbanded at Aberdeen. On the escape of Napoleon from Elba war again broke out in Europe, and in the spring of 1815 the 42nd sailed for Belgium.

At Quatre Bras—prelude to Waterloo—the Royal Highland Regiment was drawn up in a field of wheat. A large force of French infantry attacked, but were driven back by the compact squares of the 42nd. Two days later, at the Battle of Waterloo, on June 18, 1815, the Highlanders again crossed bayonets with the French.

In the frenzied defensive fighting with masses of enemy infantry an Ensign of the 92nd Highlanders (Gordons) was killed, and the French came on intending to seize the Colour he bore. A grenadier of the 42nd rushed forward through the fire and carried the Ensign —still clutching the flag—to safety. The gallant Colonel of the French Imperial Guard was so impressed that he ordered his men not to fire. The magnificent bearing of the

Highlanders of the 42nd under the concentrated fire of the French artillery, their calm and courage when they faced the charging cavalry squadrons, and their desperate unyielding defence when attacked by the close-packed lines of infantry won The Royal Highland Regiment special mention in the Duke of Wellington's Waterloo dispatch.

After several months with the occupation forces in Paris, the 42nd returned to the U.K. towards the close of 1815, and, until the outbreak of the Crimean War, in 1854 the regiment served in Ireland, and then at Gibraltar and other Mediterranean stations. In 1842 establishment was raised from 10 to 12 companies, and in the same year a second battalion was once more formed. The 2nd Battalion joined the 1st at Malta, and the two formations were ordered to Bermuda in 1847. While on this station, in 1850, the 2nd Battalion merged with the 1st. In 1851 the 42nd left for Nova Scotia en route for Scotland.

The Royal Highland Regiment landed at Scutari, Turkey, early in June, 1854, and joined the Highland Brigade, which distinguished itself during September in the fighting by the Alma. The Highland Brigade put to flight eight Russian battalions and forced the retiral of other four. A month later, in October, the Highland Brigade again clashed with the Czar's hordes at Balaclava, and after stiff fighting the Russians again retreated.

In May, 1855, the 42nd was included in the two expeditions dispatched against Kertch. On returning from the second, the regiment took up position before Sevastopol. After the failure of the British assault on the Redan in September, the Highland Brigade took over a section of the trenchworks. The Highlanders were to attack the following day, but during the night it was found that the enemy had abandoned the Redan. Mines were sprung, and with a shattering roar this key bastion in the Russian defence system went up in smoke. The enemy also evacuated Sevastopol, and the Crimean War ended with the rumble of explosions.

In July, 1856, The Royal Highland Regiment returned to the homeland, but in the summer of the following year it was ordered to India. Arriving at Calcutta in November, 1857, H.Q. and five companies were rushed to the relief of Cawnpore. It was the rainy season and the advance was slowed down. En route there were several clashes with large bodies of mutineers, which caused further delay.

REGD. TRADE MARK

Morton's
LIQUEUR
Old Scotch Whisky

Also Proprietors of :—
MORTON'S ★ ★ ★
SPECIAL RESERVE
SCOTCH WHISKY

Scotland's Finest
Established 1838

GEORGE MORTON LTD. · DUNDEE · SCOTLAND

When the Highlanders fought through to Cawnpore and battled along the streets with rifle and bayonet under heavy fire from mutineers concealed in buildings and houses, it was only to find that all the British residents and troops had been overwhelmed and massacred. The 42nd fought a spirited action at Seria Ghat, where the mutineers were overtaken, hammered, and 17 guns and a large quantity of equipment and baggage captured.

During 1858 The Royal Highland Regiment experienced further severe fighting, principally in the siege and capture of Lucknow—where Captain F. E. H. Farquharson won the Victoria Cross—and in the attack on Fort Rooyah. In this assault Quartermaster-Sergeant John Simpson, Lance-Corporal Alexander Thomson, and Privates James Davis and Edward Spence also won this award. Another Victoria Cross was earned by Colour-Sergeant William Gardiner at the Battle of Bareilly, where he saved the life of his commanding officer.

Two more Victoria Crosses were won by men of the 42nd—Privates Walter Cook and Duncan Miller—at Sissaya Ghat, where 37 men of " F " Company held at bay over 2,000 sepoys from sunrise until sundown. When the officer and senior N.C.O.'s were killed, Privates Cook and Miller organised effective resistance. On the collapse of the Indian Mutiny, detachments from the 42nd scoured the country with mobile columns in the general mopping-up operations.

On September 12, 1861, Queen Victoria authorised The Royal Highland Regiment to be distinguished, in addition to that title, by its earliest name—The Black Watch. The full designation then became the 42nd, or The Royal Highland Regiment (The Black Watch). The 42nd served in various parts of India until, in January, 1868, it embarked for Scotland.

In early December, 1873, The Black Watch sailed for the Gold Coast, and, arriving at Cape Coast Castle, the regiment marched on Kumasi, capital of the murderous King Coffee Calcalli, the scourge of West Africa. At the beginning of February, 1874, the Ashanti Expedition entered and burned Kumasi. This short campaign was fought out in intense heat, the Highlanders hacking their way through dense jungle, and battling out of numerous ambushes as the force advanced. The native porters threw down their loads and ran at the first sign of danger.

Principal actions were at Amoaful and Ordashu. At Amoaful Lance-Sergeant Samuel

McGaw won the Victoria Cross. The Black Watch returned home in March. In November the 42nd went to Malta, where it remained for four years. Towards the end of 1878 the regiment departed for service at Malta, Gibraltar and Cyprus. In June, 1879, the Highlanders were in England.

Under the Army reforms of 1881, the regiment was styled The Black Watch (Royal Highlanders). In the same year the 73rd Regiment—which had been the 2nd Battalion of the 42nd from 1779 until it " hived off " as the 73rd Highland Regiment in 1786—returned as the 2nd Battalion The Black Watch.

The 73rd Highland Regiment was in the force which in 1791 toiled up the Ghats and pushed through dense jungles. But in spite of its efforts the expedition failed to force a successful conclusion, and had to retire through the monsoon rains beset by hordes of Tippoo's cavalry. In 1792-93 the 73rd operated in Cawnpore, Calcutta and on the Madras coast, then renewed the war against Tippoo. The Highlanders attacked his stronghold at Seringapatam, which forced his surrender. In 1793 the regiment captured Pondicherry. In 1799 Tippoo's capital, Mysore, fell and the campaign ended.

The 73rd was with the force dispatched from India against the Dutch in Ceylon in 1795. The Highlanders took part in the siege and capture of Trincomali, and a year later Ceylon came under British control.

In 1806 the regiment returned to Scotland, and the following year a second battalion was raised. In 1809 the regiment was ordered to discontinue wearing the Highland dress and adopt the uniform of regiments of the Line. Thus, until 1881, the 73rd lost its Highland identity.

In the spring of 1810 the 1st Battalion left for Australia, and, on arriving, suppressed a rising of colonists. The battalion remained in Australia for four years,. Meanwhile, the 2nd Battalion, after being stationed in several parts of the U.K., was sent to the aid of the Swedish Army in 1813. On arrival at Stralsund the battalion was dispatched to join a force in Hanover, which, in mid-September, clashed with the French at Ghorde.

The battalion arrived in time to turn the tide against the French. The Scots attacked the enemy centre, which was rolled back by their charge. After Ghorde the 2nd Battalion served in various parts of Holland, and was present at the capture of Antwerp, in 1814. The battalion was located near Soignies in June, 1814, and from there it moved up to enter the fray at Quatre Bras, on June 16, 1815.

Two days later the Scots were in the vortex of the fighting at Waterloo. The battalion withstood several charges by the French cavalry and the terrific artillery bombardment, but there were severe losses among its squares. After peace came the 2nd Battalion returned to England and was disbanded in May, 1816, 300 of its men joining the 1st Battalion in Ceylon.

The 1st Battalion had arrived in Ceylon in August, 1814, and was engaged in operations against the King of Kandy, whose capital was entered in February, 1815. Split up into detachments the men of the 1st maintained order among the natives, being employed in this role until 1816. One detachment was trapped at Badulla by a large force of natives, but help arrived in time to save it from annihilation. The battalion remained in Ceylon until 1821 then returned to England.

Service followed from 1821 to 1824 in several parts of the U.K. and in the Mediterranean stations. While in Canada in 1838 the regiment was called on to suppress political disturbances. In 1845 the 73rd left Cork and at Monte Video in December, it defended the town against the attacking Argentine forces.

The regiment later sailed for South Africa, and the transport came near to being wrecked at the mouth of the Great Fish River in a gale. Arriving at Port Elizabeth, the 73rd moved off to operate against the troublesome Kaffirs in a campaign which began in 1846 and lasted for about a year. Another expedition against the Kaffirs became necessary in 1851, and hostilities continued until 1853, when the native leaders surrendered.

It was during the Kaffir campaign that the troopship Birkenhead was wrecked near Simonstown in the early hours of February, 26 1852. Reinforcements for several regiments, including the 73rd, were on board, and their splendid discipline when the ship struck a rock and began to sink ensured the survival of all the women and children—the families of soldiers.

There being insufficient lifeboats, the troops —after assisting the women and children into the boats and getting them away to safety— silently lined up on deck and did not break ranks until the ship began to settle. And when they struck out for the shore they avoided the crowded lifeboats though in shark-infested waters. Fifty-six men of the 73rd drowned—

the largest number of deaths suffered by any of the regiments represented on board the Birkenhead.

There was further action against the Kaffirs in 1856, in which the 73rd was involved. In 1858 the regiment sailed for India to assist in quelling the Mutiny. In late 1858 it arrived at Calcutta, and, at Benares, was split up into detachments which took part in a series of punitive operations and in general pacification duties. In 1861 the formation returned to the U.K., and in 1862 it was styled the 73rd (Perthshire) Regiment.

The remainder of the 73rd's existence as a separate regiment was uneventful. It served in Ireland in 1865, and in 1867 was in Hong Kong, moving to Ceylon in 1869. After five years on this station, the 73rd arrived in India in 1874, serving there until 1881. In 1881 it returned to England and rejoined its " parent " regiment—the 42nd—as the 2nd Battalion.

On the outbreak of Arabi Pasha's rebellion against the Khedive of Egypt, the 1st Battalion The Black Watch joined the Highland Brigade in August, 1882. After a night march across the desert the battalion attacked the enemy at Tel-el-Kebir in the first light on September 13, rushing the Egyptians and Soudanese with the bayonet and clearing them from their strong entrenchments. Later The Black Watch entered Cairo to the skirl of the pipes.

In February, 1884, the 1st Battalion went to Saukim as part of the force assembled for operations against the hostile tribes of the Eastern Soudan. Principal actions were at El Teb and Tamai. In the fierce fighting with the dervish warriors at Tamai, Private Thomas Edwards won the Victoria Cross for bringing in during the heat of the battle the body of a naval lieutenant and a machine-gun in danger of falling into the hands of the enemy.

In late September the 1st Battalion set out to the relief of General Gordon besieged and cut off at Khartoum by the fanatical hordes of the Mahdi. The Black Watch fought with great dash at Kirbekan in February, 1885, driving the enemy before them with their bayonets. A detachment was engaged in a sharp action at the Abu Klea wells. During the fighting advance news came in that Khartoum had fallen and that General Gordon was dead. The relief column then headed for Cairo. The 1st Battalion remained there until May, 1886, when it left for Malta. It proceeded to Gibraltar in August, 1889.

While the 1st Battalion was engaged in campaigns in Egypt and the Soudan, the 2nd Battalion had also been active. Stationed in Ireland from 1882 until 1892, it was employed for a time in dealing with outbreaks of political strife. The battalion returned to Scotland in 1892.

A detachment of the 1st Battalion was dispatched against the natives of Matabeleland, who were attacking the settlers. This trouble dealt with, the battalion arrived in India in 1896, after picking up en route companies which had been ordered to the Mauritius. The 1st Battalion served in India until 1901. In December of that year the 1st Black Watch embarked for South Africa, landing at Durban towards the end of the month to participate in the war against the Boers of the Transvaal and the Orange Free State.

The 2nd Battalion, located in England, was also ordered to South Africa, landing at Cape Town in November, 1899, to join the Highland Brigade, serving with the 1st Division. In its first major action in this campaign—the dawn attack at Magersfontein Hill, in December,— the battalion sustained very heavy casualties. In January, 1900, the Highland Brigade again clashed with the Boers at Koodoosberg Drift, and had another success at Paardeberg, on the Modder River, where a large force of the enemy was surrounded and forced to surrender.

The battalion took part in the action at Poplar Grove, and two days later attacked again at Driefontein, and marched into Bloemfontein, capital of the Orange Free State. The Black Watch was also prominent in the bitter engagements at Baviaan's Berg and at Retief's Nek. The action at Retief's Nek led to the surrender of about 4,000 Boers under Prinsloo.

The 2nd Battalion was employed on detachment duties and operated with mobile columns in Natal. When peace was signed in the summer of 1902, the 2nd was sent on to Harrismith, where the 1st Battalion was already established. Both battalions remained there until October, when the 1st left for Scotland— and moved to Ireland in 1906—while the 2nd departed for India. The 3rd (Militia) Battalion sent out a number of drafts to South Africa during the fighting, and the Volunteer battalions dispatched three Service Companies.

The battle-honours of the regiment at this time were:—The Sphinx superscribed " Egypt ", Guadaloupe, 1759, Martinique, 1762, Havannah, North America, 1763-4, Mangalore, Mysore, Seringapatam, Corunna, Busaco, Fuentes d'Onor, Pyrenees, Nivelle, Nive, Orthes, Toulouse, Peninsula, Waterloo, South Africa, 1846-7, 1851-2-3, Alma, Sevastopol, Lucknow, Ashantee, 1873-4, Tel-el-Kebir, Egypt, 1882, 1884, Kirbekan, Nile, 1884-5, Paardeberg, South Africa, 1899-1902.

Twenty-seven battalions of The Black Watch served during World War 1. Men who wore the Red Hackle fought in France, Belgium, Macedonia, Egypt, Mesopotamia and Palestine. Sixty-eight battle-honours were awarded, the ten emblazoned on the Colours being:— Marne, 1914, '18, Ypres, 1914, '17, 18', Loos, Somme, 1916, '18, Arras, 1917, '18, Lys, Hindenburg Line, Doiran, 1917, Meggido, Kut el Amara, 1917.

On the outbreak of war in August, 1914, the 1st Battalion was at Aldershot, and the 2nd at Bareilly, India, with the 21st Brigade of the Meerut Division. The 1st Battalion, forming part of the 1st Guards Brigade of the 1st Division, arrived in Belgium in mid-August, and, after several desperate encounters with the onrushing German Army, took part in the Retreat from Mons, ending the retiral within 50 miles of Paris.

The 1st Black Watch was heavily engaged in the Marne and Aisne battles during the autumn, and then experienced the hard fighting around Ypres at the first battle there. In this sector the unit put a battalion of the Prussian Guards hors de combat.

The 2nd Battalion arrived in France early in October, entering the line near Givenchy. Both battalions were frequently engaged in this area until the spring of 1915. The 2nd distinguished itself at Neuve Chapelle in March, and the two battalions were in the thick of the fighting at Festubert. At Rue de Bois, Corporal John Ripley, of the 1st, and Corporal David Findlay, of the 2nd, each won the Victoria Cross for conspicuous gallantry. Then came the Loos bloodbath in September, with the 1st and 2nd Black Watch locked in deadly combat with the Germans. In December the 2nd Battalion, with the Meerut Division, was ordered to Mesopotamia.

The 1st Battalion fought on the Somme in July, 1916, and the names Contalmaison, Delville Wood, Longueval, Bazentin, Mametz and High Wood will revive Black Watch memories. The 1st was in several desperate actions at the Third Battle of Ypres, in August, 1917, and on the Lys, in the spring of 1918. At Zonnebeke Lieutenant-Colonel L. P. Evans, D.S.O., won the Victoria Cross. Moving to

Arras, the battalion took part in the successful assault on the Drocourt-Queant switch line in September, and, later in the month, crossed the St. Quentin Canal and entered the final victorious advance.

The 1st Black Watch ended the war on the banks of the Oise-Sambre Canal, near the location where, in 1914, the battalion had concentrated with the 1st Division of the British Expeditionary Force. After the Armistice the 1st Battalion occupied Cologne, and remained in Germany until August, 1919.

The 2nd Battalion was in the force which made the valiant but unsuccessful attempt to relieve Kut-el-Amara. It fought at the Battle of Sheikh Saad in early January, 1916, suffering heavy casualties from the concentrated Turkish fire. The survivors were amalgamated with the 1st Seaforths, this battalion having also been seriously depleted. The combined unit was styled " The Highland Battalion ", but a few months later, on the arrival of reinforcements, the two battalions resumed their separate identities.

For over a year the 2nd Black Watch held the trenches in front of Kut-el-Amara, and in March, 1917, took part in the advance on Baghdad, the men of the 2nd being the first troops to enter. Later that month the battalion was engaged in operations to the north of the town, and in April went into action at Istabulat, where Private Charles Melvin won the Victoria Cross for heroism under fire. A few days afterwards the battalion entered Samarra. The 2nd Black Watch formed part of the expedition sent to capture Tekrit in November, after which the formation left Mesopotamia for Palestine.

Entering the line north of Jaffa, in April, 1918, the battalion had an important role in the Battle of Sharon, in September. The Black Watch broke through the Turkish line, taking many prisoners, and advanced to Tripoli in the wake of the defeated retreating enemy. Here news of the Armistice with the Turks was received in October, and the 2nd Battalion moved to Beirut, then on to Alexandria and Port Said. In June, 1919, the 2nd Black Watch was homeward bound.

The 3rd (Special Reserve) Battalion provided drafts for the combatant battalions throughout the war. The 4th, 5th, 6th and 7th—all Territorial Army formations—served on the Western Front. Of the Service battalions, the 8th and 9th were in France; the 10th operated in France, and later, in Salonika; the 11th had the role of a " feeder " battalion; the 12th (Labour) Battalion functioned in France; the 13th (Scottish Horse) served in Macedonia, and later, on the Western Front; and the 14th (Fife and Forfar Yeomanry) campaigned in Egypt, then in Palestine, and later, in France. The 13th and 14th Battalions—originally Scottish yeomanry formations—became battalions of The Black Watch while they were in Egypt. Thirty thousand men served in the 1914-18 campaigns; 8,000 were killed, and over 20,000 wounded.

In 1920 the 1st Battalion was in India and the 2nd Battalion with the Army of Occupation in Germany. The 2nd returned to the U.K. in 1922. In 1936 the 1st moved to the Soudan—a stage on the voyage home. The 1st Battalion arrived back in Britain in March, 1938.

A great honour was paid to The Black Watch when His Majesty King George V became the Colonel-in-Chief, later to be succeeded by Her Majesty Queen Elizabeth—The Queen Mother. In 1922 " The Auld Forty-Twa " was designated The Black Watch (Royal Highland Regiment).

The 1st Black Watch, after serving in the north of France and in the Maginot Line defences, with the 4th Division, joined 154 Brigade of the 51st (Highland) Division early in March, 1940. The Highland Division took over a section of the " Maginot ", near Metz. In these days of desultory rifle fire and machine-gun fire, occasional raids, and patrol actions, our American cousins called it " the phoney war ".

Then came May 10, and " blitzkreig " became an English word. German aircraft, tanks and infantry flowed across Holland, Belgium and France like the deluge released by the collapsing wall of a dam. Three days later a heavy bombardment was sprung on the division area, and furious fighting developed. But the Highland Division held on to its positions and gave as good as it got. On May 15, however, the division was ordered to withdraw in conformity with the French defence plan. The fighting retiral commenced, which was to end in the German tank-trap at St. Valery-en-Caux.

March, dig in, and fight . . . . March, dig in, and fight . . . . For a month this went on amid chaos, killing, and havoc. Rumours of disaster and surrender came in daily. But, for the Highland Division, it was still march, dig in, and fight. Brigades changed position; battalions moved forward; companies attacked, deployed, defended, retired, other units moved up, lost contact, and were never heard of again;

orders, fresh orders, countermanded orders followed in quick succession . . . . the crash of shells, the drone of enemy aircraft, the whistle of bombs, the chatter of machine-guns, the crack of rifles . . . . smoke, flames, confusion, ruined villages, fleeing refugees . . . . MARCH ! DIG IN ! FIGHT !

On reaching Etain and Varennes it was learned that the Germans had broken through, the French armies were disintegrating, and that a deep wedge of fast-flowing German armour was between the Highland Division and the other B.E.F. formations. The 51st retired on Paris, and news came in that King Leopold had capitulated.

March, dig in, and fight—no " phoney war " now ! The exhausted battle-weary men of the Highland Division sweated, they toiled, they swore—but they marched, dug in, and fought. The 51st Division changed direction, and retired to a new defence line stretching from the north of Abbeville to the sea. By this time the British Expeditionary Force was being evacuated from Dunkirk.

Attacking the enemy bridgehead south of Abbeville, " A " Company of the 1st Black Watch took its allotted objective, but, to conform with the action of troops on its flank, had to retire. The brigade held grimly on to the defensive positions nearest to the sea, but had to retire under heavy enemy pressure to an area around Beauchamps, and then to the line of the River Bethune. For a time the 1st Black Watch held up the German advance on the Varenne before retiring to St. Pierre-le-Viger, within a few miles of St. Valery. The German tank ring drew closer.

They were bombed, they were battered, they were shelled, they were shattered ; the artillery thundered, the rifles cracked, and the machine-guns rattled. The divisional guns were silent now—no shells; the rifle-fire slackened—no bullets; men staggered with exhaustion—no food.

But The Black Watch closed their ranks, as they did in days of yore, and fought on among the wounded, the dead and the dying. Many heard the shrill of the pibroch amid the din of battle as they went down before the rain of shot and shell in that ever-narrowing circle of fire and steel at St. Valery. Maybe the " wee folk " of the mountains, glens, woods and lochs played a dirge for those wounded and dying Scots. As consciousness lapsed, the valiant soldiers of Am Freiceadan Dubh heard the elfin pipes lament the passing of the Highland Division . . . . .

The skirl of the pipes ushered in a new 51st (Highland) Division, and, in May, 1941, that popular soldier, General Douglas Neil Wimberley—later to be known among the troops as " Tartan Tam "—took over the command. At 21.30 hours on October 23, 1942, the roaring reverberating thunder of the British barrage, from batteries of guns stretching at intervals for some six miles across the desert, was the prelude to the Battle of Alamein. The reconstituted 51st (Highland) Division went into action.

With the pipes sounding shrill and clear, the reformed 1st Battalion The Black Watch advanced, the bayonets gleaming under the desert moon. Soon they were red with German and Italian blood. In its first battle the new 51st avenged the disaster of St. Valery, and hurled Rommel's Afrika Korps back into the open desert. The prison cages rapidly filled with gesticulating excitable Italians, glad to be out of the war, and sullen dejected Germans.

To the Hills of Tripoli ! Forward the 42nd ! The 1st Black Watch advanced towards Mersa Brega and cut the road behind it in a duststorm followed by torrential rain. Soon the battalion was nearing Homs, engaging in a series of clashes with the enemy rearguard. Four miles to the east was a fort—dubbed " Edinburgh Castle "—which was the hinge of the German defence system. " Edinburgh Castle " was evacuated as the 1st Black Watch moved forward. The sharp engagements fought out in this area became known as the Battle of the Hills.

Tripoli fell in mid-January, 1943, and the pursuit continued westward, towards Tunisia. The 51st Division attacked the Mareth position in March, and, fighting through the Gabes Gap in April, advanced on the enemy, now established at Akarit. The assault on Wadi Akarit and the desperate battle for the Roumana feature followed. Sfax was entered by the Eighth Army, and the drive went on for Sousse and Enfidaville, both falling in April. The massed Pipes and Drums of the Highland Division took part in the Victory March through Tunis in May.

With 154 Brigade, the 1st Black Watch landed on Sicily in mid-July, 1943. The Italian gunners manning the coastal batteries discreetly retired inland, and the battalion quickly advanced on Vizzini and on to Palagonia. The crossings of the Dittaino secured, the brigade went over and moved against Gerbini, where stiff opposition was encountered. After initial success, a withdrawal had to be made, but the enemy was

later made to pay dearly for his stand here when the advance once more rolled forward.

Fighting into the olive groves, the 1st Black Watch hammered the enemy up the Sferro Hills to Pietraperciata Ridge, and fought on towards, Cocola. The battalion, crossing the Simeto, skirmished in the direction of Biancavilla. The 1st Black Watch had fired its last shots on the bullet-swept hills under blue Sicilian skies, and it was withdrawn to rest. The Highland Division, sailing from Catania, returned to the U.K. to train for another campaign—across the Channel in German-occupied France.

Landing on the Normandy beaches in the early hours of D-Day plus 4, the 1st Black Watch, with 154 Brigade, took part in the bitter fighting which raged along the containment area, around the Bois de Bevant, on the Orne. The battalion moved against St. Aigan—the Caen stalemate was over. The brigade carried its objectives, dug in, and the inevitable German counter-attack was repulsed with heavy losses. After clearing the woods near St. Sylvain, 154 Brigade ran into intense machine-gun fire, and there was fierce fighting ere the Germans were cleared out of their vantage points among the trees.

The brigade went forward again to establish a bridgehead on the Dives, and attacked St. Julien, the 1st Black Watch skirmishing through in the wake of the enemy. The Highland Division advanced on the Seine as the German rearguard formations splashed across in full retreat. The 51st then battled eastward, pushing hard for St. Valery.

Garlanded, kissed, cheered and wined, the Highland Division came back to St. Valery-en-Caux, clearing the enemy from a score of picturesque little villages in the rapid advance. The pipes skirled, and St. Valery was en fete. But "C'est la guerre"—the 51st's stay was short. A dangerous enemy "pocket" was holding out at Le Havre. After taking part in operations which culminated in the liberation of Dunkirk, 154 Brigade arrived at Zeelst airfield as a precautionary measure for the arrival of His Majesty King George VI. The brigade later rejoined the division in the Nijmegen "corridor", where one company was involved in repelling a German raiding party.

The 1st Black Watch was soon engaged at the Battle of the Maas, in October, 1944. Bridgeheads were established on the Dommel and Halsche rivers, south of s'Hertogenbosch. The battalion crossed the Halsche at Halder under a smoke screen, and led the brigade's advance to the west, moving on Hooge Bridge. There was a short sharp action at Waspik.

The 1st Black Watch arrived in s'Hertogenbosch early in November, and, crossing the water barriers of the Lowlands of Holland, fought onward to Leveroi, and then on to Bong and Baarlo. When the Germans made their last offensive, breaking through in the Ardennes, the 51st Division was rushed south to plug the deep gap torn between the British and American armies.

The Highland Division went into the attack down the snow-covered Ourthe Valley, 154 Brigade moving on Laroche with armoured cars. The 1st Black Watch went through the town and attacked an enemy-held ridge beyond, and, clearing it, pressed on to Erneuville to contact the Americans coming up from the south.

The Black Watch entered Roupage and Ortho to continue the advance. Then, the danger over, the 51st moved north, away from the thick snow of the Ardennes, to join battle and clear the enemy from the Maas to the Rhine. The 154 Brigade spearheaded the sweep to the Reichswald. The Black Watch were now fighting on German soil, and progress became slow and costly.

The battle raged into the Siegfried Line, and 154 Brigade tackled the German defenders at Hekkens and threw them out after a stiff action, to mount an assault across the Niers in the face of stubborn opposition. Passing through Hassum, 154 Brigade pushed hard for Goch, a Siegfried Line bastion, and the 1st Black Watch forged on to Winkel and Robbenhof. Major-General T. G. Rennie, C.B., D.S.O., M.C., commanding the Highland Division, was killed by a mortar bomb, and was succeeded by Major-General G. H. A. MacMillan, C.B., C.B.E., D.S.O., M.C.

The brigade advanced along the road to Isselburg and took Empel before making an assault on Dinxperlo. The thrust went on to the south of Lingen, and Badbergen and Dinklage were captured. The brigade led the division's advance on Delmenhorst, Ippener and Annen, with the enemy on the run. The Germans were cleared from the opposite bank of the Wumme, the 1st Black Watch taking Ottersberg, Otterstedt and Vorwerk.

The 1st Black Watch moved into Grossenham, and here the Germans initiated overtures for surrender. VE Day dawned on May 8, 1945, and, on May 12, the 51st (Highland) Division staged its great Victory March through Bremerhaven. The Massed Pipes and Drums of The Black Watch, Seaforths, Gordons, Camerons, Argylls, Scottish Horse and Royal Corps of Signals made a brave show, and there were thousands of interested German spectators lining the route. The kilts and sporrans swung in rhythm with the bare knees, the bayonets gleamed and glinted, and metal flashed—and the Red Hackle was prominent.

The 2nd Battalion arrived in Palestine in the autumn of 1937, and was soon operating against bands of elusive Arab raiders who supported the Mufti of Jerusalem. The battalion provided escorts for convoys, and took part in patrols and " sweeps " over the rugged stony hills of Judea and Samaria, and carried out a number of searches of villages for wanted men and arms. The men of the 2nd had their full share of guard and communication duties in the sweltering heat, and experienced several exchanges of fire with Arab marauders. The battalion was so engaged when war broke out in September, 1939.

Early in May, 1940, the 2nd Black Watch arrived in Egypt's Canal Zone, and, towards the end of June, set out for Aden. At the beginning of August the battalion left Aden for Berbera to defend British and French Somaliland against the anticipated Italian attack. The defection of the French, however, allowed the Italians to cross the frontier near Jibuti, and The Black Watch battalion moved to block the enemy in a defile at Tug Argan, about 60 miles from Berbera.

The battalion arrived at Laferug, several miles north of Tug Argan, on the Berbera road. On August 11 came an Italian air attack. There were no casualties, but small arms fire downed one plane in a formation of bombers and fighters. First blood to the 2nd Black Watch !

The Italians were in great force, and the defenders—Indians, East Africans, North Rhodesians and Somalis—had to give way. The Black Watch took up a position on a long low range of hills called Barkasan. The battalion moved to Abdal on August 11, but on the 13th it was ordered back to the Barkasan position and dug in.

First clash with the enemy occurred on the 13th at Tug Argan. " A " Company ran into an ambush while taking ammunition, rations and water to the defenders in this area. A brisk fire—anti-tank mortar, machine-gun and rifle—was opened, but the company successfully extricated itself with a few casualties.

When the decision was taken to evacuate the Protectorate, the 2nd Black Watch was given the task of holding Barkasan to cover the withdrawal of the forces from Tug Argan and their embarkation at Berbera. There was no armoured support or air cover, artillery was weak, and the Italians then had freedom in the skies. The prospect was grim and smacked of disaster.

But the withdrawal and embarkation operations proceeded according to plan. Italian reaction was limited to an air raid on Berbera. Mussolini's army, though possessing great numerical superiority, did not force the issue. As later events proved, the Italian Army was more skilled in avoiding action than seeking it.

On August 17, after being cut off, two platoons of Punjabis came back with the enemy close behind. The Black Watch opened fire. The enemy trucks reversed into one another and made off leaving about 100 Italian and native troops, which " D " Company engaged and quickly sent scampering for cover. The enemy then began crawling along wadis in an attempt to infiltrate.

A larger force, comprising a battalion of native troops, entered the fray and launched an attack, which was soon beaten back. The enemy again went to earth to escape the lashing hail of Black Watch bullets. Another battalion came up and attacked with artillery support, and succeeded in penetrating the position. All mortar " ammo " expended, and communications cut by shell-fire, The Black Watch went at the enemy with bayonet and Bren, and the Italians and their native troops were chased back beyond their starting point.

But the enemy build-up continued. The bayonets came out again, and 50 men of The Black Watch made a daring exposed downhill charge while the right flank poured in supporting fire. The Italians rose in their hundreds and ran like March hares, discarding rifles and equipment as they fled before the yelling Scots. This charge earned several valuable hours respite, but it was observed that the enemy was still gathering strength, and that tanks were now arriving. A few probing attacks were made on the flanks, but the spirited reaction encountered was too much for the enemy, who again sought cover with alacrity.

To escape the mortaring and sniping when the Italians got on to higher ground, outlying platoons were withdrawn. Tanks opened fire, and another enemy attack came in, " C " and " D " Companies being heavily engaged. A dangerous situation was developing with the rapid build-up of Italian strength. Small arms and machine-gun ammunition was running low, and the mortars were all silent now. Communications were still cut, and the enemy was working round the flanks in an enveloping move. The Italians were seen urging on their native troops while they themselves brought up the rear. Possibly they did not relish being too close to the bayonets of The Black Watch. More tanks appeared, but several were destroyed by fire from a Bofors.

The battalion was ordered back behind Laferug. The enemy attempted a half-hearted follow-up, but made no attempt to renew combat. The evacuation at Berbera having been successfully completed and the advancing enemy checked by The Black Watch rearguard, the battalion retired to Berbera, and, a few hours later, it was under way for Aden, arriving on August 19. From there it moved to Suez, disembarking a week later.

Black Watch casualties had been very light in the fighting against tanks, artillery, aircraft and infantry—seven killed, 16 wounded. Enemy losses at the hands of the Indians, East Africans, Northern Rhodesians, Somalis and The Black Watch were close on 2,000. Five enemy brigades had been engaged and held up for several days by five battalions with weak artillery support and no air cover—and sporting " fans " in the 2nd Black Watch were convinced that the Italian challenge in running events at the post-war Olympic Games would be serious.

There followed a spell of guard duty in Cairo, at the Citadel, and, towards the close of the year, the 2nd Battalion embarked at Port Said—destination Suda Bay, Crete. In the spring of 1941 the battalion was heavily engaged with invading German paratroops flown in from occupied Greece.

After concentrated bombing and machine-gunning by enemy aircraft, score after score of large Junkers troop-carrying planes came over. Every available gun was brought to bear on them, and a heavy fire was opened. Aircraft hit by Bofors fire plunged down in flames and smoke, and parachutists hurtled earthwards in blazing harness. Planes were seen turning round and making off with paratroops draped over their wings. Other aircraft, driven out of formation by the defensive fire, flew in among the descending parachutists, Germans were now obligingly slaughtering Germans.

Descending paratroops fell on telegraph wires and were quickly dispatched, while others became tangled up in trees and were similarly dealt with. But the enemy rained down reinforcements, and there were heavy supporting raids by bombers. The Black Watch defenders were bombed and machine-gunned from high and low level, but, from their slit trenches, they replied with well-aimed machine-gun and rifle fire, and many of the parachutists were riddled with bullets when they touched earth.

This carnage went on for three weeks. The Black Watch battalion denying the enemy the use of the vital airfield they were defending, and there was bitter disappointment when the evacuation order was received. But it was at least some consolation to know that the position had not deteriorated in The Black Watch sector of Heraklion.

In June the Royal Navy brought off the defenders of Crete under great difficulty and with appreciable loss owing to numerous and concentrated air attacks. The resulting casualties among the troops were much heavier than those incurred in the fighting on the island. The evacuation ships had to run the bomber gauntlet across the " Med " to Egypt. But the 2nd Black Watch survived to fight another day.

Early in July, 1941, the 2nd Battalion left Cairo and arrived in the Plains of Sharon. The battalion was stationed for a time near Damascus, then went to Zahle, in the eastern foothills of Mount Lebanon. A series of hard training programmes was carried out, but the battalion was not committed to battle against the Vichy French in Syria.

The scene changes to Tobruk—shelled, bombed, attacked, battle-scarred, isolated and besieged—but defiant. The 2nd Black Watch embarked on destroyers for Tobruk on October 22 and joined the beleagured garrison.

General Wavell's army had to retire to the Egyptian frontier before the weight of the powerful German armoured formations which had arrived in North Africa. But at Tobruk he purposely left behind a brigade of the 7th Australian Division—which the 2nd Black Watch reinforced. The Scots and Australians held on grimly and proved an exceedingly sharp thorn in the side of the enemy.

At Tobruk and its perimeter the 2nd Battalion stoically endured the air raids, shelling, sniping, mortaring and machine-gunning. In the epic sortie of November 20 the pipes skirled in the determined assault on the German positions at " Jill " and " Tiger ", but for so many of The Black Watch it was a dirge.

Without tank support, the battalion attacked the two objectives, suffering very heavy casualties from the storm of artillery, mortar,

machine-gun and small arms fire unleashed on it by the enemy from well dug-in defences. But the positions fell to the survivors, who fought through, and then held the salient created under a deluge of fire.

Instead of relieving Tobruk, formations of the Eighth Army poured in to join the garrison, and, for a time, there was a serious food shortage. Early in the New Year the remnants of the 2nd Battalion left Tobruk and arrived in the Delta. The battalion was later sent to Syria to meet the expected Axis onslaught through Anatolia, but success in the Western Desert ended this threat, and, in February, 1942, the 2nd Black Watch departed from Syria and disembarked at Bombay.

The battalion went to the Deccan for training in jungle combat, and later arrived at Ranchi, in Bihar, where it maintained order during civil unrest. In early September, 1943, while at Bangalore, in the south, the men of the 2nd learned that they were to serve against the Japanese in a Chindit role—long-range penetration, with supplies dropped from aircraft.

At the beginning of October the 2nd Black Watch arrived in the Central Provinces and joined General Orde Wingate's Special Force in hard training. The battalion was organised in two columns, each of about 400 strong—the 73rd and 42nd—taking the old numbers of the regiment. Fully trained and equipped, The Black Watch Chindits moved to Assam on March 15. The two columns arrived at Lalaghat on the 21st. On the 22nd, the senior formation —73 column—flew into "Aberdeen", a Dakota airstrip in the Meza Valley, near Manhton. The other column was flown in on the 25th. The 73rd moved out, and the 42nd, while gathering, was bombed and sustained several casualties.

Moving south on its way to the Banmauk-Indaw road, 73 Column had its first exchange of fire with the Japanese near Sittaw at the close of the month. Both columns ambushed an enemy force at night on this road on April 5. The leading truck was attacked and most of its occupants killed. Those in the second dismounted and were engaged and a number of casualties inflicted. The third truck made off.

Following a reconnaissance on the 9th, at first light on the 10th, 42 Column, with three platoons of 73 Column, carried out an attack with direct air support. Bombers and fighters were brought on to their target by wireless communication, and, as a result, a Japanese dump at Singgan was set ablaze and destroyed, and the defenders shot up as they ran through the exploding ammunition and bombs into the jungle.

Early in May the Chindits of 73 and 42 Columns advanced along the broad shallow waters of the Nami Chaung, and, on the 3rd, were within sight of "White City"—several hills on the edge of the Indaw-Myitkyina railway. "White City" had been held by Brigadier Calvert's force since the middle of March in the face of several determined Japanese attacks. A patrol from "White City" contacted the two Black Watch columns on the 4th and led them across the open valley without incident. Soon they were ascending the Kachin Hills and heard the din of battle at "White City".

An ambush was laid to the north of Nathkokyin on the 5th. Three platoons of 73 took up position in the gathering darkness. A few hours later a long line of Japanese troops appeared, led by a mounted officer. The Black Watch men had them in their sights and opened fire. Scores of the enemy went down in their tracks, and the remainder ran into the jungle discarding equipment as they fled from the death spitting-rifles.

On the night of the 7th a larger and much more ambitious ambush was sprung south of Nathkokyin. Six platoons, totalling about 200 men, engaged well over 1,000 Japanese, and fierce fighting ensued. The enemy, recovering from his surprise, counter-attacked strongly, but the Chindits succeeded in inflicting heavy casualties before retiring. While the action was in progress, this diversion allowed Brigadier Calvert's command to evacuate "White City" without interference.

Following operations in the Kachin Hills towards the close of May, the columns met 111 Brigade retiring from "Blackpool"—a position straddling the railway about eight miles south-east of the top of Kyusunlai Pass. There were numerous bitterly-fought actions in the pass, and a determined Japanese onslaught to drive the Chindits from the crest was repulsed early in June. Further enemy attempts to break out were also frustrated, and there was a sharp patrol engagement at Kontha.

Relieved, the two Chindit formations headed north and toiled up the Nawku Pass early in July in torrential rain. Several swollen fast-flowing rivers had to be crossed, and there was a spirited patrol action at Latang. Three platoons of 73 Column surprised the enemy at Loikum Bum, and the Japanese had the worst of the encounter. The other column had a hectic brush with the enemy at Pungan, and, after indecisive fighting, the enemy withdrew, leaving The Black Watch masters of the area.

Exhausted, sodden, ragged, foot-sore, ravaged by typhus, their clothes and equipment rotting on their bodies, the last engagement of the battalion was an attack on enemy-held Labu, on August 4. The Chindits mortared the enemy out, and gleaming bayonets and fire-spitting tommy-guns completed the elimination of the Japanese in a strong defensive position in front of the village. The survivors got up and made a run for it as The Black Watch charged with pipes skirling—played by a Sassenach named Lark !

For the Chindits of " The Auld Forty-Twa " the campaign was over. On the 9th a patrol went down into the railway valley, and there was a rendezvous with forward troops of the British 36th Division. On the 17th, Piper Lark leading, played his Scottish comrades down the main road on the first stage of the long journey by train and air back to Assam.

During the Burma Campaign The Black Watch Chindits moved unseen and unheard in front of, among, and behind the enemy, and literally " stole " several important positions from the Japanese. They lived almost like animals, creeping silently, stealthily through the jungle in exhausting heat, or monsoon downpour, worming over scrub-covered hills, snaking among arid rocks, and wading quietly through evil-smelling swamps and across fast-flowing rivers and torrents. Frequently they moved swiftly through the blackness of the jungle night to surprise and rout the enemy.

These Black Watch Chindits caused havoc, confusion and heavy losses among the Japanese, who prided themselves on their jungle " creep craft " and infiltration tactics, which early won them an easy conquest. But later they were out-generalled, out-manoeuvred and out-fought, starved of vital supplies, shelled, machine-gunned, mortared, bombed, ambushed and attacked from the most unexpected quarters.

The 4th (T.A.) Battalion was with 153 Brigade during the 1940 retreat of the 51st (Highland) Division. Detached to form Ark Force, it was evacuated from Le Havre, thus escaping the encirclement of the 51st at St. Valery-en-Caux. The 5th and 7th (T.A.) Battalions joined the reconstituted Highland Division and took part in the advance from El Alamein to Tunis, fought in Sicily, and, landing in Normandy, battled across the Continent and forded the Rhine to end the war deep in Germany. The 6th (T.A.) Battalion operated in Tunisia and Italy.

Such is the Odyssey of The Black Watch—France, Belgium, Holland, Palestine, Syria, Aden, Somaliland, Crete, Egypt, North Africa, Tripoli, Tunisia, India, Burma, Gibraltar, Sicily, Italy and Germany.

By permission of Archibald Ramsden, Esq.

" FORWARD FORTY-SECOND ". An episode at the Battle of the Alma, from the picture by Robert Gibb, R.S.A.

Battle-honours awarded to the regiment were:—Defence of Arras, Ypres-Comines Canal, Dunkirk, 1940, Somme, 1940, St, Valery-en-Caux, Saar, Breville, Odon, Fontenay le Pesnil, Defence of Auray, Caen, Falaise, Falaise Road, La Vie Crossing, Le Havre, Lower Maas, Venlo Pocket, Ourthe, Rhineland, Reichswald, Goch, Rhine, North-West Europe, 1940, Aart, Barkasan, British Somaliland, 1940, Tobruk, 1941, Tobruk Sortie, El Alamein, Advance on Tripoli, Medenine, Zemlet el Lebene, Mareth, Akarit, Wadi Akarit East, Djebel Roumana, Medjez Plain, Si Mediene, Tunis, North Africa, 1941-43, Landing in Sicily, Vizzini, Sferro, Gerbini, Adrano, Sferro Hills, Sicily, 1943, Cassino II, Liri Valley, Advance to Florence, Monte Scarlati, Casa Fortis, Rimini Line, Casa Fabbri Ridge, Savio Bridgehead, Italy, 1944-45, Athens, Greece, 1944-45, Crete, Heraklion, Middle East, 1941, Chindits, 1944, Burma., 1944.

After the war the 1st Battalion served in Germany with the occupation forces. The 2nd Battalion left Pakistan in February, 1948, bound for Perth. When all infantry regiments (except the Guards) were reduced to one-battalion strength under the Army reorganisation policy in 1947, a cadre from the 2nd Battalion joined the surviving 1st Battalion in 1948. In 1952, however, it was announced that The Black Watch was one of the seven infantry regiments authorised to raise a second battalion. The new 2nd Battalion was duly raised at Colchester, Essex, in the spring of that year. In February, 1952, the 1st, after a " stint " in Germany, returned to Crail, Fife, its place in Germany being taken by the 2nd.

The Korean War began in July, 1950. The 1st Black Watch arrived at Pusan in June, 1952, to enter the fray with the Commonwealth Division under United Nations command. In flooded dug-outs and trenches in the Korean hills the battalion operated despite a continuous downpour of torrential rain, which turned the red clay into thick, clinging slippery mud. But it did not bog down patrol activity, and there were several successful clashes with enemy prowlers and raiding parties.

The principal action of the 1st Black Watch was the defence of The Hook. In November, 1952, the North Koreans and their Chinese allies were on three sides of the crest of the ridge. The Hook was the key to the Samichon Valley, on the road to Seoul, capital of South Korea. The enemy heavily shelled the area and attacked in great strength. General Winter took a hand too, and the Scots fought this battle in 18 degrees of frost.

With their horns and trumpets blowing, the enemy swarmed across the hills and poured into the assault, coming on through their own bombardment and the United Nations counter-barrage. They were mown down in swathes, and long gaps were torn in their lines. But the attacking waves closed up and still came on —and met the bayonets of the 1st Black Watch. The cold steel stopped them, and there was a crazy pattern of bodies hanging on the wire entanglements in front of the United Nations positions. The desperate fighting for The Hook continued into 1953.

In the furious Imjin River fighting, Private William Speakman, a 6ft. 7½in. stalwart of The Black Watch, attached to The King's Own Scottish Borderers, won the Victoria Cross. At the critical stage of the battle he fought a heroic one-man action, showering the enemy with grenades as his comrades re-grouped to resume the fray.

The " Cease Fire " came on July 27, 1953, and in the same month the 1st Black Watch left Pusan for Kenya to operate against the Mau Mau. Black Watch Hill is a permanent memorial to the endurance and heroism of the battalion during its 13 months in Korea. Battle-honours awarded were The Hook, 1953, and Korea, 1952-53.

Arriving at Nairobi, Kenya, in August, the battalion was at once employed in seeking out and tracking down marauding gangs of murdering plundering Kikuyu tribesmen. The battalion scoured the jungles of the Aberdare Mountains and had a number of clashes with the Mau Mau. After " Operation Anvil " the members of this cult of barbarism were considerably less. The 1st Battalion came home in the autumn of 1955.

In September, 1954, the 2nd Battalion was dispatched to British Guiana to relieve The Argyll and Sutherland Highlanders, and the 2nd continued the pacification duties initiated by the Argylls during a period of political tension and unrest. In 1955 the 2nd Black Watch returned home and was disbanded. A contingent joined the 1st Battalion.

The 1st Black Watch left Crail for Berlin in January, 1956, and served in Germany until November, 1957, when it returned to the homeland. At the end of the following year the 1st Battalion sailed from Southampton, bound for Cyprus, to combat EOKA's campaign of murder and sabotage. " The Auld Forty-Twa " is still making Empire history and adding to Scotland's glory.

LORD SEAFORTH

After Sir Thomas Lawrence. From a copy by
W. Dyce, R.A., 1837. Bequeathed to the Officers,
2nd Seaforth Highlanders, by Lord Seaforth's
grand-daughter, Miss Florence Mackenzie, 1910

The Seaforth Highlanders

(ROSS-SHIRE BUFFS, THE DUKE OF ALBANY'S)

THE 1st Battalion The Seaforth Highlanders—the old 78th and later the 72nd Highlanders—was raised in 1778 by Kenneth, Earl of Seaforth, Chief of the Clan Mackenzie. The Earl rallied round him many of the clan from his Ross-shire estates, also a number of the Macraes from Kintail. In May, 1778, at Elgin, General Skene subjected the muster of over 1,000 Highlanders to a thorough inspection. He then described them as "stoute men, hardy and active, and in a short time will make a remarkably fine regiment". Prophetic words!

The Mackenzies of Seaforth fought in support of the Jacobite cause in the 1715 Rising, and the 5th Earl of Seaforth was deprived of his title and estates. His son was later permitted to re-purchase the lands from the Crown, and, in 1771, the grandson took the title. To show his gratitude the Earl offered to raise a Highland regiment for service in North America. King George III readily accepted. The formation was originally styled the 78th Regiment, Seaforth's Highlanders, and the Mackenzie tartan was adopted.

The regiment's badge of a stag's head with the motto "Cuidich'n Righ" (Help the King) is the crest of the Seaforth family. Crest and motto were granted to Colin Fitzgerald, founder of the family, in 1255 by King Alexander III of Scotland, whose life he saved from a hunted stag. The motto "Tulloch Ard" on officers' full-dress sword-belts is a war-cry of the Clan Mackenzie. It means the high hill, or hillock, and the allusion is to the hill which was the meeting and council-place of the clan.

Three months after embodiment the 78th Highlanders arrived in Edinburgh, where the regiment was placed under orders to proceed to India. As the regiment was raised for service in North America, this news caused immediate resentment. The angry Macraes formed up, and with two plaids on poles as their "colours", and led by pipers, they marched defiantly out of the barracks to Arthur's Seat, where they strongly entrenched themselves.

The Macraes had kinsmen and numerous sympathisers in the city, and numbers of them climbed Arthur's Seat to provide the Highlanders with food. Through the efforts of Lord Dunmore and General Skene a settlement was reached, and a few days later the Highlanders marched back to barracks. The order dispatching the 78th to India was countermanded, and the regiment was sent to the Channel Islands.

In 1781 the French launched a surprise attack on Jersey with the intention of regaining the Channel Islands. St. Helier was captured, but the Highlanders and the local Militia engaged the invaders, and after sharp fighting the French were cleared out of the town and driven back to the sea. In the same year the regiment embarked at Portsmouth for India, this time without incident.

The voyage was a disastrous one, lasting over ten months. The Colonel, Lord Seaforth, died off St. Helena, and by the time the regiment disembarked at Madras over 200 men had succumbed to scurvy and other illnesses. Only 369 men could carry arms. The 78th's first action in India was against the fort of Cuddalore, in the Carnatic Campaign against the ruler of Mysore.

Detachments from the 78th Highlanders served on the fighting ships of Admiral Sir Edward Hughes, which engaged the French in August, 1782, in Indian waters. The Highlanders, serving as sailors and marines, were encouraged by their pipers, who played during the action. The battle raged all day before the French were defeated. Continuing the war in India, the regiment took a prominent part in the capture of Palghautcheri, and operated until peace was concluded in 1784. Owing to a reduction in Army establishment, the regiment was re-numbered the 72nd in 1786.

During the Carnatic Campaign, which was resumed in 1789, the 72nd Highland Regiment was heavily engaged in the assaults on the hill forts at Coimbatore, Morglee, Savendroog, Outradroog, Outra Durgam, Dindegul and Seringapatam. Bangalore—an important fortress which Tippoo thought impregnable—was stormed and captured in 1791. In 1793 the regiment was included in the expedition sent against the French settlement at Pondicherry, which the enemy surrendered.

From 1795 until 1797 the regiment operated against the Dutch in Ceylon, capturing all the enemy's strongholds. The island was surrendered to Britain in 1797. The 72nd Highland Regiment returned to Scotland in 1798, and also served in Ireland. A second battalion of the 72nd was formed in 1804, and this formation acted as a "feeder" for the 1st Battalion until its disbandment was ordered in 1816.

The 72nd was included in the British force which was dispatched to capture the Cape of Good Hope from the Dutch in 1806, owing to the importance of its situation on the route to India. The 72nd Highlanders formed part of the Highland Brigade, which overcame stiff resistance on the Blaauberg, or Blue Mountains. Later the Dutch surrendered Cape Colony.

The Government decreed in 1809 that five regiments should be taken off the Highland establishment and assume the uniform of the infantry. The 72nd ceased to wear the Mackenzie tartan kilts and yellow facings on their doublets, and reluctantly donned the white facings and pantaloons of the Infantry of the Line. From 1806 to 1821 the regiment served in the Cape, Mauritius and India.

In 1822 the regiment returned to the U.K., and that year received the welcome news that King George IV had approved of the 72nd again becoming a Highland regiment, but that trews should be worn instead of the kilt. As a further mark of esteem, and with the King's approval, the Commander-in-Chief, H.R.H. The Duke of York and Albany, gave permission for the 72nd to bear his Scottish title, cypher and coronet, and to assume the Prince Charles Stewart tartan. Thus the 72nd took the title "The Duke of Albany's Own Highlanders", and was the only Highland regiment to wear the feathered bonnet with trews.

After being stationed in Scotland, Ireland and England, the 72nd again went to the Cape in 1828, and in 1832 was engaged in the Kaffir War, which lasted until 1835. The regiment operated in detachments to check cattle-raiding along the frontier, and the units took part in numerous punitive expeditions. The regiment returned to the homeland in 1840.

The 72nd went to Gibraltar in 1844, after which it was ordered to the West Indies in 1848, serving at Barbadoes and Trinidad.

The regiment served in Canada from 1852-54, being stationed at Nova Scotia and New Brunswick. The 72nd returned to the U.K. in 1854, and was stationed in Ireland.

The 72nd next experienced active service in the bleak, ghastly, disease-ridden Crimean Peninsula. In May, 1855, the regiment joined General Sir Colin Campbell's Highland Brigade, and took part in the bitter trench warfare and assaults which preceded the capture of Sebastopol. The Highlanders came home in 1856.

On the Indian Army Mutiny breaking out in 1857, the 72nd Highlanders were despatched to deal with the rebels. Landing at Bombay, the 72nd joined the column advancing on Kotah, a fortified town in Central India. Kotah was carried by assault, with the Highlanders in the spearhead. With the battle-cry "Cabar Feidh gu Bragh!" the Highlanders charged through a rain of bullets and stormed in among the enemy. Lieutenant Cameron won the Victoria Cross for his part in a desperate hand-to-hand encounter on a staircase.

In the autumn of 1858 the arrival of the regiment with its brigade saved the State of Bhopal from falling into the hands of the mutineers. The Highlanders were almost continually employed in engaging, pursuing and dispersing bands of rebels after they had been driven from the principal centres of insurrection. At the beginning of 1866 the 72nd Highlanders returned to Britain, remaining until 1871, when they were again sent to India for another tour of service.

In 1878 the 72nd Highlanders were in the force sent against the Amir of Afghanistan. The right wing of the Highland regiment fought well in the stiff battle for the Peiwar Kotal. The enemy were strongly entrenched in a pass near Kohat, but the Highlanders, by a sharp flank attack, dislodged the tribesmen. Peace came in 1879, but after the murder of the British Embassy staff at Kabul, operations were at once resumed.

The 72nd marched to Kabul and joined battle at Charasiah, and was engaged in the severe fighting in this area towards the end of the year. Sergeant Sellar was later awarded the Victoria Cross for his gallantry on the Asmai Heights in mid-December, 1879.

In August, 1880, after the British disaster at Maiwand, the regiment formed part of the column which made the historic advance to Kandahar to relieve the besieged garrison, covering 320 miles in 22 days.

The Afghan position at Kandahar was vigorously attacked in September, the 72nd assailing the enemy right and threatening the tribesmen's line of retreat. The Afghans withdrew, slowly at first, but the retiral soon became a headlong flight before the cracking rifles and gleaming bayonets of the Highlanders. Thus ended the hard-fought Afghan War in the high scorched passes and eternal snows of the mountains.

In 1881 the 72nd, The Duke of Albany's Own Highlanders, became the 1st Battalion Seaforth Highlanders. In the same year the 78th Highland Regiment, Ross-shire Buffs, became the 2nd Battalion, Seaforth Highlanders—a highly desirable union, as both regiments had a similar origin. On its return from foreign service in 1882 the 1st Battalion again adopted the Mackenzie tartan kilt, the dress which it had to discard under the unpopular order of 1809. From 1881 the two battalions were identically garbed.

The 2nd Battalion Seaforth Highlanders, formerly the 78th Highland Regiment, was raised, over 1,000 strong, in 1793, by Francis Humberston Mackenzie of Seaforth (later Lord Seaforth). By an odd coincidence 78 was the original number of the other regiment, which was re-numbered the 72nd in 1786. About three-quarters of the men came from the Ross-shire estates of the Seaforth family, but since these far-off days the recruiting area of the regiment has been extended to include Caithness, Sutherland, Moray and Nairn.

The first parade of the 78th Highland Regiment was at Fort George in July, 1793, after which it left for Guernsey in October. The 78th Highlanders began their overseas service with a short stay in the Netherlands in 1794, and in that year a second battalion was raised. It was granted the title of The Ross-shire Buffs. The new formation took part in the capture of the Cape of Good Hope in 1795. After this success the battalion amalgamated with the 1st Battalion and sailed for India in 1797.

In the campaign against the Mahrattas—who were assisted by the French—the 78th formed part of the forces commanded by General Sir Arthur Wellesley (later the Duke of Wellington). Marching from Poona, the regiment was in action at the capture of the fortified town of Ahmednugger, in August, 1803. The advance continued southwards, and in September came the historic Battle of Assaye. Here a British force, including Indian troops, defeated a Mahratta army six times its own strength after bitter and costly fighting.

The 78th Highlanders strode forward through a gruelling enemy bombardment and routed the gunners, in addition to standing firm and repelling several cavalry charges with their reddened bayonets. The King honoured the regiments which broke the power of the Mahrattas at this battle by ordering that an elephant superscribed " Assaye " should be borne on their colours and appointments. And the Honourable East India Company presented a special " Assaye " colour to these regiments. The 78th carried its third colour for many years afterwards until the War Office—for the sake of uniformity in the Army—ordered that this practice be discontinued.

The 78th Highlanders took part in the remainder of the Mahratta Campaign in 1803 and 1804, and were in action at the battles of Argaum and Gawal Ghur. In 1811 the regiment arrived in Java to eject the French from the island, which belonged to the Dutch. After the action at Weltervreeden, the enemy occupied the fortified lines of Cornelis, which fell in August. They made another unsuccessful stand at Samarang, in September, then evacuated the island. Clashing with the forces of the rebellious Sultan of Djocjocarta, the Highanders participated in the capture of his stronghold in 1812.

Returning to India in November, 1816, the transports conveying the 78th Highland Regiment were wrecked in the Bay of Bengal. All the regimental baggage, records and funds of £2,000 were lost, also several men. The Highlanders were marooned on the lonely island of Preparis for about a month, suffering considerable hardship through lack of provisions. After their rescue the Highlanders sailed for home in March, 1817.

In 1804 a second battalion of the 78th was again raised. It was inspected the following year at Fort George by the Marquis of Huntly, and after service at home and at Gibraltar, the 2nd Battalion experienced its " baptism of fire " from the French at Maida, in Calabria, Italy, in July, 1806. In this battle the new battalion charged the French with the bayonet, driving them back with great loss. Heartened by this success, their Italian allies soon cleared Napoleon's forces out of Southern Italy.

The following year, 1807, the 2nd Battalion formed part of a force which was dispatched to Egypt to engage the Turks, who were in a strong position at Rosetta, near Alexandria.

The Highlanders sustained heavy casualties in an onslaught against greatly superior numbers, and the survivors of one detachment, cut off at El Hamet, were forced to surrender. The expedition evacuated Egypt later that year, and the 2nd Battalion returned home early in 1808.

In 1809 the battalion was engaged on an ill-fated badly conducted expedition to Holland. Sickness was rife, and the whole expedition was withdrawn in 1810. In 1814, though depleted by drafts sent out to the 1st Battalion operating against the French in Java, the 2nd Battalion was again employed in Holland, but on this occasion with outstanding success.

In a reconnaissance in force towards Antwerp, the 2nd Battalion attacked Merxem, held by four French battalions. The assault was pressed with vigour and determination, and the enemy was cleared out of the village. The 2nd Battalion remained in the Netherlands as part of the Allied Army of Occupation until 1816, when it returned to Britain to be disbanded. The officers and other ranks then joined the 1st Battalion. The 1st served in the U.K., Ceylon, India and Aden, and early in 1857 proceeded with a division under Brig.-General Havelock to join the Persian Expeditionary Force.

Disembarking at Bushire, in the Persian Gulf, the 78th entered on a difficult campaign. The Highlanders operated in the heavy rains and made long forced marches to engage the enemy. After a night march the 78th assisted in the decisive defeat of the Persians at the Battle of Kooshab, and later, at Mahommerah.

But much stiffer battles were to be joined in " The Mutiny ". The 78th arrived in Bombay in May, 1857, with news of uprising and massacre on every side. The regiment was at once ordered to proceed by sea to Calcutta, where it disarmed several battalions of disaffected Indian troops. Then the Highlanders pressed on to Allahabad.

Here the 78th formed part of General Havelock's small column which clashed with the mutineers at Futtehpore. The enemy were hurled from the town with heavy casualties, and were again defeated at Aong and Pandu Nuddi. On July 16 the column arrived before Cawnpore, where a handful of Europeans had put up a stout resistance against fearful odds. General Havelock at once engaged and defeated the mutineers. He entered Cawnpore only to find the men of the little garrison, his troops had fought so hard to relieve, had been massacred along with their womenfolk and children two days earlier.

General Havelock advanced on Lucknow to relieve the garrison besieged in the Residency, but he had twice to fall back owing to sickness and casualties. On September 23, after receiving reinforcements, his troops, battled on to the Alumbagh, a walled enclosure about two miles from their objective. At Lucknow a few hundred British troops and loyal sepoys, and a number of armed civilian volunteers, held out against the press of mutineers under constant fire, and enduring great privations. It was " no surrender ", for the lives of many women and children were at stake.

The bridge on the canal at Charbagh was stormed and taken, and the relieving force, though suffering heavy casualties, fought its way into the narrow streets. The Highlanders were assailed by a murderous fire from windows and rooftops on every side, but late in the evening the Residency was reached, and General Havelock's column, with its numerous wounded, joined the men of the garrison in their gallant resistance until finally relieved by the advance of General Sir Colin Campbell in mid-November.

In 1859 the regiment took part in numerous mopping-up skirmishes, pursuits of fleeing mutineers, and routine pacification duties. With the Rohilkund Field Force, the 78th was engaged in the fighting at Bareilly, and in further operations against the rebels in Rohilkund. In " The Mutiny " campaign eight Victoria Crosses were awarded to officers and other ranks of the 78th Highland Regiment. Recipients were:—Lieutenant and Adjutant Macpherson, Lieutenant Crowe, Lieutenant Bogle, Surgeon Jee, Assistant-Surgeon MacMaster, Colour-Sergeant Macpherson, Private Ward, and Private Hollowell. In May, 1859, the regiment embarked for home. After arriving at Fort George in September, the Highlanders were feted in Nairn and Inverness.

The 78th Highland Regiment, after a tour of service at home and in Canada, embarked for India early in 1879, and though it operated in the Afghan War of 1879, the Highlanders were not committed to battle. In 1881 the 78th became the 2nd Battalion Seaforth Highlanders.

After the fusion the 1st Battalion Seaforth Highlanders—formerly the 72nd The Duke of Albany's Own Highlanders—was dispatched to Egypt to suppress the Egyptian Army mutiny led by Colonel Arabi Pasha. The Highlanders were prominent in the bayonet charge which shattered the rebels in the dawn battle at Tel-el-Kebir, in 1882. The battalion returned to the U.K. in the autumn of the same year, and in 1897 it took part in the international occupation of Crete. In March, 1898, the 1st Seaforths went overseas to form part of General Sir Herbert Kitchener's forces in the Sudan Campaign.

The Dervishes occupied a fortified position on the Atbara River, but this was carried by assault early in April, 1898. Four months later the battalion marched in the advance against the enemy capital of Omdurman. The Khalifa now took the offensive, matching his 60,000 warriors against the Anglo-Egyptian Army of 20,000.

The enemy's advance in close formation met with disaster on meeting the concentrated well-directed fire of the British and Egyptian troops, and the Khalifa fled, leaving his capital in British hands. The Seaforths skirmished forward and entered Khartoum. Throughout the South African War the battalion remained in Egypt, but sent strong drafts to the 2nd Battalion in the field, also two companies of mounted infantry. The 3rd Militia Battalion, on volunteering for active service, was stationed near the 1st Battalion in Cairo for about 18 months. In 1903 the 1st Seaforths left Egypt bound for India.

In February, 1908, the 1st Battalion formed part of the punitive force sent against the Zakka Khel Afridis on the North West Frontier. The campaign was short but severe, and the Seaforths had several sharp encounters with the tribesmen. Three months later the battalion again crossed the frontier, this time to operate against the Mohmands. This six weeks' campaign was also a trying one, fought out in extreme heat with a fierce enemy.

Following the amalgamation of 1881, the 2nd Battalion Seaforth Highlanders saw further service on India's North West Frontier during the Hazara expeditions of 1888 and 1891, and in the Chitral Campaign of 1895. The battalion returned home in 1897, and in the autumn of 1899 mobilised for service in South Africa.

Arriving at Cape Town the 2nd Battalion joined the Highland Brigade on the Modder River. In mid-December the brigade suffered appalling losses at Magersfontein Hill, the key Boer position. The Highlanders attacked into a withering hail of fire from the well-entrenched Boers. Action followed at Koodoosberg and Paardeberg early in 1900, and the Highland Brigade again came under heavy close fire from concealed enemy positions. But, after stubborn fighting, General Cronje was forced to surrender towards the close of February. Then the march on Bloemfontein commenced.

The Highland Brigade skirmished forward to Heilbron in the spring, and it was in the attack on Retiefs Nek, which resulted in another Boer surrender. For the remainder of the year the Seaforths were employed in various mobile columns, and there was much hard marching on short rations. Further clashes with the enemy occurred in the Orange Free State and in the Transvaal, notably at Jagersfontein, Fauresmith and Philippolis. Men from the 2nd Battalion also served in several mounted infantry companies.

Towards the close of 1901 and until peace was signed in May, 1902, the Seaforths occupied a number of blockhouses. These blockhouses were constructed in order to divide the country into areas, and the Boers were then cleared out, sector by sector.

Three companies of Volunteers—forerunners of the present-day Territorials—were sent out from the Volunteer battalions of the regiment, and the " amateurs " acquitted themselves creditably alongside their comrades in the Regular battalion. The 2nd Seaforths returned to Britain in January, 1903.

The battle-honours of the regiment at the beginning of the century were:—The Elephant, superscribed " Assaye ", Carnatic, Hindustan, Mysore, Cape of Good Hope, 1806; Maida, Java, South Africa, 1835; Sevastopol, Koosh-Ab, Persia, Lucknow, Central India, Peiwar Kotal, Charasiah, Kabul, 1879; Kandahar, 1880; Afghanistan, 1878-80; Tel-el-Kebir, Egypt, 1882; Chitral, Atbara, Khartoum, Paardeberg, South Africa, 1899-1902.

At the outbreak of World War I the 1st Battalion Seaforth Highlanders was stationed at Agra, India. With the 7th (Meerut) Division of the Indian Expeditionary Force, the battalion arrived in France in October, 1914. The 1st Seaforths was the only British battalion in the Dehra Dun—the 19th Indian Brigade. The Seaforths took over a series of trenches in the Richebourg-St.Vaast-Neuve Chapelle area, and beat back several German attacks, notably at Givenchy, in mid-December.

Early in March, 1915, the Indian Army Corps launched an attack on the German positions at Neuve Chapelle, capturing two lines of trenches and repelling several powerful enemy counter blows. There was fierce fighting to clear

Aubers Ridge on 9th May, 1915, and the 1st and 4th Battalions suffered more than 400 casualties in less than one hour. During the onslaught of other formations on Loos, in September, the Indian Corps created a diversion on the flank.

The Seaforths were withdrawn from the Western Front in November, 1915, and dispatched to Mesopotamia. In an effort to break through the Turkish lines and relieve the isolated beleagured garrison at Kut-el-Amara, the 7th (Indian) Division attacked Sheikh Saad, Wadi and El Hannah, in January, 1916. Casualties were so heavy that the 2nd Battalion The Black Watch and the 1st Seaforths were amalgamated as " The Highland Battalion ".

In April the enemy position at El Hannah was pierced, and the key stronghold at Sanniyat attacked, and after further fierce fighting the Turks were forced to yield ground. In these operations several decorations for gallantry were awarded, Corporal S. W. Ware receiving the Victoria Cross. But, with the fall of Kut-el-Amara to the Turks at the end of the month, these costly efforts proved to have been in vain. In the autumn The Highland Battalion was resolved into its original elements.

In mid-February, 1917, the Dehra Dun Brigade captured three lines of trenches at Sanniyat, Sergeant T. Steele winning the Victoria Cross. A fortnight later the Seaforths arrived before Baghdad, which was captured early in March, after light resistance. The Highlanders later advanced north, fighting spirited actions at Moushahdieh, Beled and Istabulat. In November there was another sharp clash at Tekrit. The " Mespot " campaign over, the 1st Seaforths arrived in Egypt early in 1918.

The 7th (Indian) Division joined the 21st Army Corps in Palestine and took its place in General Allenby's final victorious advance in the wake of the beaten retreating Turkish Army. The Seaforths, after marching over 30 miles in two days, assaulted and captured Beit Lid, in mid-September. After spells at Beirout and Tripoli, the battalion proceeded to Egypt in March, 1919, and in June the Seaforths sailed for home and Fort George.

The 2nd Battalion Seaforth Highlanders arrived in France from the South of England in August, 1914, as part of the 4th Division of the British Expeditionary Force. With the 10th Brigade, the Seaforths were in the Retreat from Mons, and, after the German reverse on

the Marne, the battalion was heavily engaged in grim fighting at Meteren and Frelinghien during October. The Seaforths then entered a ghastly winter of trench warfare.

At the close of April, 1915, the Highlanders were committed in the Second Battle of Ypres. They attacked St. Julien, sustaining numerous casualties. Early in May the Germans attacked, using gas. With handkerchiefs tied round their mouths, the Seaforths beat them back. Several further enemy assaults were similarly repelled.

The battalion arrived in the Albert-Arras area in July. This was a comparatively quiet sector on the Third Army's front, but the Seaforths took part in several successful minor operations. In the British Somme offensive launched early in July, 1916, the Highlanders attacked near Beaumont Hamel, and captured a number of trenches. For his gallantry in the Battle of the Somme, Drummer W. Ritchie was awarded the Victoria Cross.

The Seaforths fought in this onslaught throughout the summer and autumn. In the spring of 1917, after another grim winter in the trenches, the battalion entered the Battle of Arras, early in April. The Seaforths attacked and captured Roeux in May. Lieutenant D. Mackintosh won the Victoria Cross in this battle. Though wounded, he organised and led a spirited attack into a hail of fire. But the award was posthumous, as Lieutenant Mackintosh was killed the same day.

In October the Seaforth Highlanders were heavily engaged at the final battle for Ypres and blood-soaked Passchendaele Ridge. After its third winter of privation in the frozen water-logged trenches, the battalion faced the massed German spring offensive of 1918 at Arras. The Seaforths, with the 4th Division, fought like men possessed to stem the advancing shoulder-to-shoulder German hordes, and later the battalion was rushed to La Bassée to check a possible enemy breakthrough.

The impetus of the offensive gone, the Allied Armies counter-attacked hurling the Germans back to the Meuse, and the advance to victory began. A few months after the Armistice the 2nd Battalion returned to Fort George. In the autumn of 1919 the Seaforths sailed for India.

The 3rd (Special Reserve) Battalion—" descended " from the old Ross-shire Militia—was employed throughout the war as a training battalion for the two Regular battalions. The three Territorial Army battalions—the 4th, 5th, and 6th—joined the 51st (Highland)

Division, and operated until the Armistice on the Western Front.

The Service battalions were the 7th and 9th—which joined the 9th (Scottish) Division and served in France—and the 8th, which was included in the 15th (Scottish) Division. The 15th Division also served throughout the war on the Western Front. The 10th (Reserve) Battalion was a " feeder ", or draft-supplying unit. The 1st Garrison Battalion operated in the Balkans. In all, 19 battalions of The Seaforth Highlanders were embodied during World War I.

The lengthy and impressive list of battle-honours awarded to the regiment for its deeds of valour in the 1914-18 campaigns is as follows: Le Cateau, Retreat from Mons, Marne, 1914, '18, Aisne, 1914, La Bassée, 1914, Armentieres, 1914, Festubert, 1914, '15, Givenchy, 1914, Neuve Chapelle, Ypres, 1915, '17, '18, St. Julien, Frezenberg, Bellewaarde, Aubers, Loos, Somme, 1916, '18, Albert, 1916, Bazentin, Delville Wood, Pozieres, Flers, Courcelette, Le Transloy, Ancre Heights, Ancre, 1916, Arras, 1917, '18, Vimy, 1917, Scarpe, 1917, '18, Arleux, Pilckem, Menin Road, Polygon Wood, Brood-seinde, Poelcappelle, Passchendaele, Cambrai, 1917, '18, St. Quentin, Bapaume, 1918, Lys, Estaires, Messines, 1918, Hazebrouck, Bailleul, Kemmel, Bethune, Soissonais-Ourcq, Tardenois, Drocourt-Queant, Hindenburg Line, Courtrai, Selle, Valenciennes, France and Flanders, 1914-18, Macedonia, 1917-18, Megiddo, Sharon, Palestine, 1918, Tigris, 1916, Kut-el-Amara, 1917, Baghdad, Mesopotamia, 1915-18.

In addition to the Victoria Crosses won by Lieutenant Mackintosh, Sergeant Steele, Corporal Ware, and Drummer Ritchie, Sea-forths in other battalions of the regiment who were awarded the supreme decoration for heroism were:—Sergeant A. Edwards, at Ypres, in September, 1917; Sergeant J. Meikle, M.M., near Marfaux (France), in September, 1918; and Lance-Corporal R. McBeath, at Cambrai, in January, 1918.

Between the two world wars the 1st Battalion The Seaforth Highlanders operated in Palestine, and the 2nd Battalion on India's North West Frontier, in maintaining the " Pax Britannica ". In the Second World War six battalions of the regiment were committed to battle on widely-separated fronts.

The 2nd, 4th and 5th Battalions were part of the 51st Highland Division holding a stretch of the Maginot Line east of Metz. There was active patrolling in this sector at night,

and the Highlanders usually had the better of the exchanges. The 2nd and 4th Battalions were in 152 Brigade.

On May 10 the Germans invaded Belgium, and three days later a heavy barrage fell on the divisional lines. Bitter fighting ensued. On May 15 the 51st Division was ordered to retire to new positions, but a wedge of German armour had already been driven between the 51st and the other British Expeditionary Force formations. The Highland Division joined the line of the 9th French Army, taking station north of Abbeville. The position was pre-carious, as the enemy had established two firm bridgeheads—at St. Valery-sur-Somme, and south of Abbeville. And by this time the evacuation of the shattered B.E.F. had begun from the Dunkirk beaches.

The Highlanders and their French allies attacked the Abbeville bridgehead on June 4, and their determined onslaught wrested con-siderable ground from the success-flushed Wehrmacht. But, without reserves, and thinly-spread, the assaulting formations had later to retire to their original positions, and on the following day a heavy German attack broke, several forward posts being overrun. Dive-bombers joined in, and it became a fight for survival.

A withdrawal was decided upon, the 152nd Brigade retiring from the Blangy-Monchaux area to the Forêt d'Eu. Fighting back desper-ately, the Highland Division retired to the line of the River Bethune, and the 152nd Brigade took over positions from Dieppe to Arques. The great German breakthrough in the Netherlands continued, the enemy driving hard for the Channel ports. The offensive gathered momentum from St. Quentin to the sea, and split the 10th French Army. German armour penetrated to Rouen, and their line of retreat cut, the Highlanders fought on alone, exhausted, battle-weary, and suffering heavy casualties.

When the Germans established bridgeheads across the Seine, the Highland Division was gallantly fighting its last battle in the short disastrous campaign of 1940, withdrawing into the narrowing defence perimeter, ringed about by Rommel's forces to the south and west and the sea to the north.

After a week of withdrawal actions and failure to evacuate the division from St. Valery-en-Caux the Divisional Commander, Major-General Victor Fortune, knew his men had done all that was expected of them—and much

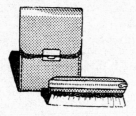

more. The General gave his final order—to surrender—on that fateful morning of June 12, 1940. The din of battle stilled, and the silent tattered, exhausted, blood-stained columns filed past him and began the march into Nazi prison camps.

Scotland was stunned, but proud—proud of the heroic defiance of her Highlanders in the face of such overwhelming odds. But it was her saddest day since Flodden Field. . . . The survivors of the 51st were few, but they were destined to fight again in a new Highland Division, into which Scotland again sent her best and bravest. The new 51st (Highland) Division was formed in the U.K., the surviving brigade—the 154th—evacuated from Le Havre, forming the nucleus. New 2nd, 4th and 5th Battalions were raised and the soldiers of the new 51st trained hard, for they were men with a mission. This mission took them out to Egypt in August, 1942, when Rommel's Afrika Korps and Panzertruppen were nearing the gates of Alexandria and Cairo.

At El Alamein the Highlanders hurled themselves into battle and silenced the chattering German machine-guns. The pibroch skirled eerily amid the artillery's roar and the metallic clanging rumble of the tanks, like the banshee's wail. Shelled and mortared, grenades bursting, shells whistling and crashing, the new Highland Division pushed through to the throat of the enemy—and red were the bayonets of the Highlanders under the desert moon.

Back streamed columns of prisoners—gesticulating Italians and sullen Germans. Then the pursuit began, with the Highlanders in the lead. The Seaforths advanced from Mersa Brega to enter Misurata, and grappled with the enemy at Corradini and El Nab. The fighting flowed towards the Mareth Line, and in the fierce battle at Wadi Akarit the Seaforths carried their objective with a bayonet charge.

The Seaforths were ordered to take Djebel Roumana, several hundred feet high, with precipitous slopes intersected by wadis. Machine-gun, mortar and anti-tank gun emplacements had been hewn from the solid rock and were well camouflaged. The Seaforths attacked across two miles in the open, and were among the foothills when the British barrage burst on the enemy. The Highlanders stormed up the steep slopes, and after several hours of close fighting Djebel Roumana fell, and about 1,000 Italian prisoners were herded

back. German forces then counter-attacked strongly, but the reinforced Highlanders held on to their gains.

From Buerat to the hills of Tripoli the Seaforths with the Eighth Army harried the retreating Germans and Italians, giving them no respite to reorganise. From Tunisia the 2nd, 4th and 5th Battalions crossed to Sicily and were joined by the 6th Battalion, part of 5th Infantry Division. There were violent battles around Lentini, Scordia, Militello, Francofonte and Vizzini, Bridgeheads established over the various rivers, the Seaforths pushed into the Sferro Hills to enter Biancavilla and Fleri.

With the fall of Messina, the flight of the Germans to the Italian mainland, and the surrender of large numbers of Italians, the brief hard-fought campaign in Sicily was over. The 51st Division was sent back to the homeland to prepare for the greater battles which lay ahead; leaving the 6th Battalion to fight on in Italy until the German surrender.

The 51st (Highland) Division returned with the invasion forces to France in June, 1944. The 152nd Brigade was given the task of reducing the enemy-held villages of St. Honorine and Demouville, which it did most thoroughly, and hammered its way down the Troarn road. There was further fierce fighting at the approaches to Tilly-la-Campagne, Favieres and Lisieux.

The Seaforths were represented in the Normandy campaign by the 7th Battalion in the 15th (S.) Division, as well as those in the 51st (Highland) Division. The 7th Battalion was involved in several very hard battles on the west side of Caen at the end of June and July, 1944, and eventually took a major part in the " break-out " at Caumont which led to the overwhelming victory at Falaise.

The 51st Division crossed the Seine to liberate a string of picturesque little French villages, and, after hard fighting with the German rearguard formations, the men of the 51st (Highland) Division poured into St. Valery-en-Caux. The pipes skirled in the square, and there was laughter, flags, ceremonies, wine, flowers, singing, dancing, kisses. . . . And so the Highland Division—via the battlefields of North Africa, Sicily, and Normandy—returned to St. Valery by the misty sea. Thus the 51st kept faith with the Auld Alliance between Scotland and France—and kept faith, too, with the creed of the clans—

" Na diobair caraid 's a charraid " (Forsake not a friend in the fray).

A troublesome German " pocket " was still holding out at Le Havre—another task for the Highlanders—and within 24 hours the enemy was hammered into surrender. In the Battle of the Maas the 152nd Brigade had the task of clearing the woods around Boxtel and Olland, and the Seaforths thrust towards Vught and on to s'Hertogenbosh. There was a sharp encounter with the enemy at the Drunen cross-roads. The brigade arrived at Nederweert and forded the canals under heavy fire.

When Hitler launched his Ardennes winter offensive to drive a wedge between the American and British forces, the 51st Highlanders came down from the Nijmegen area into the Louvain-Maastricht region, but the enemy was checked before they reached the Meuse. The Highland Division attacked down the Ourthe Valley, with the 2nd Seaforths engaged in a series of mopping-up operations. The battalion occupied Halleux, then moved on to Ronchamps.

In the Reichswald battle progress was slow and costly. The Seaforths fought their way deep into the Siegfried Line defences, and there were violent tussles around Hekkens. After pushing through Goch, one battalion turned south to capture Boeckelt. Over the Rhine at Rees, the 152nd Brigade attacked Mittelburg, then, crossing the Issel, delivered an assault on Isselburg. On the fall of Dinxperlo the Highlanders arrived in Lingen. The brigade made a fighting advance into Goldenstedt, and took several villages on the road from Quakenbrück to Visbek. The 152nd pushed on from Ippener and Annen to Delmenhorst, with the enemy still in flight.

The Germans made a stand at Ganderkese, but the Seaforths went in with the bayonet covered by artillery fire, and the opposing paratroopers were ejected. They moved on to Selsingen, and launched an assault on Bremervörde through enemy shelling, but on engaging the German infantry there was only fitful resistance.

The 51st (Highland) Division had fought its last battle deep within Germany. And in the closing hours of the war it received the unconditional surrender of the 15th Panzer Grenadiers—their old adversaries of the desert campaign in North Africa.

While the 4th and 5th Battalions were taking toll of Rommel's forces in the Western Desert, and later in the orange groves and hills of Sicily, the 1st Battalion was battling with the Japanese. When Mahratta troops attacked a Japanese camp in the Kaban Valley from the front, Seaforths took the enemy by surprise from the rear. Completely encircled, the Japs came at the Seaforths in desperation with their bayonets, and ran into a deadly blast of fire which levelled them rank after rank.

The men of the 1st Battalion The Seaforth Highlanders were no strangers to conditions in the Far East, as, for 14 years they had served in Palestine, Egypt, Shanghai, Hong Kong, Singapore, Penang and India. In the Burma Campaign they operated in extreme forward positions for long periods in intense heat, and then under the monsoon deluge. Frequently, owing to isolation, they were short of rations, and mail was often four months late.

The battalion was rushed into defensive positions shortly after the British forces retreated into India. The Seaforths operated over sodden territory during the 1942 monsoon, and in the winter they assisted in covering the emergence of Major-General Orde Wingate's expedition from Burma, and fought on through the torrential rains of 1943.

The Seaforths were engaged on a round of constant patrols whatever the weather, and had numerous brushes with the enemy. In the early disastrous days of the Burma Campaign they faced up to heavy odds and gave as good as they got during the advance of the Japanese towards India.

The 1st Battalion was among the most advanced British formations in the series of deadly actions fought out around Imphal. To the east of the town the Seaforths distinguished themselves in jungle fighting and in operations which ranged over mountain peaks between 5,000 and 6,000 ft. high. At Kasom the Seaforths were under heavy attack, but, after a stiff engagement, they repulsed the Japs, and went on to mop-up the enemy around Sokpao and hasten the enemy withdrawal in this area.

After skirmishing over the densely wooded hills and mountains, the Seaforths clashed with the enemy at Lamu, some 25 miles north-east of Imphal, and the Highlanders harried the Japs in a series of hectic actions which lasted for several days. In the battle for Kohima the Seaforths rushed the Japs and tore them from their jungle lairs—slit-trenches, fox-holes, and cunningly camouflaged hideouts. The Japanese soldier was no superman now. The leadership of General Slim had helped to explode that unfortunate myth.

British and Indian troops, using rubber boats, attacked the enemy in the waterlogged bunkers of the Imphal area following two days' incessant rain, which flooded the defences. The Japs took another heavy knock in this " naval engagement " with the British and Indian infantry, and once more Seaforth bayonets went for the throats of the enemy.

The 1st Battalion The Seaforth Highlanders was given special mention in the official story of the 23rd (Indian) Division—which lived and fought for two years in the hills and valleys round Imphal. Three times this division— in which the 1st Seaforths served—helped to cover British and Indian formations in fighting withdrawals from Burma.

First, it held the gap in 1942, when our forces crossed the Chindwin River on the way back to India before the powerful Japanese offensive. The following year the division covered General Wingate's men returning from their first successful mission deep in the heart of enemy-held territory, and, in 1944, the 23rd (Indian) Division played an important part in assisting the 17th (Indian) Division's fighting withdrawal from Tiddim.

The 23rd (Indian) Division's story tells how the Seaforths of the 1st Battalion were the first troops of the division to arrive on this front. In 1942 the battalion manned the gap when the retreating Burma Army came through. The Seaforths watched the strategic Ukhrul road and patrolled the Chindwin. The battalion helped to slow down the enemy crossing the river, then, when the Japs succeeded in cutting the withdrawal route of part of the 17th (Indian) Division, the Seaforths, with the men of the 23rd (Indian) Division, beat off determined enemy attacks intended to annihilate the " tail " of the hard-pressed 17th.

The end of the Japanese War in August, 1945, terminated the Seaforths' contribution to the victories in the 2nd World War. Six battalions had been actively engaged against the enemy and had added much to the distinguished history of the regiment.

In 1947, when all infantry regiments (except the Guards) were cut to one battalion, the 2nd Battalion The Seaforth Highlanders were amalgamated into the 1st Battalion. In May, 1951, the 1st Seaforth Highlanders sailed from Singapore, and arrived in Scotland in June,

after 18 years of overseas service, the last six of which had been spent in Malaya and Java. During World War II The Seaforth Highlanders were represented in France, Belgium, Holland, Germany, Egypt, Tripolitania, Cyrenaica, Tunisia, Sicily, Italy, Burma, Madagascar, Malaya and Java.

The Territorial soldiers of The Seaforth Highlanders operated in all theatres of war, and their pluck, fortitude and splendid fighting qualities—as in World War I—enriched the saga of the regiment.

Battle-honours of the regiment for the campaigns of 1939-45 are:—Ypres-Comines Canal, Somme, 1940, Withdrawal to Seine, St. Valery-en-Caux, Odon, Cheux, Caen, Troarn, Mont Pincon, Quarry Hill, Falaise, Falaise Road, Dives Crossing, La Vie Crossing, Lisieux, Brest, Nederrijn, Le Havre, Lower Maas, Meijel, Venlo Pocket, Ourthe, Rhineland, Reichswald, Goch, Moyland, Rhine, Uelzen, Artlenberg, North-West Europe, 1940, '44-45, El Alamein, Advance on Tripoli, Mareth, Wadi Zigzaou, Akarit, Djebel Roumana, North Africa, 1942-43, Landing in Sicily, Augusta, Francofonte, Adrano, Sferro Hills, Sicily, 1943, Garigliano Crossing, Anzio, Italy, 1943-44, Madagascar, Middle East, 1942, Imphal, Shenam Pass, Litan, Tengnoupal, Burma, 1942-44.

The Seaforth Highlanders returned in May, 1954, from a spell of duty in Germany, and in June of the same year set out for the Middle East. The 1st Seaforths served in Egypt in the Canal Zone until, in July 1955, the regiment was flown from the Canal Zone to the Aden Protectorate. Their presence here was made necessary as a result of repeated attacks on convoys and Protectorate forces by rebel tribesmen.

The Seaforths took part in several punitive expeditions, directed principally against the warriors of the Shamsi section of the war-like Rabizi tribe. They were engaged in " Foreign Legion " operations among the desert sands, rocks and hills, protecting convoys from ambush, tracking down the rebels, going to the assistance of Protectorate troops and levies isolated in beleagured forts, and in pacification duties. The battalion left Aden in the spring of 1956, for eighteen months in Gibraltar and was posted to Germany in the autumn of 1957.

When the Royal Assent was given to the Order that The Seaforth Highlanders and The Cameron Highlanders should unite under the War Office scheme to reduce the number of regiments in the Army, members and ex-members of the two regiments had naturally much to regret. But there is an affinity between the Seaforths and the Camerons. They recruit in virtually the same areas, their depots are a dozen miles apart—the Seaforths at Fort George, and the Camerons at Inverness—and there has always been a fine stimulating healthy rivalry between them.

On many a battlefield Seaforths and Camerons have charged together, with similar rally-cries, and their bagpipes sounding in unison—and their blood has mingled. If there has to be a union, then a union of these two Highland regiments is an excellent one, and, once the problems of name, tartan, badge, depot, and certain other difficulties have been resolved, the future of the combined regiment is assured.

Photograph by courtesy Camera Press Ltd.

H.R.H. THE DUKE OF GLOUCESTER

COLONEL-IN-CHIEF—THE GORDON HIGHLANDERS

The Gordon Highlanders

THE GORDON HIGHLANDERS have a romantic origin. The regiment was raised in 1794, principally by the charm and efforts of the lovely Jean, wife of the 4th Duke of Gordon. The comely Duchess donned a regimental jacket and Highland bonnet, mounted her horse, and, accompanied by six pipers, toured her husband's estates and country fairs. She gave a kiss to all recruits coming forward to enlist—and some were the richer by a golden guinea. The regiment came into existence in a year of crisis, for the French Revolutionary Government had declared war on Britain.

In 1794 the Government accepted the offer of the Duke of Gordon to raise a Highland regiment on the Gordon estates—which extended across Scotland from Speymouth to the shores of Loch Eil. Though three-quarters of the recruits came from the family estates, the City of Aberdeen, Aberdeenshire, Banffshire and Moray were well represented, and among the many clansmen on the roll, the Macdonalds and the Camerons were particularly numerous. A number of recruits came, too, from the isles of the west—Skye, Barra and Uist.

The Letter of Service authorising the Duke to raise the regiment conferred on his son, the Marquis of Huntly, the commission of Lieutenant-Colonel Commandant. The Marquis, a captain in the 3rd Foot Guards (later The Scots Guards), had also served in The Black Watch. On June 24, 1794, the first parade of the new Highland regiment took place at Aberdeen. The formation was numbered the 100th Regiment. The men wore full Highland dress, with feathered bonnet and belted plaid; the facings on the red coat were yellow; the hose were red and white, with scarlet garters and buckled shoes.

The distinctive Gordon tartan kilt was worn. This was not a clan tartan. It was designed for the Duke of Gordon by William Forsythe, of Huntly, Aberdeenshire, for use by the Gordon Fencibles, one of four regiments raised by the Gordon family. The tartan, however, was later adopted by Clan Gordon.

In the year of its origin the regiment first experienced overseas service at Gibraltar, and later arrived at Bastia, Corsica, where it was employed in occupation duties. A detachment took part in a highly successful raid on the island of Elba. In 1798 it was re-numbered and styled the 92nd, The Gordon Highlanders. The regiment was ordered to Ireland that year to repel a French invasion, but was not committed to battle.

In their first engagement, in 1799, on the sandhills of Egmont-op-Zee, in Holland, the Gordons won their first battle-honour. They were escorting a number of guns along the beach when an attack by about 6,000 French troops burst upon them. The Gordons went at the enemy with the bayonet, and the French were forced to give way before their impetuous charge. In this action the Commanding Officer —the Marquis of Huntly—was wounded, and there were close on 300 casualties.

During the fighting two Gordons came upon the body of a general lying on the field. They bore him quickly to a dressing-station and immediately rejoined their unit. On recovering General Moore (later Sir John Moore) offered a reward of £20—a deal of cash in these days—to the two Highlanders who had probably saved his life, but no one came forward to claim the money.

As a result of the severe casualties inflicted by French riflemen on the sand-dunes of Holland in 1799, a Rifle Corps was raised in 1800, which later became the 95th—now The Rifle Brigade. At first an experimental corps, it was formed by detachments of picked men from 14 regiments, including The Gordon Highlanders. The Gordons contributed a kilted Highland Company.

The Gordon Highlanders next saw service in Egypt, where they again distinguished themselves, on this occasion at the Battle of Mandora, in 1801. The 92nd was one of only two regiments—both Scottish—which were later awarded " Mandora " as a battle-honour. The Gordons were also in action at Aboukir, Alexandria and Ramalieh, and they acquitted themselves valiantly against the French, who were forced to evacuate their troops. The Sphinx superscribed " Egypt " is a proud campaign honour of The Gordon Highlanders in the Land of the Pharaohs.

When it was learned that Napoleon planned to seize the fleets of the Baltic nations in an attempt to wrest supremacy of the seas from Britain, an expedition—which included The Gordon Highlanders—was dispatched with a squadron of men o'war to Copenhagen in 1807. The surrender of Denmark's fleet was asked, and it was promised to return all fighting ships once the danger was over. The Danes refused to appreciate the position, rejected the British undertaking, and resolved to defend their neutrality, but, after a fierce engagement, they were forced to accept the offer.

In the war against Napoleon in Spain, General Sir John Moore advanced to join battle with the enemy, his force including the Gordons. It was intended to link up with the Spanish and launch a full-scale attack, but by the time he had concentrated at Salamanca his Spanish allies had been decisively defeated, and over 100,000 enemy troops were converging on the British force. On Christmas eve, 1808, General Sir John Moore embarked on the historic 200 miles winter retreat over the grim fastness of the Cantabrian Mountains with the French in pursuit of his ill-clad numbed, starving columns.

When they reached Corunna it was found that the transport ships had not arrived, but the exhausted ragged British soldiers attacked the French with such fury that, when the ships did arrive, the enemy were content to become spectators of the evacuation. Among the killed at the Battle of Corunna, in mid-January, 1809, were Sir John Moore and the Colonel of the 92nd. Corunna was another battle-honour of the Gordons.

But The Gordon Highlanders were soon back in Spain taking part in the second stage of the war against Napoleon, which dragged on until 1814, with all its long train of assaults, sieges, exhausting marches, reverses and victories. In the hard fighting, which ended with the advance north to the French frontier, The Gordon Highlanders won a number of battle-honours—Fuentes d'Onor, Almaraz, Vittoria, Pyrenees, Nive, Orthes, Peninsula.

At Vittoria the 92nd went to the aid of the 71st (H.L.I.) when they were suffering heavy losses and in danger of being surrounded owing to mistaking French troops for their Spanish allies. In this onslaught the Gordons, too, sustained severe casualties, but they successfully extricated the hard-pressed men of the 71st.

The battle ended with the rout of the French, who abandoned most of their guns, baggage, equipment, and an assortment of loot—also their pay-chest. Joseph Bonaparte, Napoleon's brother—who had been installed as King of Spain—had a narrow escape from capture as he fled from the field. In the fighting during the pursuit of the French forces north and through the Pyrenees in 1813, the 92nd made a decisive bayonet charge at Maya, which shattered the fleeing enemy and speeded up their retreat. There was fierce fighting for the Gordons on the Nivelle, and in the advance to Bayonne. At St. Pierre their pipers played to the death. When one fell, another took up the air, and when he went down a third continued it.

At Quatre Bras, on the eve of Waterloo, The Gordon Highlanders took station near a farmhouse. In front was a ditch, which they were ordered to defend. Ere long the High-landers were being raked by the French artillery and charged by their cavalry, whom the Gordons repulsed with their bayonets in a savage action. Then the Highlanders charged the infantry at the farmhouse and inflicted another sharp reverse on the French, but lost their Colonel, John Cameron of Fassiefern, in the desperate close fighting.

Of Colonel Cameron Sir Walter Scott later penned these lines:—

" *Through shot and shell he leads no more,*
Low laid 'mid friends' and foemen's gore;
But 'long his native lake's wild shore
And Sunart rough and high Ardgour
And Morven long shall tell,
And proud Ben Nevis hear with awe
How upon bloody Quatre Bras
Brave Cameron heard the wild hurrah
Of conquest, as he fell."

On the retreat of the Dutch-Belgian Brigade at Waterloo, the French infantry made for the gap thus created, and a critical situation quickly developed. Two brigades were at once moved forward, and, as the enemy paused before making the final onslaught, The Royal Scots, Black Watch, Camerons and Gordons were ordered to charge. Their volley crashed out, and as the wild Highland rush with the bayonet commenced, up came the Union Brigade, which included The Royal Scots Greys.

The pibroch was sounding its defiant challenge as the Gordons grasped the stirrups of the Greys and they charged together. The shout went up, " Scotland For Ever ! " The enemy, reeling before the shattering volley of the Highlanders, were now ridden over by the cavalry and attacked by the infantry. In a few minutes it was all over, and the ground was littered with French infantrymen. About 3,000 prisoners were brought back.

The charge of The Royal Scots Greys and The Gordon Highlanders at Waterloo is immortalised by Lady Butler's famous picture. And the battle-honour " Waterloo " was later awarded to both regiments. The 92nd Highlanders marched on Paris and were engaged in occupation duties. There followed stretches of duty at home and overseas, including a lengthy term in the West Indies, where the ranks were depleted by tropical diseases.

While stationed at Gibraltar in 1854, the 92nd sent volunteers to the Crimea, and several hundred served with the Highland regiments. The Gordons were eventually ordered to the front, but a few days after their arrival the war ended. One Gordon volunteer, Private Thomas Beach, of Forfar, rejoined the regiment with the newly-instituted Victoria Cross adorning his tunic. He won the first Gordon V.C. at Inkerman. Private Beach attacked several Russians who were plundering Lieutenant-Colonel Carpenter, 41st Regiment, who was lying wounded. He accounted for two of the enemy, and protected the officer until help arrived.

The regiment went to India in 1859, and was employed on pacification duties towards the close of the Sepoy Mutiny. The Gordons operated with mobile columns engaged in taking the surrender of bands of rebels, and in hunting down wanted men, and parties of mutineers who had become bandits. In 1872 the 92nd adopted the now familiar Stag's Head badge with the motto " Bydand " (Stand Fast) as its crest, replacing The Sphinx with the word " Egypt ", which had been in use since 1805.

The murder of the Viceroy's envoy at Kabul was followed by the Afghan War of 1878-80, fought out in the high passes. There was stiff fighting and several reverses in this campaign against the fanatical hill tribesmen. The Gordon Highlanders were in General Sir Frederick Roberts' column in the march from Kabul to the relief of Kandahar, which restored the position after the disaster to General Burrow's force at Maiwand.

No wheeled transport and no camels were taken, and pack-guns—carried by mules— were the only artillery. Kit and supplies were cut to the last ounce, and this historic march— a notable feat of organisation and endurance— was made in stifling heat. The long winding column covered over 300 miles in 20 days, advancing across rough stony tracks—and frequently there were no tracks—in arid, rugged, mountainous terrain, through suffocating dust-clouds, and on tight rations. It was a long climb as well as a long march.

General Roberts' column snaked its way deep into Afghan territory to reach Kandahar at the end of August, 1880. Battle was joined, and the tribesmen were rooted from their strong entrenchments and eyries among the rocks and crags and decisively beaten. The enemy had artillery and made good use of it, employing the defensive features of their country to the maximum. They showed no mercy to the wounded and took no prisoners. They were skilled in ruse and ambush, and their snipers took heavy toll ere they were located and silenced.

The Afghans fought to the last when cornered in their mountain retreats and strongholds, and when they charged *en masse* it was always a bloody close-fought engagement. The Gordons ended their historic march to Kandahar by charging and capturing the enemy guns. Major George Stuart White (later Field-Marshal Sir George Stuart White) led a charge by the Gordons at Charasiah which won him the Victoria Cross. He was again conspicuous in the final charge at Kandahar.

Another Gordon won the Victoria Cross in this campaign—Lieutenant William Henry Dick-Cunyngham. In full view of the enemy and under heavy fire in the Sherpur Pass, this officer rallied his men on an exposed bullet-swept hilltop, and, as a result of his example and encouragement, the Gordons held on to their position at Takht-I-Shah. Charasiah, Kabul, 1879, Kandahar, 1880, Afghanistan, 1878-80, were later added to the regiment's battle-honours.

A contingent of The Gordon Highlanders was with General Sir George Colley's force of about 350 men, which seized the summit of Majuba Hill, in the South African Campaign of 1880-81. Previously this General had had the worst of the exchanges with the Boers at Laing's Nek, on the Natal Transvaal border.

The troops made the difficult ascent, scrambling over rocks and gullies in the darkness to reach the summit. They were ordered to hold it against the expected enemy attack, but not to dig any entrenchments. This was a most unfortunate decision, as the bare exposed plateau afforded no cover for the defenders, but ample to the attackers, crawling up the hillside from several angles.

Boer marksmen picked off the troops at their leisure, and, when they thought they had thinned them out sufficiently, they attacked. But they were facing the Gordons. Though many of the Highlanders went down, killed or wounded, they came at the Boers with the bayonet. Then, standing shoulder to shoulder, the last 150 men held out until the order was given to retire. General Colley was killed in this action.

Less than 100 men left that bullet-swept hill alive. The blame for this debacle rested with the Government, whose weak policy brought disgrace to British arms in South Africa. It was in London that Majuba Hill was lost—and so many Gordons. A discreditable peace was signed—while General Sir Frederick Roberts was on the way to Cape Town with considerable reinforcements.

The 92nd became the 2nd Battalion The Gordon Highlanders in 1881, when the regiment was linked with the 75th, or Stirlingshire Regiment—which became the 1st Battalion The Gordon Highlanders. There was a feeling of regret in the ranks of the 75th and the 92nd at the loss of their respective numerals, but they accepted the inevitable.

A humorous epitaph was composed by the armourer-sergeant of the 75th when the regiment was stationed at Floriana, Malta. It ran:—

" *Here lies the poor old Seventy-Fifth,*
But, under God's protection,
They'll rise again in kilt and hose,
A glorious resurrection !
For by the transformatory power
Of Parliamentary laws,
We go to bed the Seventy-Fifth
To rise the Ninety-Twas ! "

And the men of the 92nd, while in South Africa, staged a full military funeral for a flag bearing their numbers. In the still of the night the Gordons paraded with all solemnity. There was an oration, and three volleys rang out over the grave. But next morning, when the flag was " exhumed " and hoisted it was found to bear the inscription in the doric of North-East Scotland, " Ninety-Twa No' Deid Yet ".

The 75th was raised as a Highland regiment under the colonelcy of Robert Abercromby of Tullibody. The regiment was embodied at Stirling in June, 1787, and first smelt powder in India, where it served from 1787 until 1807. In the campaign against Haider Ali, the 75th was in action at Chowghaset and Trincalore forts.

The regiment was in the force which crossed the Ghats in the indecisive operations of 1791. In the next attempt, though out of ammunition, the 75th stood firm before a furious charge by Tippoo's " Tiger " Battalions. When war broke out again the regiment was in the final assault upon Seringapatam, in 1799, forming one of the attacking columns.

The Highlanders stormed and captured an important redoubt, as a result of which the success of the main attack was ensured. About 1,000 enemy guns were taken and Tippoo was killed. The regiment was present at the unsuccessful assault on the strong Jat fortress of Bhurtpore in 1805. After their campaign in the jungles of Mysore, the 75th voyaged home in 1807.

The 75th—which discontinued wearing the Highland uniform in 1809—was operating against the troublesome Kaffirs in South Africa during 1835. Then the regiment returned to India to fight in several savage actions during the Mutiny.

The Stirlingshire Regiment was included in the column which skirmished forward to lay siege to and capture Delhi. A few miles from the city the 75th charged a battery of guns which barred the advance. Rushing through a storm of fire, they routed the mutineers to open the road to Delhi.

Forming part of a flying column, the 75th was instrumental in saving Agra from the Mutiny terror and massacre. The regiment also took part in the historic Relief of Lucknow. It fought its way through the narrow streets under heavy close-range fire from mutineers established in buildings and houses on all sides, and suffered severe losses. But the 75th won through with bullet and bayonet and again hammered the enemy.

Three Victoria Crosses were awarded to men of the regiment. At Koodsia Baugh, Delhi, Private Patrick Green engaged the rebels and rescued a wounded comrade. Lieutenant Richard Wadeson, at Subjee Mundee, Delhi, saved the life of a private soldier when he was attacked by enemy cavalry, and later similarly rescued another private of the regiment, who was wounded and being attacked. Also at Delhi, Colour-Sergeant Cornelius Coghlan, under heavy fire, went with three men into an enemy-held serai and brought out a wounded soldier. The sergeant later rallied and led a charge at Subjee Mundee, and then successfully evacuated the wounded under cross-fire. The regiment came home in 1862, to be followed by the 92nd.

In operations against the Mahdi's desert warriors, the Gordons were in the brisk engagements at El Teb and Tamai, and they were with the desert and river columns which made the dash to the aid of General Gordon, cut off and under siege at Khartoum. They arrived two days too late. The Gordons also took part in the sharp actions at Abu Klea and Kirbekan. The battle-honours Tel-el-Kebir, Egypt, 1882-84, and Nile, 1884-85, were later awarded.

In 1888 the 1st Battalion arrived in India, and, in 1895, it formed part of the punitive Chitral Relief Force, which was heavily engaged in the high frontier passes. Two years later the battalion was again operating on the North West Frontier. The Afridis had to be taught a sharp lesson after a number of attacks on military posts and ambushes of convoys and parties of troops.

Beyond the Khyber and Malakand passes British and Indian troops took part in strenuous operations, which necessitated fording freezing mountain torrents, hurling snipers from lofty perches among the crags, manhandling guns, ammunition and supplies across gorges, up precipitous slopes, and over fast-flowing rivers, and dealing with the sudden onfalls of the hillmen, skilled in guerilla tactics and the art of ambush.

The 1st Gordon Highlanders fought a spirited action at Dargai. The enemy had to be cleared from a vital hill, which meant the scaling of gullies and crags while the pack-batteries shelled the tribesmen on the heights above. The artillery fire had little effect, as the enemy sheltered among the rocks and boulders. In front of them was a long uphill stretch devoid of cover, and the tribesmen opened a murderous fire on the assaulting troops.

The order was received, " The hill must be taken ". The Gordons rushed up the bullet-swept body-littered slope with levelled bayonets. As the Highland charge broke upon them the tribesmen gave way and made off down the reverse slope. In this desperate engagement Piper George Findlater, though shot through both ankles, propped himself up among the rocks and continued to play the Regimental March, " Cock o' The North " to " brosnachadh " his comrades. Piper Findlater was awarded the Victoria Cross. Private Edward Lawson carried badly-wounded Lieutenant K. Dingwall to safety, then went back and brought out a wounded comrade. Private Lawson was wounded twice in these rescues. He, too, was awarded the Victoria Cross.

The fighting over, the exhausted Gordons carried their wounded, and those of the Dorsets and Ghurkas, down the rocky tracks and gullies to receive medical attention, as there were no stretcher-bearers available. News of the charge of the Gordons at Dargai got round quickly, and, as the weary Highlanders toiled towards the bivouac site, the troops in the camp came out to meet them and cheered in the Gordons, many of them coming forward to offer their water-bottles—when water was strictly rationed. For their outstanding service in India, The Gordon Highlanders were awarded the battle-honours Chitral and Tirah. In 1898 the heroes of Dargai came home.

In the South African War, 1899-1902, The Gordon Highlanders made another fine contribution to the success of British arms. The 2nd Battalion arrived in Ladysmith from Bombay, and took part in the thrust to stop the Boer invasion of Natal. The 2nd Gordons were heavily engaged at Elandslaagte, and suffered serious losses in clearing the enemy from strong entrenchments on a disputed ridge.

At Elandslaagte Captain Matthew Fontaine Maury Meiklejohn rallied a party of leaderless Gordons in a galling fire and delivered an attack, in which he was wounded four times. In the same battle Lieutenant William Robertson led several successive rushes against the enemy positions in the final advance, and later headed a small party in seizing the Boer camp. Lieutenant Robertson was twice wounded. The captain and the lieutenant were awarded the Victoria Cross.

After the Battle of Elandslaagte the 2nd Gordons returned to Ladysmith and were under siege until a relieving force broke through at the end of February, 1900. The 2nd distinguished itself in the fighting at Wagon Hill.

The 1st Battalion, coming out from Britain, was in time to take part in the bid to relieve Kimberley. This battalion was in the disastrous attack on Magersfontein Hill, in which the Highland Brigade was shattered by the murderous close-range Boer fire.

At Magersfontein, on April 11, 1899, Captain Ernest Beachcroft Beckwith Towse won the Victoria Cross for trying to assist mortally-wounded Colonel Downman, and, at the end of the month, this officer, with 12 men, held Mount Thaba against a strong force of Boers.

The 1st Gordons were in the stiff battle for Paardeberg—which avenged Magersfontein.

Here Cronje surrendered with 4,000 of his men. The advance then swept on to Bloemfontein and Pretoria. Both battalions took part in numerous long marches and in a number of lesser engagements in this hard-fought campaign—at Laing's Nek, Rooi Kopjes, Frischgewagd, Belfast, Machadodorp, Lydenburg, Reit River, Poplar Grove, Driefontein, Sannah's Post, Hout Nek, Zand River, Doornkop, Diamond Hill and Wolverkranz.

At Leekoehoek, near Krugersdorf, Captain William Eagleson Gordon won the Victoria Cross for his gallant attempt to save a gun. He called for volunteers, and, when the bid failed, he ordered the survivors to take cover. Having seen the wounded to safety, he himself then retired. Captain David Reginald Younger also won the Victoria Cross in this epic. But the award was posthumous, as Captain Younger was mortally wounded. Another Victoria Cross was won by a Gordon Highlander at Doornkop, near Johannesburg. Corporal John Frederick Mackay braved a hail of bullets to attend to wounded comrades lying in exposed positions, and, in addition, he brought one man back to safety under heavy fire. For its splendid service in South Africa the regiment received the battle-honours Defence of Ladysmith, Paardeberg, South Africa, 1899-1902.

After the South African War the 2nd Battalion returned to India, and in 1914 was stationed in Cairo. The 1st Battalion left South Africa for the U.K., and in 1914 was at Plymouth. The 1st Gordons, with the 8th Brigade, 3rd Division, were with the British Expeditionary Force which joined battle with the German invaders of Belgium on the Mons-Conde Canal in mid-August, 1914. Heavy casualties were inflicted on the Kaiser's advancing hordes, but the arrival of fresh enemy troops caused a fighting withdrawal to the Cambrai-Le Cateau area.

After the eight days of retreat from Mons the 1st Battalion could only muster one weak company. But the non-stop fighting with the enemy—who had great numerical superiority and an abundance of artillery—went grimly on. The Germans were thrown back from the Marne, and the exhausted depleted B.E.F. advanced to the Aisne.

Meanwhile the 2nd Battalion had taken the field with the 7th Division, and, at the First Battle of Ypres held the line against a force several times its own strength. A few score survivors came out of this great battle, in November, 1914—but the all-out German drive for the strategic Channel ports was stemmed.

Then followed the 1915 holocaust at Neuve Chapelle, in March, Festubert in May, and Loos, in the autumn. A year later came the shambles on the Somme, with the 2nd Gordons distinguishing themselves at Mametz, and the 1st at Delville Wood. So the war dragged on—High Wood, Flers and Pozieres.

For the Gordons it was attack and counterattack, outpost, patrol and raid, living like animals in freezing waterlogged trenches and holes in the ground, little rest, and half-cooked meals—and often the food was eaten raw—assaults with rifle, bayonet and grenade, artillery bombardments lasting for hours—sometimes days—sickness, vermin, disease, wounds and death, the whistle and crash of shells, the rattle of rifle and machine-gun fire, the thundering rumble of mines exploding under the trenches, mud, blood and bodies, and the cries of the wounded and dying . . .

In 1917 the Gordons were on Vimy Ridge and Bullecourt. Then they grappled once more with the enemy at Ypres—in the third battle there—and, later, at Cambrai. At a critical stage in the war in Italy, the 2nd Gordons were dispatched from the Western Front to the help of our allies after their defeat at Caporetto. The 2nd Battalion went into action against the Germans and Austrians during 1917-18, and for their outstanding contribution to the successful outcome of the fighting along the Piave, the Gordons won the battle-honour Vittorio Veneto.

In France the Gordon battalions—Regular, Service and Territorial—were all heavily engaged at the Second Battle of the Somme, and there was more grim fighting on the Lys. Then came the last German offensive which forced the Aisne and reached the Marne, only to be hurled back to end in retreat and surrender.

Twenty-one battalions of The Gordon Highlanders served in the 1914-18 campaigns. The principal battle-honours awarded to the regiment were:—Mons, Le Cateau, Marne, 1914, '18, Ypres, 1914, '15, '17, Loos, Somme, 1916, '18, Ancre, 1916, Arras, 1917, '18, Cambrai, 1917, '18, Vittorio Veneto.

Victoria Crosses were awarded to the following:—Captain James Anson Otho Brooke, at Gheluvelt; Lieutenant Allan Ebenezer Ker, at St. Quentin; Drummer William Kenny, at Ypres; and Private Gordon McIntosh, also at Ypres.

Captain Brooke's award was made " For most conspicuous bravery and great ability "

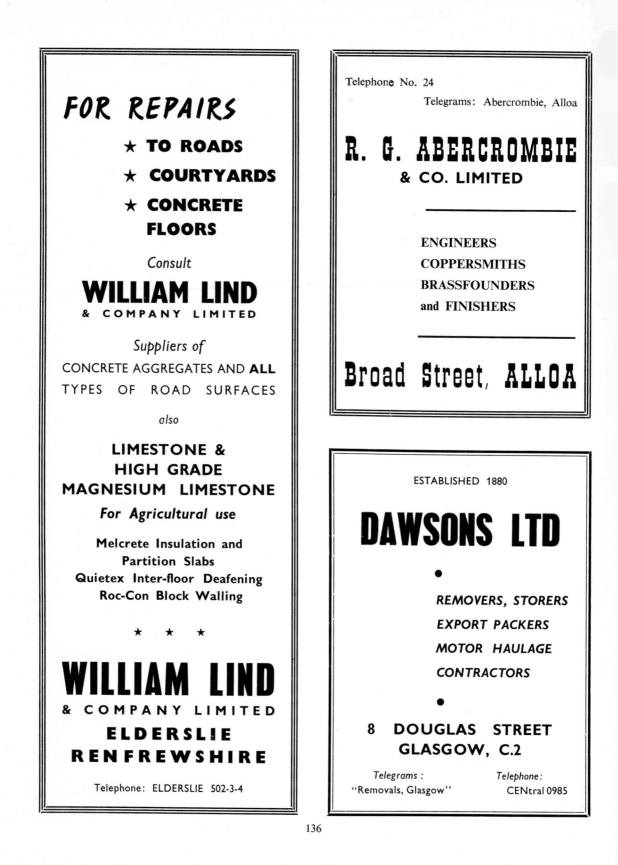
136

in leading two attacks on German trenches under heavy fire, and regaining a lost trench at a very critical moment. Captain Brooke prevented an enemy breakthrough, but he was killed on the day of his triumph.

Lieutenant Ker, on an exposed flank, engaged the enemy with a Vickers machine-gun and held up their attack. A sergeant and several wounded men rallied round him, and when the Vickers was destroyed and all their ammunition spent, they continued to keep the enemy at bay with revolvers, though attacked from behind with bombs, machine-gun fire and bayonets. Lieutenant Ker got the badly wounded together and resolved to defend them to the last. He and his little band of Gordons were finally overwhelmed and disarmed by a strong force of the enemy. But he had held up over 500 Germans for three hours.

Drummer Kenny rescued wounded men on five occasions under very heavy fire. Twice he saved machine-guns from capture by carrying them out of action, and conveyed urgent messages over fire-swept ground. While a position was being consolidated, Private McIntosh's company came under close-range machine-gun fire. He rushed forward, threw a Mills bomb, killing two of the enemy and wounding a third. He brought back two light machine-guns, and the consolidation proceeded unhindered.

After the war the 1st Battalion served in Cologne. Early in 1920 the 1st Gordons landed at Constantinople as part of the Army of the Black Sea. Internal trouble in Turkey and quarrels with Greece necessitated this move. The 1st Battalion later arrived at Malta, but two years afterwards the Gordons were again sent to Turkey. This crisis also passed. The battalion left Malta in 1924, and arrived in Egypt, where there was Nationalist activity. After a month near Cairo, the battalion sailed for Bombay. Service followed in the Deccan, Delhi, and on the North West Frontier. After 10 years in India the battalion went to Palestine, and after a short stay there the Gordons returned home. The 2nd Battalion arrived in Ireland after its war service, and was at several home stations before leaving for Gibraltar. September, 1939, found the 2nd at Singapore, while the 1st was located at Aldershot.

The 1st Gordons went to France with the 1st Division in September, 1939, but in March, 1940, the battalion was switched to the 51st (Highland) Division. The 1st Battalion joined 153 Brigade, which already included the 5th Territorial Battalion. On May 10 the Germans invaded Belgium, and a few days later the 51st Division's section of the Maginot Line, near Metz, was subjected to a heavy bombardment. Bitter fighting ensued.

On May 15 came orders to retire, but there was a wedge of German armour between the Highland Division and the remainder of the British Expeditionary Force. The enemy bridgehead at Abbeville was attacked on June 4, but, after achieving success, the Highlanders had to retire before a powerful German counterattack which overran their forward positions. By this time Belgium had capitulated to the invaders, and the B.E.F. was being rescued from the Dunkirk beaches.

Operating with the 9th French Army, defensive lines were held in turn in the Monchaux-Gamaches area and along the River Bethune, but the Wehrmacht tidal wave—crested by tanks—came on. Dive-bombers joined in, and the Highland Division retreated fighting desperately for survival. The Gordons were making a fight to the finish, and enemy casualties mounted steeply. When the French surrendered the 1st Gordons still battled on in the west of the shrinking defence perimeter round St. Valery, with the 5th Battalion heavily engaged on the south-east.

Without food, ammunition running low, the divisional artillery silent, with no hope of evacuation, and many wounded, it was only a matter of time. St. Valery was under heavy artillery bombardment and air attack, some rescue ships in the harbour were forced to put to sea, and German tanks were closing in on the doomed division. Major-General Victor Fortune, commanding the 51st, gave the order to surrender on the morning of June 12. The enemy commanding general was Erwin Rommel.

The Highland Division went out fighting—and at El Alamein, in October, 1942, the men of the new Highland Division entered the lists against Rommel. And vengeance was theirs in the first great battle of the resuscitated 51st. With the 1st Gordons in the reconstituted 153 Brigade was the 5/7th Battalion. Both formations had been re-formed.

The pipes skirled, the massed British artillery thundered, and the Highlanders attacked across the sands. For the Germans it was defeat, disaster, havoc and death, and the Afrika Korps turned tail and fled. The ponderous rumbling tanks floundered before the lashing fire of the guns, and many became blazing death-trap infernos. The remainder clanked round and made a run for it over the desert hills, their noses pointed towards Tripoli, with the Highlanders in close pursuit.

Early in January, 1943, the 1st Gordons, mounted on tanks, burst into Tripoli, and the chase continued. " Desert Fox " Rommel was the quarry, and the Highlanders the hunters. Things had changed in North Africa. The arrival of the 51st had turned the tide in the war across the sands.

The Gordons, again catching up with the enemy, were in the bitterly-contested attacks at Wadi Akarit and in the grim assaults on the Mareth Line. Their onslaught at Wadi Cheffar opened the road to Sfax, and the 1st Gordons led the Eighth Army in. Cheerily, defiantly, inspiringly the pibroch skirled that morning in May when the massed Pipes and Drums of the 51st (Highland) Division marched in the Victory Parade through Tunis.

The Highlanders crossed to Malta early in July, and a few days later landed in Sicily. The 1st Gordons attacked Vizzini and pushed on to Sferro. There was savage fighting at the various river crossings and in the drive into the hills. The 51st was withdrawn and dispatched to the U.K. In mid-November the Highlanders lined the troop ships as they sailed up the Clyde.

Landing in Normandy on D-Day plus one. 153 Brigade moved into the " Triangle " area, and in the subsequent fighting for the coastal villages the 1st Gordons came up from the River Orne to make an assault on Colombelles. After the break-out from the containment area early in July, the battalion moved into the woods around St. Sylvain, then advanced to take Doux Marais, and enter the chateau at St. Marie-aux-Anglais. The Gordons came under heavy fire as they crossed the River Vie. The battalion moved into La Forge Vallee before pushing on to Lisieux.

The Highland Division crossed the Seine after the German rearguard formations, and then raced for St. Valery. The pipes skirled in the square and the town was en fete for the return of the 51st. The Massed Bands of the Division beat " Retreat " at nearby Cailleville, where the H.Q. was established. The pipes wailed in the lament " Flowers O' the Forest " in honour of the men of the 51st who fell in the epic retreat of 1940. In St. Valery-en-Caux it was a day of gladness with sadness.

The enemy fortress at Le Havre was attacked, but it quickly surrendered, and the Gordons brought back many prisoners. In the stubborn fighting on the Maas the 1st Gordons penetrated into Schijndel and advanced to operate with the brigade around Nieuwkuijk, Vlijmen and Haarsteeg. The Wessem Canal was forded in Buffaloes under intense mortar-fire, and the Zig Canal was crossed.

Hitler launched his desperate gamble in the Ardennes in December, 1944, and the Highland Division was moved south. After initial success the German offensive was checked and thrown back with heavy loss. The 1st Gordons moved through Verdenne to make the climb to Laroche, and had a brush with the enemy near Hubermont. Advancing on Nisramont the battalion discovered the enemy had evacuated the village. The Germans decisively repulsed, the 51st went north, away from the frost and snow of the Ardennes.

The Gordons were engaged in mopping-up operations in a string of war-shattered villages, including St. Martensberg and Grafwegen during the Reichswald assaults. The battalion fought across the Niers and hammered the enemy at Gennep, where it hurled back a counterblow. Goch fell, and the advance rolled steadily on to Thomashof and Rees.

Over the Rhine and on to Isselburg. The 1st Gordons were now on the last lap. Crossing the Ems, the battalion moved forward to Goldenstedt and cleared the enemy from Hockensburg and Brettorf. Orel was reported strongly held by the enemy, but the Gordons quickly cleared the Germans out of the town to advance on Barchell, where a counter-attack was successfully beaten back. The battalion advanced through Bremervörde, Ebersdorf and Waterbeck, and, on the morning of May 4, overtures for a local surrender were made by the Germans which soon developed into negotiations for a general capitulation.

The great day dawned on May 8, 1945— VE-Day. On May 12, Major-General G. H. A. MacMillan, C.B., C.B.E., D.S.O., M.C. (later Lieutenant-General Sir Gordon MacMillan, G.O.C.-in-C., Scottish Command) led the Highland Division in the Victory March through Bremerhaven. The Scottish " Lion " regiments were all represented—The Black Watch, Seaforths, Camerons, Gordons and Argylls of 152, 153 and 154 Brigades, and their supporting Corps troops. And right proudly did they follow their leader—Chief of the Clan MacMillan. It was a field day for the tartan and the Massed Pipes and Drums of the valiant 51st.

The 2nd Battalion, The Gordon Highlanders, like their comrades of the 1st Battalion, went down fighting in 1942, when the Japanese overran Singapore in overwhelming strength.

But the same year a new 2nd Battalion was formed, and, as part of the 227th (Highland) Brigade of the 15th (Scottish) Division, the 2nd Gordons landed on the Normandy coast in that eventful June of 1944.

Towards the end of June, the 2nd Gordons were in the fierce fighting which raged around Cheux in the First Battle of the Odon. In mid-July the battalion was again committed in the Second Battle of the Odon, and fighting reached a peak of vehemence at Evrecy. Then followed the break-out from the salient known as the "Scottish Corridor", which set the 15th Division on the advance to Victory over the Seine, the Rhine and the Elbe.

Crossing the blood-stained Odon, the Scots hurled back several determined counter-attacks, and at Caumont they encountered a hurricane of fire. Many were laid low, but the remainder pressed on, and, at Estry, Scot and Teuton again clashed. The Gordons of 227 Brigade pushed on past Louviers, and the advance rolled on across France and towards the Belgian frontier.

In mid-September the division was established on the Albert Canal, and hard fighting was experienced on the Escaut Canal. Enemy opposition stiffened, and the tempo of the advance was slowed down. Furious counter-attacks were launched by the Germans, but they were repelled with considerable loss. The 2nd Gordons were once more in the thick of the fray.

During October the enemy made a determined stand along the Dutch frontier, but Best was captured, and the 15th (Scottish) Division fought on to S'Hertogenbosch, where the forward sweep was again checked by stubborn defensive fighting, and static conditions ensued.

Tilburg fell, and the Gordons of 227 Brigade were in a fierce action in the Meijel-Liesel area in mid-November. Once more the Germans were prised out of their strong defence works. The advance to the Maas commenced, and Blerick was captured in wintry weather, The waterlogged condition of the ground bogged down further progress, and the 15th Division held the Maas line.

In late January, 1945, the Scots were on the move again, and the Gordons bit deeply into the Siegfried Line defences in February. The Scottish Division moved north of the Reichswald, skirting flooded Nijmegen, and after the assault and capture of Cleve and Goch, the great "mop up" of the shattered German formations west of the Rhine commenced. On March 24 the division crossed the Rhine below Wesel, and the brigades carried all their objectives.

Over the Issel went the Scots, and during the early part of April they pushed forward, driving hard for the Elbe, via Celle, on the River Aller. They met and overcame stubborn resistance at Belsen and Uelzen. The 2nd Gordons forged ahead in the clearing of Artlenburg, and now across the Elbe, the division raced for Hamburg, which surrendered on its approach.

Isolated German battle-groups fought on, but these were systematically cleared from the Sachsenwald, and the 15th (Scottish) Division arrived in the Ahrensberg area early in May. Came May 8—the day so many had lived and fought for—and so many had died for. The roar of the guns and the metallic clank and rumble of the tanks was stilled. Stilled too was the deadly chatter of machine-guns, the crump of mortars, and the sharp crack of rifles. The Scots heard the song of the birds and saw the glorious bloom of the spring flowers. But many found it hard to believe that the holocaust was over.

The 5th Battalion was lost with the 51st (Highland) Division at St. Valery, but a new 5/7th Battalion served with the reconstituted 51st in North Africa, Sicily and Germany. The 4th and 6th Battalions were evacuated from Dunkirk in the 1940 campaign in France. The 6th later joined the First Army and served in Tunisia and Italy. This battalion distinguished itself at Anzio and on the road to Rome.

The 4th and 8th Battalions became respectively the 92nd and 100th Anti-Tank Regiments, R.A. (The Gordon Highlanders). The 9th also changed its role, becoming the 116th Regiment, Royal Armoured Corps (The Gordon Highlanders). The 100th Anti-Tank Regiment and the 116th Regiment, R.A.C. defended Kohima and North-East India, and were in the final drive which cleared the Japanese out of Burma.

The battle-honours of The Gordon Highlanders in World War II are:—Withdrawal to Escaut, Ypres-Comines Canal, Dunkirk, 1940, Somme, 1940, St. Valery-en-Caux, Odon, La Vie Crossing, Lower Maas, Venlo Pocket, Rhineland, Reichswald, Cleve, Goch, Rhine, North-West Europe, 1940, '44, '45, El Alamein, Advance on Tripoli, Mareth, Medjez Plain, North Africa, 1942-43, Landing in Sicily, Sferro, Sicily, 1943, Anzio, Rome, Italy, 1944-45.

After the war the 1st Battalion served with the British Army of the Rhine, and the 2nd in

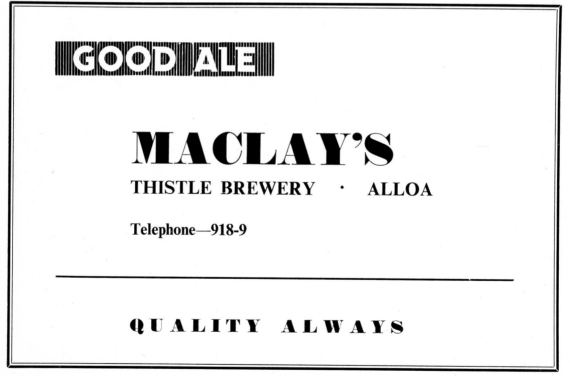

Tripoli. On all infantry regiments (except the Guards) being cut down to one battalion in 1947, the 1st and 2nd Gordons amalgamated in the 1st Battalion. The Battalion returned to the U.K. from Germany in mid-December, 1950, but a few weeks later the Gordons were under orders for Malaya, where they were to serve for three years.

In sweltering heat, and plagued by myriads of insects, fighting patrols penetrated into and scoured large areas of dense jungle and scrub, operated over arid hills and a maze of rocky gullies, and skirmished through green, slimy treacherous reptile-infested swamps. Over 70 bandits fell to their guns for the loss of 19 Highlanders. The battalion returned home in April, 1954.

The 1st Gordons were flown out to Cyprus in October, 1955. After their jungle-fighting role in Malaya from 1951-54, they were well prepared to combat the EOKA terrorists. The Gordons guarded vital areas, Government buildings, and police posts, and sought out the terrorists and bomb-slingers in their hide-outs in the grim fastness of the Trodoos Mountains, high above the snow-line. They located arms dumps, set up road-blocks, formed anti-riot squads, and dispatched anti-smuggling patrols along the rugged northern coast. They also provided escorts for convoys passing through the danger areas. Sixteen Gordons were killed in operations in Cyprus.

The Gordon Highlanders did not again see " The Northern Lights of Old Aberdeen " until they returned to Scotland early in January, 1957—in time to " first-foot " their relatives with gifts from Cyprus.

Photograph by courtesy " Daily Express "

H.R.H. THE DUKE OF EDINBURGH

COLONEL-IN-CHIEF—THE QUEEN'S OWN CAMERON HIGHLANDERS

The Queen's Own Cameron Highlanders

FROM misty isles beloved of artist and poet, from shieling and clachan, thatched croft, and windswept moorland, from mountains of the eagle, glens, peat-bogs, and rugged sea coves, from the great silences where are heard strange bird calls, from lochs, heather hills, brown ploughlands, and green pastures came the men who marched behind the pipes and drums of The Cameron Highlanders. Hardy sons of the sea and soil, these, whose forebears had followed the standards of the Old Pretender and Bonnie Prince Charlie, but, whose loyalty once won for the new Royal House, fought gallantly and gloriously on many a foreign field and around the lonely outposts of the Empire.

The regiment was raised on August 17, 1793, at Fort William, by Major Alan Cameron of Erracht (later Lieutenant-General Sir Alan Cameron, K.C.B.), son of Ewen Cameron of Erracht. Unfortunately young Cameron killed a man in a duel and fled the country. He was captured by the Americans in the winter of 1775, while on his way from Norfolk to join The Queen's Rangers, then forming at Detroit. He was imprisoned at Philadelphia, but, with the aid of an American Loyalist, he succeeded in escaping, though badly injured in the process.

Alan Cameron reached the New Jersey coast, only to be betrayed again to the Americans. On re-capture he was placed in an underground dungeon. After another attempted escape, he was finally liberated under an exchange of prisoners scheme arranged between Britain and the American Colonist forces. He left New York for England in 1778, with his health much impaired by the privations he had endured.

In consequence of the war with Revolutionary France, regiments were being formed in many parts of the country. Alan Cameron, anxious to prove that old sores of the Jacobite risings were now healed and that there were no more loyal subjects in the realm than the clansmen of Lochaber, Appin, Morven and Mull, made several applications to the War Office for permission to raise a regiment. Eventually he received a Letter of Service authorising him to proceed. In the letter there was a clause specifying that the soldiers would not be drafted into other corps.

The regiment came into being as The 79th, or Cameronian Volunteers, but the following year —1794—the title was changed to The 79th Regiment, or Cameron Highlanders. Clan Cameron rallied as it had seldom done before, and in recruiting the new regiment Alan Cameron received considerable help from his brother, Captain Ewen Cameron—" Eoghainn Mor " (Big Ewen) as he was locally known— and from Macdonell of Keppoch, whose father was slain at Culloden

Alan Cameron received financial support from his father-in-law, Nathaniel Phillips, a Pembrokeshire landowner, whose daughter, Ann, he married in 1779. In his native Lochaber, Alan Cameron asked, and received, the support of the inhabitants, and promised several commissions to the near relatives of the man whose life he had taken in the duel.

As it was considered that the prevailing colour of the Cameron tartan—red—would not harmonise well with the scarlet coatee, the Macdonald sett was selected for the regiment, with the addition of the yellow stripe of the Clan Cameron and the omission of three of the thin red lines of the Macdonald tartan. This design has since been known as the Erracht tartan.

The Letter of Service authorised the raising of the regiment within three months, and decreed that it should consist of one company of grenadiers, one of light infantry, and eight battalion companies. The regiment was recruited to a strength of 750 in less than two months, and the first muster was in December, 1793. The Highlanders paraded under Major Alan Cameron at Fort William, where it was inspected and passed as efficient. A few days later the new formation marched for Stirling.

When the Camerons left Lochaber the pipes were playing " Gabhaidh Sinn An Rathad Mor " (We Will Take The High Road), and they were accompanied for several miles by a large number of their kinsmen and womenfolk. In

June, 1794, at Belfast, the regiment was issued with its first full-dress uniform, the facings of the red coat being green. And proudly wearing kilts of Cameron of Erracht tartan, the Highland soldiers attracted much attention and admiring comment.

In the same year the Camerons first saw active service as a British regiment in the Duke of York's ill-conducted campaign in the Netherlands. The 79th served until 1795 against the French Republican forces, and had no opportunity to distinguish itself as it was not committed to battle. But the regiment lost 200 men from privation, principally due to the severity of the winter. Starved and poorly-clad, the British troops took part in the miserable retreat across Hanover and Westphalia to Bremen and the mouth of the Elbe.

On the return of the 79th to the U.K. it was proposed to disband the regiment and draft the Highlanders into other formations in violation of the promise given to Alan Cameron —now a Colonel—when he raised the regiment. Alan Cameron sought an interview with the Duke of York, the Commander-in-Chief, and legend has it that he angrily informed him that " to draft the 79th is more than you or your Royal father dare do."

The Duke, just as heatedly, replied: " The King, my father, will certainly send the regiment to the West Indies ", and Colonel Cameron stormed back: " You may tell the King, your father, that he may send us to Hell if he likes, and I'll go at the head of them—but he daurna draft us."

The Duke of York was impressed by the vehemence of the Cameron. The drafting order was rescinded, but the decision to dispatch the regiment to the West Indies was unfortunately implemented. The 79th was sent to the island of Martinique, where, within two years, the regiment lost over 260 men from yellow fever and other tropical diseases. The regiment was so reduced that the survivors were illegally drafted into The Black Watch and other corps, while the officers, senior non-commissioned-officers and band returned to England in 1797, and, arriving at Inverness in 1798, recruited up to strength.

In 1799 the reconstituted regiment took the field again in Holland against the French, gaining its first battle-honour on October 2 at Egmont-op-Zee. Colonel Cameron was wounded in this severe engagement. The day after the battle the Duke of York, the C.-in-C., rode up to The Cameron Highlanders, and, removing his hat, said to the Commanding

Officer: " Major Maclean, nothing could do the regiment more credit than its conduct yesterday ". So the Duke of York made his peace with the Camerons . . . . .

Eighteen months later, after participating in the unsuccessful attempt on Ferrol, where it was hoped, with the aid of a naval squadron, to destroy Spanish shipping and the arsenal, the 79th joined Lieutenant-General Sir Ralph Abercromby's expeditionary force, and in March, 1801, landed at Aboukir Bay.

After defeating the French at Mandora and Alexandria, the Camerons marched on Cairo. Here the enemy was compelled to surrender and evacuate Egypt. For its outstanding part in dispelling the fear of French interference in India and the East, the 79th was granted the Royal authority to inscribe upon its colours and appointments the badge of the Sphinx superscribed " Egypt ".

A Rifle Corps was formed in 1800, which later became the 95th—now the Rifle Brigade. Originally raised on an experimental basis, it was formed from detachments of picked men from 14 regiments, including the Camerons, who contributed a kilted Highland Company. In 1804 a second battalion of The Cameron Highlanders was raised, and acted as a " feeder " but on the conclusion of peace with the French, it was disbanded at Dundee towards the close of 1815.

The 79th was engaged in the joint naval and military operations undertaken against Denmark in 1807. It was feared that if the Danish Fleet fell into Napoleon's hands this would upset the balance of sea power. The Danes naturally refused to surrender their fleet, but, after bombardment, Copenhagen capitulated, and, the object of the expedition accomplished, the troops returned.

At the close of 1808 the Camerons were advancing from Lisbon into the heart of Spain to engage the French. The regiment was led by Colonel Phillips Cameron, the founder's eldest son, Alan Cameron having been promoted major-general. Soon the Highlanders were fighting in the epic Retreat from Corunna, which began at Christmas before three powerful enemy columns, each superior in numbers to Lieutenant-General Sir John Moore's force. The Battle of Corunna, in January, 1809, in which Sir John Moore was killed, ensured the successful evacuation of the British troops on the transports after their disastrous winter retreat over the mountains.

Later in the year the 79th took part in the expedition to Walcheren, in the attempt to capture Antwerp and destroy French shipping, but little progress was made after the siege and occupation of Flushing. The troops were ravaged by fever, and, on the operation being abandoned, were withdrawn to England.

In the protracted Peninsular War, which eventually liberated Portugal and Spain from the French yoke, the Camerons were in the defence of Cadiz, the battles of Busaco, Fuentes d'Onor and Salamanca, the occupation of Madrid, the siege of Burgos, the battles of the Pyrenees, Nivelle, Nive and Toulouse. A detachment of 49 men from the regiment entered the fray at Talavera. Only 12 came out. At Busaco Captain Alexander Cameron, with an outlying picquet held on though surrounded by the enemy, and went down fighting against overwhelming odds.

In the bloody fighting for Fuentes d'Onor, Colonel Cameron, son of the founder of the regiment was killed. The shout " Thuit an Camshronach " (Cameron has fallen) went up. The Highlanders in their grief and fury charged the French Imperial Guards, decimated them, and swept the enemy from the disputed village, turning looming defeat into victory.

At Burgos the only success achieved was by the 79th in the capture of the outlying Horn-work. At the Battle of Toulouse the 79th stormed and carried the Colombette Redoubt and the Tour des Augustins—the two strongest features of Marshal Soult's defenceworks.

Sadly depleted, the Camerons arrived at Cork in December, 1814. The regiment was stationed there until March, 1815, awaiting transport to North America, but, on the escape of Napoleon from Elba, a renewal of the war with France was inevitable, and the sailing order was cancelled. The Cameron Highlanders were dispatched to Belgium in May, 1815. The regiment arrived at Ostend and went on to Brussels. The officers were attending the Duchess of Richmond's ball on the night of June 15 when news was received that Napoleon had crossed the Sambre and an attack was imminent. Bugles sounded and pipes skirled. The Camerons fell in on the Place Royale and marched to Quatre Bras.

Stationed on the left of the British line at Quatre Bras, the 79th was heavily engaged, suffering severe casualties in the French on-slaught. The Camerons scattered the enemy advancing on the guns, and entered on a spirited pursuit. Then, forming square, the Highlanders stood firm and repelled several cavalry charges by the Cuirassiers.

From Quatre Bras the British Army retired to the field of Waterloo. In this decisive battle, on June 18, the Camerons formed square in the centre of the Duke of Wellington's position and threw back assault after assault by dense columns of French infantry with great slaughter. Hour after hour the Highlanders braved the terrific enemy cannonade, then faced the surging charges of Napoleon's massed cavalry squadrons—and triumphed.

Within the compact square the pipes skirled defiance, and Piper Kenneth Mackay, of Tongue. Sutherlandshire, stepped outside the levelled rifles and bayonets of the Camerons to play " Cogadh na Sith " (War or Peace), and, despite the onrush of the famous Old Guard veterans — Napoleon's " invincibles "—continued to inspire his comrades.

Then came the wild Highland charge which routed Napoleon's bloodied shattered formations and sealed the doom of the Emperor. Close on 500 Camerons were killed or wounded, and the remnant of the 79th ended the battle commanded by a subaltern—Lieutenant Alexander Cameron—a nephew of the founder.

The Cameron Highlanders entered Paris, and for three years served with the Army of Occupation in France. The regiment then had spells of duty in the Channel Islands, Ireland, England, Scotland, Gibraltar, and was twice stationed in Canada. On the outbreak of war with Russia in 1854, the Camerons were at Portsmouth. Arriving in the Crimea the regiment, forming part of the Highland Brigade, had their full share of all the privations and bitter fighting in this grim hard-fought campaign. The Camerons were at the battles of the Alma and Balaclava, in the expedition to the Sea of Azov, and in the siege of Sevastopol.

There was stubborn fighting on the slopes by the River Alma. The Camerons crested the hill in battle array, colours flaunting in the breeze, and the pipes strindently sounding their stirring call, and ere long the Highland Brigade had a fine panoramic view of the Russians hastily retreating on Sevastopol.

The 79th were undaunted by the thundering, flashing, fire-belching Russian cannon and the endless dense-packed ranks of the Czar's infantry, and red were the bayonets of the Camerons at Balaclava. At Sevastopol, on the failure of the assault on the Redan Redoubt, the Camerons were ordered to attack with their brigade at dawn. During the night, however, the Russians evacuated the fortifications, blowing up many of the defenceworks as they retired, and the Highlanders quickly moved into the silent Redan. But service in Turkey, Bulgaria and the Crimea cost the regiment dear in casualties and sickness. Three hundred and eighty-seven officers and other ranks did not return.

After a short period of home service the regiment was ordered to India, then in the throes of The Mutiny. The Camerons landed at Calcutta towards the close of 1857, and marched to the relief of Lucknow. In the narrow winding streets the Highlanders engaged the mutineers. It was a day of the bayonet. House after house was cleared of the enemy, and when the rebels made a run for it, the Camerons at once took up the pursuit, capturing the colours of the 7th Oude Irregular Infantry and four of the enemy guns. Further stiff actions followed at the Battle of Bareilly, and the storming of Rampore Kussia, and in the subsequent operations in Oude and Rohilkund.

In 1863 the regiment was represented by a contingent in an expedition sent against disaffected tribesmen on the North West Frontier, and there were several sharp clashes with the enemy in the Shubkudder Pass. The 79th remained in the East until 1871, when it returned to the U.K. after 13 years service in India. But 349 Camerons were left behind—glory's price had once again been dearly paid.

The fiery Camerons and their impulsive leaders had in the past incurred the Royal displeasure, but on their return from India the 79th came under the appraising eyes of Queen Victoria. At Osborne, Isle of Wight, in February, 1872, Her Majesty expressed the desire to see The Cameron Highlanders in marching order, and, the following year, at the same place, the regiment furnished a guard of honour.

In April, 1873, Queen Victoria personally presented new colours to the 79th at Parkhurst Barracks, Isle of Wight, and, in July of the same year, the Queen commanded that the regiment should in future be styled " The Queen's Own Cameron Highlanders ", and that the facings on the uniforms be changed from green to blue, as befitted a Royal regiment. Throughout her long and eventful reign there were numerous other occasions on which Queen Victoria showed her marked interest in the 79th, which she frequently referred to as " My Own Cameron Highlanders ". One of Her Majesty's last public appearances was to present the first colours to the newly-raised 2nd Battalion in October, 1898, in front of Balmoral Castle.

The 79th furnished a detachment of two officers and 135 other ranks to accompany The Black Watch to the Gold Coast for the Ashanti expedition, led by Major-General Sir Garnet Wolseley, in 1873. These Camerons—who volunteered for this campaign in the jungle and bush—were engaged in the fighting at Amoaful and the capture of the barbarous King Coffee's capital, Kumasi. The detachment on its return joined the regiment at Aldershot.

In 1881 The Queen's Own Cameron Highlanders had a narrow escape from extinction. In that year a scheme of Army reorganisation was framed whereby infantry regiments of two battalions would be formed by linking together two regiments. It was proposed to make the 79th the 2nd Battalion of the 42nd (The Black Watch).

On being asked if this would be acceptable, the Commanding Officer of the Camerons sent firm refusals by wire and by letter. Nothing more was heard of the matter until the Secretary of State for War announced in the House of Commons in April, 1881, that the 79th would continue as the only single-battalion regiment in the Army. And so the regiment remained until the 2nd Battalion The Queen's Own Cameron Highlanders was raised from a nucleus provided by the 1st Battalion in 1897.

For this continuance of its existence as a distinct unit, Queen Victoria was mainly responsible. Under the Army reorganisation plan The Queen's Own Cameron Highlanders were, appropriately enough, associated with the Inverness-shire Militia and Volunteers, as the county's regiment, but the old numeral " 79 " was dropped.

Early in August, 1882, The Queen's Own Cameron Highlanders left Gibraltar and disembarked at Alexandria, where the regiment joined the Highland Brigade. It was conveyed by transport ship to Lake Timsah, and, on landing, the Camerons marched across the open desert to attack the Egyptian mutineers, led by Colonel Arabi Pasha, who were strongly entrenched at Tel-el-Kebir.

The wild Highland charge at dawn stormed over the thorough enemy defences, and after a short but fierce hand-to-hand engagement, the enemy fled in rout with " The March of the Cameron Men " skirling in their ears. The Camerons remained with the Army of Occupation in Egypt, and in 1884-5 the regiment served with the force which ascended the River Nile for the attempted relief of General Gordon, who was surrounded by the dervish warriors at Khartoum. When news was received that Khartoum had fallen and that General Gordon ad been murdered, the operation was abandoned.

The Camerons operated against the dervishes who had followed up the retiring Nile Expedition to Wadi Halfa, about 800 miles down the river, and, at Koseh Fort, with the help of 250 Soudanese, a detachment of Egyptians, and an armed steamer, the Highlanders held at bay during December, 1885, 7,000 of these desert fanatics. When reinforcements came up the enemy was shattered at Ginnis.

The regiment returned to the U.K. in 1887 to enter another troubled period in its existence. That year—and again, in 1893—it became known that the authorities were contemplating the conversion of The Cameron Highlanders into a third battalion of The Scots Guards. Consternation and dismay prevailed, and a storm of protest was launched, which was successful in saving the regiment from virtual extinction. And once again Queen Victoria championed the cause of her Cameron Highlanders. In 1897 the 2nd Battalion of the regiment was formed at Fort George.

After a few years of home service, the 1st Battalion arrived at Malta, and later went on to " Gib ". In 1897 the Camerons returned to the Land of the Pharaohs. The battalion received orders early in 1898 to join the expeditionary force assembling at Berber for the re-conquest of the Soudan.

At the Battle of Atbara, in April of that year, the bayonet charge of the Camerons tore great gaps in the enemy's defences. When the Khalifa's warriors rose up and came at them with sword, spear and rifle, Piper Stewart continued to play a rousing march until he fell riddled with bullets. Private Cross bayonetted a huge dervish as he attempted to spear General Gatacre.

Early in September, at the Battle of Omdurman, the Camerons formed part of the British line, the men standing shoulder to shoulder to meet the frenzied massed attacks of 60,000 desert warriors led by their shrieking holy-men and standard-bearers. Within a few hundred yards of the levelled rifles and glinting bayonets they were mown down in swathes by the accurate concentrated fire of the infantry and gunners.

A last stand was made round the great black flag of the Khalifa, but the howling religious fanatics were shot, bayonetted or hacked down. The Khalifa fled, but was killed later. Khartoum was entered, and the pipers of the Camerons played a lament before the ruins of General Gordon's house. The regiment was the only one which had taken part in the Egyptian and Soudan campaigns of the 1880's. So came to an end the reign of terror, corruption, intrigue, tyranny and massacre of Arabi Pasha, the Mahdi, Osman Digna, and the Khalifa in Egypt and the Soudan.

A company of the Camerons under Captain the Hon. A. D. Murray accompanied General Sir Herbert Kitchener on his important mission to Fashoda, which brought France and Britain to the brink of war. Major Marchand and a French force had arrived on the Nile, but the British and Egyptian flags were hoisted as a sign of possession, and, after high-level political activity, tension eased.

At the end of the century the battle-honours of The Cameron Highlanders were:—The Sphinx, superscribed " Egypt ", Egmont-op-Zee, Corunna, Busaco, Fuentes d'Onor, Salamanca, Pyrenees, Nivelle, Nive, Toulouse, Peninsula, Waterloo, Alma, Sevastopol, Lucknow, Tel-el-Kebir, Egypt, 1882, Nile, 1884-85, Atbara, Khartoum.

The 1st Battalion left Cairo in March, 1900 to serve in South Africa against the Boers. The Camerons arrived in time to take part in the advance north from Bloemfontein. The Highlanders forded the Vaal River and entered Pretoria to the stirring strains of " The Pibroch o' Donuil Dhu ". The battalion was in the operations which succeeded in hemming in General Prinsloo's force in the mountains on the Basutoland border, and it was engaged in the brisk action at Retief's Nek, where 4,000 Boers surrendered. The Camerons operated around Wittebergen and skirmished forward in harassing guerilla fighting with the enemy.

At Nooitgedacht, Sergeant Donald Farmer won the regiment's first Victoria Cross. In a surprise enemy attack, with men falling on all sides, he dashed out into the heavy close-range fire and brought back a badly wounded officer with the bullets whistling round him.

By the end of the war the 1st Camerons had done more marching than any other regiment —over 3,000 miles—a record, with a goodly margin to spare. The battalion had the support of a company of hardy Inverness-shire Volunteers (later Territorials), and a number of stalwarts from the Western Isles, who joined the 1st Camerons in South Africa as Militia reservists. The battle-honour South Africa, 1900-02 was later awarded to the regiment.

The death of Queen Victoria caused deep mourning in the ranks of The Queen's Own

This is the Coach that alone, week by week, takes some of Erskine Paraplegic patients to visit the world outside the Hospital walls.

To keep it going expenses continue to rise. Will you add your contribution as one of those who do not forget.

Donations to be sent to Mr. Andrew Fraser, Hon. Treasurer, Manager, Bank of Scotland, Ibrox Branch, 418 Paisley Road West, Glasgow, S.W.1.

This space donated by—**James McLean (The Bookmaker), Ltd., 12 Woodside Terrace, Glasgow.   Tel., Douglas 7000**

Cameron Highlanders. The link with the Royal Family was restored in November, 1902, when H.R.H. the Prince of Wales was appointed Colonel-in-Chief, an honour which he renewed when he came to the throne as King George V. Meanwhile the 2nd Battalion was upholding the fine reputation of the regiment in Crete, South Africa, North China and India.

In World War I there were 13 battalions of The Queen's Own Cameron Highlanders, eight of which were committed to battle. A total of 284 officers and 5,609 other ranks made the supreme sacrifice. Fifty-two battle-honours were awarded to the regiment for its outstanding part in the campaigns of 1914-18. These were:—Retreat from Mons, Marne, 1914, '18, Aisne, 1914, Ypres, 1914, '15, 17', '18, Langemarck, 1914, Gheluvelt, Nonne Bosschen, Givenchy, 1914, Neuve Chapelle, Hill 60, Gravenstafel, St. Julien, Frezenberg, Bellewaarde, Aubers, Festubert, 1915, Loos, Somme, 1916, '18, Albert, 1916, Bazentin, Delville Wood, Pozieres, Flers-Courcelette, Morval, Le Transloy, Ancre Heights, Arras, 1917, '18, Scarpe, 1917, Arleux, Pilckem, Menin Road, Polygon Wood, Poelcappelle, Passchendaele, St. Quentin, Bapaume, 1918, Lys, Estaires, Messines, 1918, Kemmel, Bethune, Soissonnais-Ourcq, Drocourt-Queant, Hindenburg Line, Epehy, St. Quentin Canal, Courtrai, Selle, Sambre, France and Flanders, 1914-18, Struma, Macedonia, 1915-18.

At the outbreak of war the 1st Battalion was in Edinburgh Castle, and the 2nd Battalion at Poona, India. The 1st, 4th (T.A.), 5th, 6th and 7th Battalions fought on the Western Front. The 4th was later absorbed by the 1st owing to its reduced numbers.

The 2nd Camerons arrived in France and served from December, 1914, until November, 1915, when it was transferred to Salonika. This battalion became one of the mainstays in the fighting on the Struma front, distinguishing itself in the Battle of Karajaköi. The 2nd operated in this theatre of war until the surrender of the Bulgarians, then went on to Batum, and from there through the deep forests of the Caucasus to occupy Tiflis, on the shores of the Caspian Sea.

One company of the 5th (Lochiel's) Battalion was furnished by the Glasgow Stock Exchange, and another by university students. The 7th was largely recruited from the men of the City of Glasgow Police. The 3rd (Special Reserve) Battalion and the 8th Battalion acted as "feeders", while the 9th (Labour) Battalion and the 11th Battalion served in France. A home service battalion took over depot duties.

Practically the entire regimental staff of the 1st Camerons perished in the early days of the war, when, in September, 1914, the explosion of a cluster of German shells brought down the roof of a cave in which they were sheltering. Only four of the entombed men were brought out alive. The 1st Battalion experienced the ghastly trench warfare of France and Flanders, and made a magnificent fight of it, particularly at Loos, on the Aisne, and in the smashing of the mighty German offensive in the spring of 1918.

The Camerons greatest battle of the war was at Loos, in September, 1915. The 1st, 4th, 5th, 6th and 7th Battalions were all engaged, and suffered very heavy casualties. For their heroism in this historic action two Cameron Highlanders were awarded Victoria Crosses—a rare achievement for a regiment in one engagement.

Corporal James Dalgleish Pollok won his award with the 5th (Lochiel's) Battalion at Hohenzollern. This N.C.O., volunteering to attack a redoubt, went over the parapet and approached the Germans from the flank. Unseen by the enemy, Corporal Pollock succeeded in hurling his bombs with deadly effect, clearing the Germans out of the trench. Though twice wounded, he held the captured trench under heavy machine-gun and rifle fire until assistance was forthcoming.

Lieutenant-Colonel Angus Douglas-Hamilton's award for gallantry at Hill 70 was unfortunately posthumous. Though units on both flanks had been forced back, he led his 6th Battalion forward four times into a murderous fire, and the assaulting waves reached the farthest point in the attack. In the fifth and final rally he led a handful of survivors with the call, "Come on, men, and we will show them how to charge!" Then, at their head, the lieutenant-colonel fell mortally wounded.

In the desperate attack on Hill 70, the 7th Battalion carried the H.Q. flag—to which a couple of pieces of Cameron tartan had been sewn—and around it the Highlanders rallied again and again. But each time the number was fewer. The Camerons followed it through the storm of German shot and shell, and nothing but death could stop them. "Clanna nan Gaidheal ri guelibh a cheile!"

Another Victoria Cross was awarded to a Cameron in the bitter fighting on the Aisne. Private Ross Tollerton went to the assistance of

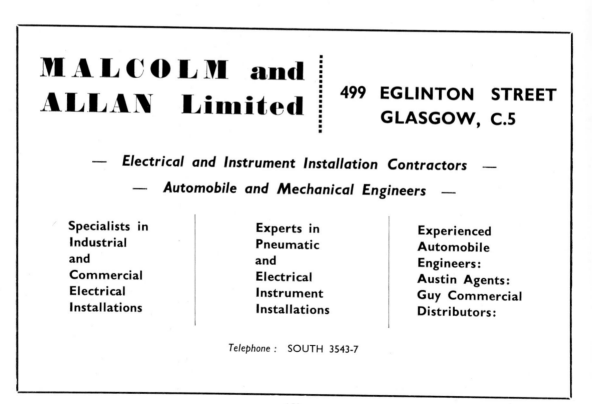

Lieutenant Matheson, who had been seriously wounded. He remained with him for three days in an exposed position, but eventually brought back the officer to safety and succour.

The 4th Battalion, which had fought hard and well at Loos, again won renown at Neuve Chapelle and Festubert. The 6th faced up to the powerful German 1918 offensive at Monchy, in the Arras sector, and its fight enriched the saga of the regiment. After the Armistice the 1st and 5th Battalions advanced to the Rhine and occupied Cologne. The 6th and 7th Battalions, as a combined unit, went to Brussels.

In August, 1919 the 1st Camerons left Scotland on a lengthy tour of foreign service in India, Burma and the Soudan. In May of the following year the 2nd Battalion went to Ireland. It spent two years operating during the Irish troubles before going on to Germany.

Marshal Graziani's army of 300,000 Italian Regular and " Blackshirt " divisions was poised on the western frontier of Egypt in 1940. General Wavell faced them with a " token " force of Empire fighting men, including the 2nd Camerons, serving with the seasoned 4th Indian Division. The position was critical, for after the chaos of Dunkirk, there was not a single fully-equipped division in the U.K. which could be sent to North Africa. But General Wavell, a former Black Watch officer, was not dismayed. He decided to attack, and thus began the short victorious September, 1940-February, 1941 campaign in the Western Desert.

Fortified towns, villages, posts and encampments were attacked and captured, while the R.A.F. kept Mussolini's air force down by bombing the airfields. At Nibeiwa, a few miles from Sidi Barrani, the Camerons, following tanks into the Italian defences in troop-carrying lorries, received the final order from a loud-speaker. It was " CAMERONS—GO ! "

The Camerons lept from the lorries, and, with bayonets fixed, made the traditional furious Highland charge against the Italians, the bagpipes shrilling through the din of guns, cries and cheers. Hundreds of Italians were downed in the mad scrambling rush, and close on 3,000 made prisoners. The classic signal came in from The Scots Guards that prisoners had not yet been counted, but estimated " about five acres of officers and 200 acres of other ranks."

The pursuit of the fleeing Italians ended with the round-up of tens of thousands of Mussolini's discomfited soldiers at Beda Fomm and well beyond Benghazi. And in invasion-threatened Britain the news from North Africa cheered the people of the " island fortress " and greatly impressed the Americans—and there was secret rejoicing in Nazi-occupied Europe.

The 4th and 5th Indian divisions were detached from General Wavell's desert army, and, via Egypt and the Soudan, dealt a crushing blow to the 250,000 Italian defenders of East Africa. Skirmishing forward, the Camerons, with their Indian comrades, rooted out the enemy from strong defensive positions in the advance towards the Keren Hills. The outlying defences were assaulted and carried, and the Camerons began the fighting ascent, scaling and battling the enemy off 1,000 to 1,500 feet high crags in the face of artillery, machine-gun and rifle fire.

The fighting in the hills went on for several weeks. The Italians showered down grenades and boulders on the ascending Highlanders, but, when the bayonets of the 2nd Camerons came winking over the crests and crags, their hands went up in surrender. A ridge in the Keren Hills is named after the Camerons. This highly successful nine weeks drive ended with the capture of the Red Sea port of Massawa. The 5th Indian Division and the 1st South African Division chased the Italians out of Abyssinia, and the fighting at Amba Alagi completed the Italian rout in East Africa. The 2nd Camerons then returned to the Western Desert.

Early in June, 1942, " Desert Fox " Rommel launched a powerful attack on the Gazala-Bir Hakeim Line. Enemy pressure increased, and Tobruk was isolated. Help could not be sent by the hard-pressed Eighth Army, and German armour broke into the defence perimeter. The Luftwaffe joined in, and there was no air cover. Tobruk surrendered—but not the Camerons and Gurkhas.

The 2nd Camerons and a battalion of The Gurkha Rifles were still fighting a day after the surrender, but, exhausted, out of ammunition and food, ringed by enemy tanks and infantry, pounded from the air, and with no hope of breaking through or of rescue, they too had to give up. The next day what was left of the battalion marched out—not as a defeated force—but under their Commanding Officer, Lieutenant-Colonel C. S. Duncan, D.S.O. Headed by pipers the victors of Nibeiwa, Agordat and Cameron Ridge marched into captivity.

But parties of Cameron Highlanders escaped to cross the desert, and a few eventually succeeded in reaching the British lines. The 2nd Battalion was resuscitated, and, arriving in

Italy, fought at Cassino and in the Gustav Line onslaughts. The Camerons crossed the Rubicon and advanced fighting northwards to battle through the German serial lines of defence. Later the Camerons were sent to Greece to preserve order, and then they served in troubled Trieste. The 2nd Battalion was officially disbanded in June, 1948.

As a result of the strict security " blackout ", some time elapsed before Scotland was told that her Cameron Highlanders were in the war against the Japanese. Then news was released that the 1st Battalion had distinguished itself in the Kohima-Imphal drive, in May, 1944. Now the scene was set for the launching of the all-out offensive which liberated Burma. In this great operation the Camerons were engaged in incessant fighting under the most exacting conditions, but the Highlanders soon established an ascendancy over the Japanese.

After a succession of gruelling attacks and counter-attacks among the hills, jungles and swamps, the assault crossing of the Irrawaddy by the British 2nd Division was a wonderful feat of arms, with casualties mounting as the crisis of the battle approached. Coming out from concealment when other units were making the crossing under a blizzard of fire, the Camerons splashed in, and the leading company gained the enemy-held bank with light casualties, and quickly dug in. Then a storm of shot and shell was unleashed upon them from the enemy artillery, machine-guns and rifles.

Their position in the small bridgehead was precarious, and, as daylight spread, the Camerons stood up to the continuing concentrated fire of the Japanese. So intense was enemy reaction that only a trickle of reinforcements managed to join them across the Irrawaddy, hissing and foaming with the splashing bullets and exploding shells and grenades.

For three days the 1st Camerons went through this ordeal of fire, wounds and death, but the Highlanders grimly retained their bloodsodden " finger-hold " on the enemy bank. Then, gradually at first, reinforcements battled through the fire and landed on the east bank, and a build-up commenced which enabled an attack to be launched in sufficient strength to smash back the enemy from a series of cunningly-concealed and carefully-prepared camouflaged defences.

With the Fourteenth Army the 1st Camerons were in the force which bore the brunt of the bitter fighting which opened the way for the capture of Chauk and Yenangyaung—Burma's largest oil centres. Sweeping down the eastern bank of the Irrawaddy from Yenangyaung and its 300 wells, Camerons and tanks fought into another important oil town—Magwe—about 240 miles from Rangoon.

In the severe fighting which raged among the derricks of this 60-mile stretch of oil country, the 1st Camerons wiped out a number of Japanese suicide defenders, who fought to the last, and the enemy sustained very heavy casualties. Now the Camerons were on the final lap of the rapid advance to Rangoon, which ended the campaign in Burma.

The 1st Battalion The Queen's Own Cameron Highlanders was the representative Scottish formation in the British force which occupied Japan. The kilted Highlanders paraded through Shiro and Kure, and the pibroch sounded in the Lands of the Samurai.

In 1943, His Majesty King George VI—who became Colonel-in-Chief on his accession to the throne—authorised the regimental pipers to wear kilts of the Royal Stewart tartan to commemorate the 150th anniversary of the raising of the regiment.

During 1947 the Camerons were stationed in Malaya co-operating with the local police in internal security. In the spring of 1948 the battalion returned to the homeland after serving overseas since 1942—when the Camerons arrived in India to train for jungle combat with the Japanese.

Previously the Camerons had fought in the short early summer campaign of 1940 in France. Pressed back by superior numbers of better-armed German infantry and armour, the Camerons retired fighting to Dunkirk for evacuation. When the regiment won its first battle-honour in 1799 at Egmont-op-Zee, the casualties totalled 79—the original number of the corps. By a strange coincidence 79 Camerons embarked at Dunkirk.

The Cameron Highlanders will probably go down in history as the last Highland regiment to wear the kilt in battle. When they were making their final heroic stand at La Bassee against overwhelming odds at the close of May, 1940, the Cameron Highlanders were wearing the distinctive Erracht tartan.

The 4th Battalion sacrificed itself with 152 Brigade of the 51st (Highland) Division at St. Valery. The 5th Battalion took its place in the reconstituted Highland Division, and, in North Africa, fought across the Western Desert from El Alamein to Tunis. Arriving in Sicily

with the 51st, the Camerons, after a series of bitterly-fought engagements, forced the Germans to evacuate the island.

Landing on the shell and bullet-swept Normandy beachheads on D-Day plus one, the Highlanders broke out of the containment area around Caen to fight forward across the Seine and race, with the other units of the Highland Division, to liberate St. Valery. Then the Highlanders hammered the Germans back from France and the Low Countries, pursued them across the network of canals and rivers to make the assault-crossing of the Rhine, and take part in the final advance deep into the heart of the Third Reich. The 7th Battalion became the 5th (Scottish) Parachute Battalion, whose fight in the Italian Campaign the Germans will remember for many a day. Thus Cameron Highlanders—Regular, Territorial, and conscript—kept faith with their ancestors and the old 79th.

After taking part in several street and desert skirmishes in the troubled Suez Canal Zone, the 1st Battalion returned from Egypt in May, 1952. In the autumn of that year the Camerons left for service in Austria and Germany. Early in 1955 the battalion came home, but, a few months later, was ordered to Korea, where it remained for over a year with the United Nations Command. A short spell of anti-terrorist operations followed in Malaya in 1956.

There was further action in 1957, when the Camerons arrived in the Aden Protectorate. They had a number of clashes with Yemeni tribesmen who had crossed the border and embarked on a campaign of attacking forts and ambushing convoys and troops in difficult rock and desert country. In the spring of 1958 the 1st Camerons returned to the homeland.

On the eve of her Coronation, Her Majesty The Queen honoured the regiment by giving orders for the appointment of H.R.H. The Duke of Edinburgh as Colonel-in-Chief.

The Seaforth Highlanders and The Queen's Own Cameron Highlanders are scheduled to amalgamate in 1961. There was a partial "amalgamation" in 1955, when 30 National Service soldiers, trained as Cameron Highlanders, were posted to the Seaforths. The men of the two regiments quickly settled down together and became good comrades—a favourable augury for the future.

The two regiments are next-door neighbours, and draw recruits from practically the same area. They have similar ancestry and traditions. and both possess distinguished fighting records. The glorious pages of Scotland's military history show that Seaforths and Camerons have soldiered together, endured privation together, fought, bled, and died together. If union there must be—and the War Office has left no doubt about this—the union of The Seaforth Highlanders and The Queen's Own Cameron Highlanders is an ideal one.

The Argyll & Sutherland Highlanders

(PRINCESS LOUISE'S)

THE name of each of Scotland's regiments is indelibly linked with some outstanding victory or feat of arms. The Argyll and Sutherland Highlanders have a battle-honour on their Colours which is immortal. It is BALACLAVA.

Here about 500 Highlanders of the 93rd, or Sutherland Regiment, stood firm and hurled back nine charging Russian cavalry squadrons. The "Thin Red Line" on that cannon and bullet-swept hill in the Crimea, on October 25, 1854, vies with the great battles of Greek and Roman mythology.

The Argyll and Sutherland Highlanders was formed by the union, in 1881, of the 91st (Princess Louise's) Argyllshire Highlanders and the 93rd Sutherland Highlanders. In that year the 91st became the 1st Battalion, and the 93rd the 2nd Battalion of the regiment.

The 91st was raised in 1794 as the 98th, or The Argyll Regiment. A Letter of Service dated February 10, 1794, from King George III to John, Fifth Duke of Argyll, authorised him to raise the regiment. Duncan Campbell, of Lochnell, Argyllshire, who had served as a captain in the 1st Foot Guards, was appointed Lieutenant-Colonel Commandant. Though recruiting in the Highlands was successful in rallying men to the regiment, parties were sent into the Lowlands—to Edinburgh, Glasgow and elsewhere—and further recruits were added. Soon the regiment had 700 men on its roll. About half were Highlanders, the remainder being Lowlanders, with a leaven of Irishmen. Later more recruits arrived from Wiltshire, Somerset, Gloucestershire and Warwickshire.

At a time when Britain was menaced by Republican France, Lieutenant-Colonel Campbell assumed command at Stirling on April 15, 1794, and a few weeks later in May, the newly-formed regiment was inspected and passed as efficient and fit for service. In June the Highlanders arrived in England, and early in July the King approved the list of 35 officers, 17 of whom were Campbells. Originally the men were dressed in the Highland military garb, with short coat or jacket, faced with yellow, and belted plaid. The tartan worn was the 42nd, with its familiar green and black colouring.

Action was not long delayed. In 1795 the 98th was dispatched to South Africa and served in the campaign which resulted in the surrender of the Dutch at the Cape of Good Hope and its temporary annexation. In 1798 the regiment was re-numbered, becoming the 91st. Early in the following year a number of soldiers in the Cape Town garrison approached the men of the 91st to join them in a mutiny. The Highlanders refused and reported the matter to the authorities.

The regiment returned to the U.K. in two contingents, the first towards the close of 1802, and the second some three months later, after taking part in the ceremony of handing back the Cape of Good Hope to the Dutch in accordance with the terms of the Treaty of Amiens. On the 91st coming home the only part of the Highland dress resumed was the feather bonnet. When supplies of tartan cloth arrived it was made into trousers. So the Highlanders reluctantly went into trews.

In 1809 the War Office ordered that the 91st—and certain other Highland regiments—must cease wearing the kilt and adopt the uniform worn by regiments of the Line. The 91st had also to discard its county title of "Argyllshire" and the appellation "Highlanders", and from 1810 until 1864 the formation was merely designated the 91st Regiment of Foot. But the officers were not long in securing that the pipers at least should march in the "Garb of Old Gaul".

When Britain's old enemy Spain, asked for assistance against Napoleon, aid was at once forthcoming. The Duke of Wellington landed forces—which included the 91st—at the Mondego River in the autumn of 1808. The French were defeated at the battles of Rolica and Vimiera. Rolica and Vimiera are listed among the battle-honours of the regiment.

General Sir John Moore advanced into Spain with four divisions. The 91st Regiment was in this force, which, on reaching Salamanca, learned that several strong French columns were closing in on them from different directions.

Napoleon said that an army marches on its stomach. The British troops began a retreat

of over 200 miles through the Cantabrian Mountains in the dead of winter with empty stomachs. The retreat went on through deep snow, in chilling torrential sleety rain, frost, slush, and mud. Transport and supply broke down, and the men were ill-clad, hungry, and without shelter.

French sharpshooters and skirmishers harried the exhausted, famished, tattered men, and by the time Corunna was reached, thousands were barefoot. But during the epic retreat discipline in battle was never lost. Seven times the 91st, in a rearguard role, turned and attacked the pursuing French, and at Corunna fought again in a furious battle lasting several hours, which gained time for the evacuation ships to arrive. The French retired to a safe distance and licked their wounds while the evacuation proceeded. Corunna is another proud battle-honour of the 91st.

In 1809 the regiment took part in the expedition to Walcheren, on the low-lying Dutch coast. Soon the British force was in the throes of a disease epidemic, and over 4,000 men succumbed. The survivors were then withdrawn. Rejoining the " Iron Duke ", in Spain, the 91st took part in the fighting advance northwards into France. Pyrenees, Nivelle, Nive, Orthes and Tolouse all appear as battle-honours of the 91st.

The regiment was with the force dispatched to Holland in 1814, and fought at Bergen-op-Zoom. The 91st was not committed at Waterloo, but came up in time to take part in the pursuit of the shattered French Army, and a drummer boy of the regiment, William Ballantine, bearing a flag of truce, led the Allied Armies into Paris to begin the occupation of the French capital. At St. Helena, in 1840, a detachment of the 91st was present at the disinterment of Napoleon's body, which was taken to France for re-burial.

About 1824 the regiment was offered the Highland dress, but with tartan trews instead of the kilt. This was declined. A Reserve battalion, formed in 1842, served in South Africa, and, with the 91st, operated in the Kaffir War of 1846-47. After the 91st left for home, the Reserve battalion fought in a further campaign against the Kaffirs from 1851-53. The battle-honours South Africa, 1846-7, 1851-2-3 were later awarded.

The discipline of the Reserve battalion saved the families of soldiers when, on August 27, 1842, the transport Abercrombie Robinson was battered by a fierce gale as she lay at anchor in Table Bay. The ship was driven ashore during the night, but the 460 Reservists, under Captain Murray Gordon, ferried the women and children through the thundering surf to safety and without loss.

The discipline of the 91st was again in evidence in another drama of the sea. Reinforcements for the 91st and other Scottish regiments were on the troopship Birkenhead when she struck a rock at night, near Simonstown, on February 26, 1852. The Birkenhead began to sink, and, as the number of lifeboats were totally inadequate for the 631 on board, all troops not engaged in helping women and children into the boats were assembled on deck and told that if any more were taken off the boats would capsize. Not a man moved.

The lifeboats safely away with their human loads, the remainder of the troops joined their comrades, lined up on deck and stood fast in silence as the ship slid under them. Then only did they strike out for the shore, through shark-infested waters, and avoiding the boats lest they should capsize them. A total of 438 men were lost, but as a result of their splendid discipline and sacrifice all the families of soldiers were saved. One survivor was an officer of the 91st—Captain Wright.

On its return to the U.K. in 1855 the Reserve battalion was absorbed in the Regular battalion. In 1864 the regiment was styled the 91st Argyllshire Highlanders. The following year the wearing of trews of their former tartan —but with a red stripe—was adopted, and, instead of the feather bonnet, a diced shako was issued. The Kilmarnock bonnet was used for " walking out ".

On the occasion of the wedding of H.R.H. Princess Louise to the Marquis of Lorne (later the Duke of Argyll), in March, 1871, the regiment furnished a Guard of Honour, band and pipers. To commemorate this event Her Majesty Queen Victoria ordered in 1872 that in future the regiment should be designated the 91st (Princess Louise's) Argyllshire Highlanders.

In 1879 the 91st served in the war against the Zulus, and in this campaign the regiment carried its Colours into action for the last time. The battle-honour South Africa, 1879 was later awarded. In 1881 the 91st became the 1st Battalion The Sutherland and Argyll Highlanders. A year later the title was changed to The Argyll and Sutherland Highlanders.

Princess Louise, as Colonel-in-Chief, designed the plaid brooch and cap badge, the former being the only one in the Army of Celtic origin. The badge included the Boar's

160

ead of the Campbells and the Wild Cat of
he Sutherlands, with a wreath of broom and
histles, and was surmounted by her coronet.
'he cypher of the Princess was also featured in
he design.

The other " partner " in the union, the 93rd—
which became the 2nd Battalion—had its
origin in 1799. The 93rd was raised under the
patronage of the Sutherland family. The
Letter of Service in this case was dated March,
1799, and was addressed to Major-General
William Wemyss, of Wemyss, nephew of the
deceased Earl of Sutherland. The regiment was
not raised by the usual method of recruiting,
but by a form of conscription.

A census was taken of all men—sons of
tenants—on the estates of the Countess. Major-
General Wemyss visited each parish, and the
eligible men were lined up for his inspection.
The General passed along the ranks, his snuff-
box in his hand, and behind him came a servant
bearing a supply of whisky. To each man he
selected for service he offered a pinch of snuff
and a dram, and his name was entered on the
roll.

After enrolling the men were dismissed to
their various occupations, principally on farms,
and crofts, and other rural industries. The
following year, 1800, the Highlanders were
summoned to join the regiment as a test of
loyalty to their Chief and to the King. This is
believed to be the last exercise on a large scale
of feudal power in the Scottish Highlands.
Not a man was absent when The Sutherland
Regiment held its first muster at Strathnaver.
Close on 650 strong, the regiment marched to
Inverness, where it was inspected and declared
fit and ready for service. The formation was
also known as Major-General Wemyss'
Regiment of Foot.

In addition to the men of Sutherland, recruits
from the other northern counties joined the
regiment, and Ross-shire was well represented.
A goodly number had already served in The
Sutherland Fencibles, previously commanded
by Major-General Wemyss. The uniform was
full Highland military dress, with feather bonnet,
and kilt and plaid of the Sutherland tartan.

The regiment—numbered the 93rd in 1800—
first experienced active service in South Africa
as part of the Highland Brigade. After fighting
on the Blaauberg, or Blue Mountains, the
Highland Brigade was instrumental in forcing
the surrender of the Dutch, and Cape Colony
came under British control. Cape of Good
Hope, 1806, was the first battle-honour of the
93rd which remained at the Cape until 1814.

In the war with America, 1812-14, the 93rd
took part in the expedition launched against
New Orleans, in early January, 1815. The
attack on the strongly entrenched position
failed, and the 93rd lost over 500 men. This
shambles was the result of a staff officer's
blunder. He gave an order halting the assault,
when the troops were under a hail of enemy fire,
without allowing them to return the fusilade.
A greater tragedy was that peace had been signed
some three weeks before and the soldiers in
the field were unaware that the war was over.

Serving in Canada in the 1830's, the 93rd was
involved in the Canadian political disturbances
of this period, and clashed with armed mobs
and bands of trouble-makers. The disorders,
however, were quickly and effectively dealt with,
and the ringleaders rounded up. In 1854 the
93rd joined Major-General Sir Colin Campbell's
Highland Brigade in the Crimea.

There was stiff fighting on the banks of the
Alma and in the hills beyond, but the bullets
and bayonets of the Highland Brigade won the
day, and repulsed a massed counter-attack by
dense columns of Russian infantry. The
enemy retreated on Sevastopol, and the British
advanced southwards to the coast at Balaclava.
This small village with its harbour soon fell,
and a base was set up for the landing of guns,
munitions and supplies.

A few days later, on October 25, 1854,
General Menschikov dispatched 25 battalions
of infantry, 34 squadrons of cavalry and 78
guns to destroy the Balaclava base. Sir Colin
Campbell faced this formidable array with
the Heavy and Light Cavalry Brigades, the
93rd Highlanders, and three battalions of
Turkish troops. The Turks were holding a
ridge, known as the Causeway Heights, at the
head of the Balaclava valley, and along which
the main road to Sevastopol ran.

The Turks on the exposed ridge were subjected to a terrific artillery bombardment,
which caused many casualties. The unnerved
men abandoned this vital position and streamed
out of their entrenchments towards the 93rd
Highlanders. The dogmatic attitude and cool
bearing of the kilted soldiers reassured them,
and a number of the Turks rallied and were sent
to reinforce the flanks of the 93rd. But now
several thousand Russian cavalry were on the
Causeway Heights.

Nine squadrons wheeled from the main
body, moved into the valley, and rode for
Balaclava. Barring their way were the two
red lines formed by the 93rd Highlanders.
General Sir Colin Campbell rode up and called

L

161

to them "No retreat from here! You must die where you stand!" The press of Russian cavalry came thundering on, and Sir Colin advanced his men to the top of the hill.

The Russian avalanche, bristling with swords and lances, tore on over the grassy downland towards the 93rd. The Turks again broke and fled. The "Thin Red Line" stood alone, silent, ready, waiting .... The order to fire was given. A volley crashed out. The first line of horsemen was shattered, and the remainder thrown into confusion. Falling men, and rearing, plunging, riderless horses checked the impetus of the charge, and the mass of cavalry reined in and wheeled away, men still toppling from their mounts.

The Russians reformed and made another charge, this time hurtling towards the right flank, bared by the retreat of the Turks. The Grenadier Company of the 93rd formed line to meet them. At close range another volley crashed forth. Again hundreds of horses and men sank to the ground, and once more the galloping cavalry was halted and broken.

The squadrons veered away and the rush continued—but in the opposite direction. The Balaclava life-line was saved. The "Thin Red Line" had triumphed over the Czar's cavalry. The 93rd Sutherland Highlanders was the only infantry regiment allowed to commemorate Balaclava on its colours. It is one of the proudest battle-honours in the British Army.

The tall bearded men of the Highland Brigade, their feather bonnets waving, kilts and sporrans swinging above bare knees, advancing through the drifting battle-smoke and shouting wild clan war-cries in the Gaelic tongue, rifles and bayonets levelled, and the pipes skirling eerily above the rumble of cannon and crackle of musketry, struck terror into the illiterate superstitious peasant soldiers of Russia. They thought they were beset by a legion of hairy demons in red coats dripping with gore, who marched to the shriek and wail of souls in torment ....

The 93rd was engaged in the siege and assault on Sevastopol and it was an officer of the regiment who was first to observe that the enemy had withdrawn from the bitterly-disputed Redan Redoubt. The Highlanders were preparing to move in when the position was blown up by the Russians. Soon peace talks were under way, and the fighting ended. In addition to Balaclava, the 93rd Highlanders also won the battle-honours of Alma and Sevastopol.

The 93rd, bound for China, was re-routed at The Cape for India, where the Sepoy Mutiny was raging. The regiment marched from Cawnpore to the relief of Lucknow. Here a British garrison was holding out against thousands of mutineers. The relief column, commanded by the veteran Sir Colin Campbell, pushed through with all speed, and arrived before Lucknow.

Palaces, mosques, domes, minarets, archways, gates, gardens, bazaars, walls, and the houses along narrow winding alleys and in foul-smelling warrens were manned by the mutinous sepoys and their adherents. The 93rd Highlanders were sent forward to clear a section of the suburbs, and stormed the Sikanderbagh, a tall fortified building enclosing a spacious courtyard. The Sikanderbagh was held by about 2,000 sepoys, who poured a withering fire on the advancing Highlanders from embrasures along the 20ft high walls.. The Highlanders were ordered to lie down, and for over an hour the artillery fired over them.

The gunners succeeded in making a breach in the walls. The loyal 4th Punjabis rushed forward, but they were cut down by the murderous fire. Then General Sir Colin Campbell coined that famous phrase "Bring on the tartan". The 93rd was "the tartan". The bayonets glinted in the sun as the Highlanders, braving the storm of fire, poured through the breach. In four hours, room by room, the building was cleared with bullet and bayonet.

The 93rd captured the Shah Nujjif. Under a hail of fire a 12-year old boy—Drummer Ross—climbed to the top of a minaret by the main gate, and, assisted by Lieutenant/Adjutant McBean and Sergeant Hutchison, unfurled the Regimental Colour of the 93rd—surmounted by a Highland feather bonnet—from a spire on the top of the dome.

House by house, street by street, Lucknow was cleared of the enemy after several days of bitter costly fighting, in which the men of the garrison co-operated with their rescuers. Sir Colin knew he was not strong enough to hold Lucknow, and, by a skilful ruse, he evacuated about 600 women and children and over 1,000 sick and wounded. The large convoy, heavily escorted, with ample food—and the treasury—was outside the town before it was observed by the enemy. One division was left behind to hold the Alambagh.

Sir Colin marched back to Cawnpore, but, en route, news came in that their destination was under strong attack. The 93rd was ordered to make a forced march to reach a bridge of boats before nightfall so that the convoy could cross the Ganges. Though exhausted by the marching and fighting under the merciless Indian sun, the Highlanders covered the distance in record time. The troops went over under fire and routed the sepoys on the other side, and the convoy crossed in safety, after which it headed for Allahabad. The Highlanders continued their march on Cawnpore.

On arrival the 93rd took part in the successful battle with over 25,000 rebels from Gwalior who had surrounded Cawnpore. Sir Colin Campbell then retraced his steps to relieve the force he had left at the Alambagh. This assault on Lucknow by the 93rd was a repetition of their previous attack. The Highlanders routed the mutineers in the courtyard of the Begum Kothi, and the palace was systematically cleared.

Bags of powder with lighted fuses were hurled into a number of the rooms, and the Highlanders got to work with bullet and bayonet. And Pipe-Major John MacLeod strode up and down the corridors playing his pipes.

Lieutenant/Adjutant McBean—who joined as a private in 1835 and was commissioned in the Crimea—burst into a room and quickly accounted for two non-commissioned-officers and nine sepoy mutineers. He received one of the seven Victoria Crosses awarded to men of the 93rd during The Mutiny. When the medal was pinned on his tunic and he was complimented, the modest William McBean replied: "Tuts, it didna tak' me twenty meenits". This stalwart Highlander later commanded the regiment.

Organised resistance broken, the 93rd was employed in a series of mopping-up operations. The Highlanders scoured the country in mobile columns, and pursued, attacked, and rounded up marauding bands of mutineers who had not surrendered. There were numerous forced marches and several sharp clashes with detachments of sepoys who sought refuge in the jungle or took to the hills and became brigands. These pacification duties continued until the autumn of 1859, when peace came again to strife-torn India. The battle-honour Lucknow was later awarded to the 93rd.

The 1st Battalion The Argyll and Sutherland Highlanders—formerly the 91st (Princess Louise's) Argyllshire Highlanders—fought with great dash in the South African War. The 1st Argylls were in the fighting advance on Kimberley, and in the severe Modder River actions. With the Highland Brigade the battalion made the disastrous attack up the slopes of Magersfontein Hill, and sustained very heavy casualties when the storm of close-range enemy fire burst upon them.

The 1st Battalion was prominently identified in the battle for Paardeberg. After a stiff engagement Cronje and 4,000 of his tough Boer fighting men were forced to surrender. The Argylls also took part in a number of minor clashes with the enemy. During this hazardous campaign the 3rd and 4th Battalions (Militia) were also engaged. For their excellent service in the open rolling veldt, limitless bush, and innumerable kopjes three battle-honours were awarded—Modder River, Paardeberg, South Africa, 1899-1902.

Twenty-seven battalions of The Argyll and Sutherland Highlanders served during World War 1. Argylls went into action in France, Belgium, Macedonia, Palestine, and Mesopotamia. The principal battle-honours for the 1914-18 campaigns are:—Mons, Le Cateau, Marne, 1914, '18, Ypres, 1915, '17, '18, Loos, Somme, 1916, '18, Arras, 1917, '18, Cambrai, 1917, '18, Doran, 1917, '18, Gaza.

Victoria Crosses were awarded to:—Captain J. A. Liddell, at Ostend-Ghent; Lieutenant W. D. Bissett, at Maing; Lieutenant J. R. N. Graham, in Mesopotamia; Second-Lieutenant J. C. Buchan, at Marteuille; Second-Lieutenant A. Henderson, M.C., at Fontaine-les-Croisilles; and Lieutenant D. L. MacIntyre, at Henin.

The 2nd Battalion The Argyll and Sutherland Highlanders was the first B.E.F. unit to land in France. In mid-August, 1914, the strident notes of their pipes and the rattle of their drums in Boulogne cheered the French, whose armies were being pressed back on Paris by the invading German hordes.

Kaiser Wilhelm referred to the British Expeditionary Force as the "Contemptible Little Army". It consisted of four divisions, later reinforced by three more. But the B.E.F. tore the guts out of the German Army during the epic fighting retreat from Mons to the Cambrai-Le Cateau line, and, though exhausted by weeks of marching and combat, the "Contemptible Little Army" attacked and hurled the numerically superior enemy back from the Marne to the Aisne.

Both battalions of the Argylls were heavily committed in the closely following engagements, and their casualties quickly mounted. Brigades went into battle and came out at battalion strength; battalions were reduced to companies, and companies to platoons. But the fight went

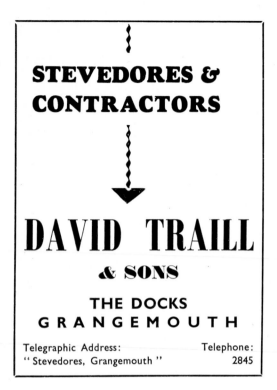

grimly on, and, though the B.E.F. ceased to exist, its survivors became the hard core of the new armies which Britain sent into the field against the aggressors.

The Argylls " soldiered it out " in the mud and slime of France and Flanders as the tide of war ebbed and flowed around Ypres and Loos, and along the Somme, and later, at Arras and Cambrai. The shattered battalions were rested, reorganised and reinforced, and again entered the fray to carry the fight to a victorious conclusion in spite of the massed German offensive, in March, 1918, launched through the dawn mists near Cambrai.

The dense, close-packed, shoulder-to-shoulder waves of German infantrymen bore down on the fire-spitting British trenches, The rifles cracked, the machine-guns rattled, and the artillery thundered, but as soon as one long line was cut down or disappeared in smoke, another took its place, as the enemy sent in reinforcements. The bayonets came into it too, but the massed onrush of the endless field-grey ranks, supported by a terrific artillery barrage, could not be stemmed in spite of the carnage they were suffering under the concentrated artillery and small arms fire.

Then the impetus of the offensive was gradually slowed down and stemmed as the Germans were fought to a standstill over a thick carpet of their dead, wounded and dying. The British counter-attack was launched, and the shattered German Army, now reduced to a famished, ill-clad rabble, was soon in full-pelt retreat before the Allies. Disturbances broke out in the Fatherland, and the German collapse was complete.

The 1st Argylls, however, ended the war in the Balkans. In Macedonia this battalion took a prominent part in the severe fighting, and won fresh renown for the regiment. The battle-honour Doiran, 1917, '18, was later granted to the Argylls for outstanding service in this theatre of war. Throughout the campaigns of 1914-18 the two Regular, three Territorial and the various Service battalions of The Argyll and Sutherland Highlanders fully maintained the great traditions of the past, and their sacrifice and stirring deeds on several fronts added fame and lustre to the name of the regiment.

In 1924 the 1st Argylls dealt effectively with a mutiny at Khartoum. In the early twenties the 2nd Battalion was engaged in Ireland during the rebellion. Later it provided anti-piracy guards on China's Yangtse river, quelled the riots in Hong Kong in 1931, and in 1935 and 1937 the 2nd Argylls operated against the troublesome Mohmand and Mahsud Wazir tribesmen on India's North-West Frontier.

Marshall Graziani's army of about 300,000 Italians was massed on the western frontier of Egypt in 1940, constituting a grave threat to the vital Suez Canal. In December of that year another " Contemptible Little Army " of a few divisions went into action. Military training in Mussolini's army must have placed considerable emphasis on cross-country running, for, when the bayonets of General Wavell's men came near, the Italians made a run for it, and even the rapidly advancing Scots had difficulty in maintaining contact with them. The Italian gunners were made of sterner stuff than their infantry, and at the Battle of Sidi Barrani they poured a murderous fire on the Argylls, alone in the open desert, without artillery support. Gallantry and discipline however triumphed, and although casualties were heavy the Argylls advanced and drove off the enemy at the point of the bayonet.

When they did overtake the Italian " harriers ", prisoners were brought in by the thousand, and Sidi Barrani quickly changed hands. Here the rifles and bayonets of the 1st Argylls had a field day. The enemy surrendered in battalions arround Beda Fomm and during the advance to and well beyond Benghazi. The Italians were still running, evidently having got their " second wind ". The glinting bayonets behind them was no doubt an added stimulus.

After the Axis invasion of Greece, the 1st Argylls arrived in Crete, and, with troops evacuated from Greece, took part in the attempt to save the island. When the Nazi paratroops " snowed " from the skies there was good shooting for the Argylls, particularly around Heraklion, but the Germans continued to pour down troops and stepped up their air attacks. The British force was brought off under great difficulty by the Royal Navy, and ferried across the " Med " to Egypt under constant air attack, which caused more casualties than the fighting on the island.

After contributing to the defeat of Rommel at El Alamein, the 1st Argylls were in the fighting advance across the rolling sand dunes and intersecting wadis of the Western Desert to the hills of Tripoli and into Tunis. Crossing to Sicily, the battalion battled inland, established bridgeheads and forded rivers under heavy fire, and pushed into the hills to clear the Germans from the island.

Fighting on the Italian mainland, the 1st Argylls were in the slow bitterly-contested advance northwards to Rome and beyond. The

battalion operated over shell-torn, bomb-pocked roads and upward-spiralling, crazily-winding mountain tracks. The Argylls established bridgeheads and forded fast-flowing rivers in a storm of enemy fire and pierced the German serial defence lines in atrocious weather conditions. They fought through orchards, gardens, orange groves and vineyards, and pushed into the hills and snow-clad mountains, and battled on through ruined shells of villages to end the campaign in May, 1945.

When the Japanese invaded Malaya, the 2nd Argylls formed part of the Singapore garrison. Trained in jungle-fighting, the battalion was sent out to cover the withdrawal of British and Indian troops from a series of threatened frontier posts over 500 miles from Singapore.

For over a month the Argylls were locked in deadly combat with the Japanese, who, in spite of overwhelming numerical superiority, by no means had things all their own way, for the 2nd Argylls hit back effectively on several occasions and took heavy toll of the invaders. The battalion suffered numerous casualties when attacked by light tanks and infantry on the Slim River, but the survivors, along with a detachment of Royal Marines, formed a composite battalion. This formation revelled in the title " Plymouth Argylls ". The Highlanders and Marines fought on, and though in retreat, succeeded in inflicting further appreciable casualties on the advancing enemy as a result of their speed and aggressiveness.

The last commitment of the 2nd Argylls was the holding of the vital water supply pipe-line to Singapore, the eventual cutting of which was followed by the surrender of the garrison. But the fight of the Argylls and Royal Marines in Malaya showed that man to man the British soldier was much superior to the Jap. Before many months had passed this was conclusively proved. Due to their gallantry and determination few of the 93rd survived death, wounds or capture and the Battalion ceased to exist. A few of the stalwarts however, remained to revive a new Battalion imbued with the indomitable spirit of the old 93rd.

With the 227th (Highland) Brigade, 15th (Scottish) Division, a reconstituted 2nd Battalion of The Argyll and Sutherland Highlanders landed in Normandy early in June, 1944. The battalion was soon engaged in the First Battle of the Odon, where fighting reached a peak of ferocity around Cheux. Further stiff fighting followed in the Second Odon Battle, particularly around Caen and Evrecy.

Arriving in the Caumont area, the 15th Division took part in the great breakthrough, and the Scottish infantry advanced on Estry and the Seine. The 15th crossed and moved up to the Albert and Escaut canals, but progress was slowed down by stubborn German defensive tactics on the Dutch frontier.

Best, Tilburg, Meijel and Liesel fell, and the division was soon established along the line of the River Maas. Blerick was captured, but further movement was checked by wintry conditions, and the infantry brigades of the 15th held on to their gains in a sector of the Maas line and waited for an improvement in the severe weather.

When this came, the 15th (Scottish) Division battled towards, into, and through the Siegfried Line, and Cleve and Goch fell. The infantry brigades crossed the Rhine below Wesel, and the 2nd Argylls, with their brigade, quickly carried alloted objectives on the enemy-held bank, and advanced with all speed to the Issel. Celle, on the Aller, was entered, and Belsen and Uelzen changed hands. The drive to the Elbe was now well under way, and the 227 (Highland) Brigade cleared the enemy out of Artlenberg.

Once over the Elbe—the last of the numerous river and canal barriers to be crossed—the infantry pushed on to Hamburg, which capitulated before an attack could be launched. Thousands of German troops were surrendering, but a number of suicide battle-groups still insisted on dying for the Fuehrer. They found the Scots infantrymen most obliging when they cleared the Sachsenwald and advanced to Ahrensberg early in May. Within a few days came news of the Armistice. The 2nd Argylls had fired their last shots in World War II.

The 5th Battalion served as an anti-tank regiment, and the 6th, after experiencing the short 1940 campaign in Northern France, fought again in North Africa and Italy as an anti-tank formation. The 7th and 8th battalions were in 154 Brigade of the 51st (Highland) Division, and during the disastrous retreat of May-June, 1940, the remnants of the two battalions formed part of " Ark " Force. This formation was detached from the 51st, and so escaped the German encirclement at St. Valery. " Ark " Force was successfully evacuated. The 7th Battalion fought an epic battle at Franlen.

When the reconstituted Highland Division joined battle at El Alamein, the 7th Battalion was there too, and in the furious fighting at Wadi Akarit, Lieutenant-Colonel Lorne Maclaine Campbell, D.S.O., of Ardrishaig

Argyll, earned his well-deserved Victoria Cross. Though wounded, he so inspired and rallied his men that they held their important bridgehead under heavy shelling and machine-gun fire, and beat off an enemy counter-attack which was supported by tanks.

The 7th Argylls battled over the sandy wastes of the Western Desert to Tripoli and Tunis, and, arriving in Sicily, in June, 1944, the battalion made a fighting advance with the Highland Division. With the " H.D." the 7th fought across France, Belgium and Holland to final victory over the Elbe, deep in the heart of Hitler's Third Reich.

The 8th Battalion, with the 78th Division, fought with outstanding gallantry in the desert war, and in Sicily and Italy. Major John Thompson McKellar Anderson, D.S.O., of Dunoon, Argyll, won the Victoria Cross in North Africa, at Longstop Hill. He led the attack through a storm of fire, and though wounded, carried the enemy position with less than 50 survivors. The Battalion gained more decorations than any other Battalion of the Regiment.

The 8th Argylls later fought in North-West Europe. Watched by crowds of silent peasants from nearby villages the pipe band of the battalion played a lament on the site of Lidice, the Czech village obliterated—with its inhabitants—by the Nazis. The 9th Battalion of the Argylls served as a light " ack ack " regiment.

The Battle-honours awarded to The Argyll and Sutherland Highlanders for operations in World War II indicate the magnificent contribution of the Regiment to the ultimate defeat of Dictatorship, and are listed as follows:—Somme, 1940, Odon, Tourmauville Bridge, Caen, Esquay, Mont Pincon, Quarry Hill, Estry, Falaise, Dives Crossing, Aart, Lower Maas, Meijel, Venlo Pocket, Ourthe, Rhineland, Reichswald, Rhine, Uelzen, Artlenberg, North-West Europe, 1940, '44, '45, Abyssinia, 1941, Sidi Barrani, El Alamein, Medenine, Akarit, Djebel Azzag, 1942, Kef Ouiba Pass, Mine De Sedjenane, Medjez Plain, Longstop Hill, 1943, North Africa, 1940-43, Landing in Sicily, Gerbini, Adrano, Centuripe, Sicily, 1943, Termoli, Sangro, Cassino II, Liri Valley, Aquino, Monte Casalino, Monte Spaduro, Monte Grande, Senio, Santerno Crossing, Argenta Gap, Italy, 1943-45, Crete, Heraklion, Middle East, 1941, North Malaya, Grik Road, Central Malaya, Ipoh, Slim River, Singapore Island, Malaya, 1941-42.

On the " pruning " of all infantry regiments (except the Guards) to one battalion strength in 1947, the 1st Argylls survived, the 2nd Battalion going into " suspended animation ". The 1st Battalion was stationed at Hong Kong when the Korean War broke out in June, 1950. The United Nations quickly took up Moscow's challenge and dispatched forces to assist the South Koreans in their conflict with the Communist-dominated North.

The 1st Argylls were the first British troops to arrive in war-torn Korea. The battalion landed at Pusan towards the end of August, 1950, to find the Americans desperately defending the Naktong perimeter. Here the Scots fought their first action in the Korean campaign. The Argylls were in the assaults on several important hill features during the push towards Songju, to the west of Taegu.

About two miles west of Hill 325 a critical situation developed. Two companies of the Argylls advanced and occupied a hill known as 282, but, without warning, artillery support was suddenly withdrawn. An air strike was requested on a nearby height from which the North Koreans were delivering a heavy and well-directed concentration of fire, and Major Kenneth Muir took command of the 282 position. His presence and example helped to turn the tide, and the approach of American planes further raised morale.

By a tragic error the pilots dropped napalm bombs on the two hard-pressed companies and raked their area with machine-guns. Fire enveloped the hilltop, destroying reserve ammunition and forcing the men below the crest. Major Muir immediately set about reorganisation, and stretcher-bearers commenced evacuating the numerous wounded. He was left with a fighting strength of less than 50, and " ammo " was down to a few rounds apiece.

Major Muir led the Argylls back to the crest, and for half an hour they held on, though their number was steadily lessening under the rain of enemy fire. He moved openly about the position rallying and inspiring the handful of survivors. The enemy broke cover and came at them. Major Muir got down behind a 2-inch mortar and planted bombs among the advancing North Koreans until he was mortally wounded.

But a few Argylls managed to fight their way out of the encirclement, and the story of Kenneth Muir's heroism became known. A posthumous award of the Victoria Cross was later announced. The first V.C. bestowed for valour in Korea had been won by an Argyll.

This action left the 1st Argylls with only two rifle companies, but they remained fully operational and advanced north after the now retreating enemy. They got to within twelve miles of the Yalu River, and the war seemed to be drawing to a close. Then the whole situation changed overnight, when China poured hordes of seasoned troops into the conflict.

During the ensuing United Nations retreat there was bitter close fighting with the massed Chinese and North Korean forces. A desperate battle raged by the Imjim River, but the enemy's powerful onslaught was finally checked and thrown back, and the Argylls and their Commonwealth comrades fought forward again towards the 38th Parallel.

Their eight months tour of duty in Korea over, the 1st Battalion left the advancing 27th British Brigade to embark at Inchon for Hong Kong, arriving there at the end of April, 1951.

In August, 1952, the 1st Argylls sailed from Hong Kong for home after three strenuous years in the Far East. The battle-honours Pakchon, Korea, 1950-51 were awarded.

Another call came in October, 1953, when the Argylls were rushed out to British Guiana to maintain order during political unrest. The trouble soon subsided, and the battalion returned to Scotland at the end of 1954. Early in 1958, after service in Berlin, the 1st Argylls were ordered to Cyprus, where they quickly administered sharp punishment to the EOKA terrorists and their sympathisers.

Her Majesty The Queen is Colonel-in-Chief of The Argyll and Sutherland Highlanders. Her Majesty has always maintained contact with the regiment, and shows a keen and appreciative interest in all its activities at home or abroad.

ERSKINE PARAPLEGIC COACH AND COMFORTS FUND
OFFICE-BEARERS

Chairman
JAMES ADAIR, O.B.E.

Hon. Secretary
Mrs. MARGT. W. FREW, M.B.E., 15 Southampton Drive, Glasgow, W.2

Hon. Treasurer
ANDREW FRASER,
Manager, Bank of Scotland, 418 Paisley Road West, Glasgow, S.W.1

Committee

WALTER GALT
JAMES GRAY
GEORGE LOWRIE
ROBERT M. TULLOCH M.M., M.A.

HUGH McCARTNEY
ROBERT McMILLAN, E.R.D.
RICHARD MITCHELL

Subscriptions will be gladly received and acknowledged by the Honorary Treasurer and for your convenience a remittance note is subjoined.

- -

I enclose $\frac{\text{cheque}}{\text{postal order}}$ value £ : : as $\frac{\text{donation}}{\text{subscription}}$ to the Erskine Paraplegic
cash

Coach and Comforts Fund and shall be obliged if you will acknowledge receipt.

To MR. ANDREW FRASER,
Manager, Bank of Scotland,
418 Paisley Road West,
Glasgow, S.W.1

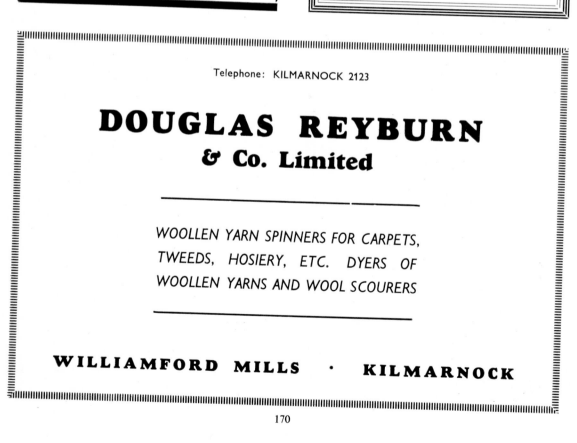

From the picture by Robert Gibb, R.S.A., by permission of Archibald Ramsden, Esq.

THE THIN RED LINE—93rd Sutherland Highlanders at Balaclava

General Sir Gordon H. A. MacMillan, K.C.B., K.C.V.O., C.B.E., D.S.O., M.C., D.L., Colonel of the Regiment from 1945 to 1958 inspecting the Regimental Mascot, CRUACHAN II, during a parade held for him when he visited the 1st Bn. in Montgomery Barracks, Berlin, in the Summer of 1956. With him is Lt. Col. B. A. Pearson, D.S.O., who was then Commanding the Battalion

ACKNOWLEDGMENTS

The Author and Publishers record their thanks to the Commanding Officers, Adjutants and other Officers of The Scottish Regiments, and to Mr. W. A. Thorburn, Scottish United Services Museum, Edinburgh Castle, for their valued co-operation in the production of this book.

List of Advertisers

ANDERSON, PETER LTD., Galashiels 72
ABERCROMBIE, R. G. & CO. LTD., Alloa 136
ABERNETHY, WM., Glasgow 160
AITKEN'S, Falkirk 160

BANK OF SCOTLAND 8
BEN ROY, Leith and Glasgow 28
BRECHIN BROS. LTD., Glasgow 30
BROWN, JOHN, & CO. (CLYDEBANK) LTD. 50
BLENKHORN, RICHARDSON & CO. LTD. 70
BAIN, WM., & CO. LTD., Coatbridge 90
BROWN, DANIEL, Restaurant 148

CHRISTIE, R. L., Edinburgh 6
CAMPBELL, ARCH., HOPE & KING LTD., Edinburgh . . . 20
CROAN, ROBT., & SONS LTD., Edinburgh 22
CRAIGFOOT TWEED CO., Edinburgh 30
COLTARTS 88
CALEDON SHIPBUILDING & ENG. CO. LTD., Dundee . . . 98
COWLEY, RONALD, & CO., Dundee 110
CHAPLIN, W. H., & CO. (SCOT.) LTD., Glasgow 124
CRAIG & ROSE LTD., Edinburgh, Glasgow 127
CALDER, JAS., & CO. (BREWERS) LTD., Alloa 156
CANNING, W., Paisley 156
CADENHEAD, Aberdeen 164
CURRIE, J. & T., Perth . . . . *Cover II*

DICK & BENZIES LTD., Glasgow 48
DAWSONS LTD., Glasgow 136
DONALDSON BROS. (ALLOA 1937) LTD. 156

ELECTRICITY BOARD—SOUTH OF SCOTLAND, Glasgow . . . 46
EDWARD & SONS LTD., Glasgow 56
EUCLID (GT. BRITAIN) LTD., Newhouse 82

FINDLAY, ALEX., & CO. LTD., Motherwell 86
FLOOR & WALL TILING CO., THE, Greenock 154

GEORGE & JOBLING, Glasgow 42
GRAY & CALDWELL LTD., Paisley 48
GOODFELLOW & STEVENS, Arbroath 98
GRAY, J. & J. LTD., Dundee 110
GREENSMITH DOWNES, Edinburgh 130
'GLEN CREE,' Newton Stewart, Scotland . . . . . *Cover IV*

HACKETT, R., Glasgow 16
HIGHGATE, JOHN, & CO. LTD., Paisley 140

LIST OF ADVERTISERS—*continued*

HOPKINS, JOHN, & CO. LTD., Glasgow 158
HARDIE, R. G., & CO., Edinburgh and Glasgow 166
HAMILTON (PAISLEY) LTD. 170

JOHNSTON, DUNCAN, LTD., Strathaven 152
JOHN, J., (COMMISSION AGENTS) LTD., Edinburgh . . . . *Colour Insert*

KIRRIEMUIR GINGERBREAD, East Kilbride 22
KEANIE, JAS. Y., LTD., Jonhstone 64
KEAY, THOS. C., LTD., Dundee 110
KERR, JAMES S., Glasgow 152

LINDSAY, BRUCE BROS., LTD., Leith 16
LEWIS'S LTD., Glasgow 64
LANARKSHIRE BOLT LTD., Hamilton 90
LOVE, THOMAS, & SONS, Perth 106
LIND, WM., & CO. LTD., Elderslie 136
LANG, DAVID S., LTD., Paisley 154
LOWE, DONALD, & CO., LTD., Perth . . . . *Cover III*

MURRAY, WILLIAM, & CO. LTD., Edinburgh 6
MACMILLAN, K. W., Bonhill, Alexandria 22
MITCHELL BROS. LTD., Glasgow 32
MEIKLEJOHN, NEIL, & CO., LTD. Glasgow 48
MARTIN, JAS., (KIRKINTILLOCH) LTD. 48
MOTHERWELL MACHINERY & SCRAP CO. LTD., THE, Motherwell . . . 86
MORTON, GEORGE, LTD., Dundee 100
MUSIC SHOP, THE, Perth 106
McKECHNIE, HENRY, & CO. LTD., Glasgow 122
MACLAY'S THISTLE BREWERY, Alloa 140
McLEAN, JAMES, (THE BOOKMAKER) LTD., Glasgow 148
MALCOLM & ALLAN, LTD., Glasgow 150
McKELLAR, ARCHD., LTD., Glasgow 152
MACKINLAY, Leith 166
MACWILLIAM, JOHN, & SONS, Glasgow 170

NEISH, ROBERT, LTD., Edinburgh 16
NELMES, H., & CO., Glasgow 42
NEILSON & CLELAND LTD., Coatbridge 88

ONE-DAY CLEANERS, Glasgow 124

PARKERS STORES LTD., Edinburgh 20
POLY TRAVEL AGENTS, Glasgow 44
PEACOCK, J. C., & CO. LTD., Glasgow 68
PEEBLES CO-OPERATIVE SOC. LTD., Peebles 72
PATERSON, J., & SON LTD., Rutherglen 90
PIRIE OF PAISLEY 154

ROLLAND, DECORATORS LTD., Edinburgh 16
ROB ROY HIGHLAND MOTEL, Aberfoyle 32

LIST OF ADVERTISERS—*continued*

RESTAURANT FERRARI, Glasgow 42
ROGANO RESTAURANT, Glasgow 56
REID GEAR CO. LTD., THE, Linwood 64
RAMSAY (PEEBLES) LTD. 72
RODERICK, IAN LTD., Glasgow 90
RAMSAY LADDERS, Forfar 110
REID & TODD, Glasgow 122
RUSSELL, W. B., LTD., Glasgow 160
REYBURN, DOUGLAS & CO. LTD., Kilmarnock 170

SMART, J., & CO. (CONTRACTORS) LTD., Edinburgh and Glasgow . . . 2
SUMMERS, JAMES (GLAZIERS) LTD., Glasgow 8
SMITH, H. V., & CO. LTD., Edinburgh 20
SCOTTISH GENERAL INSURANCE CO. LTD., Glasgow 28
SCOTTISH BREWERS LTD., Edinburgh 30
SCOTTISH GAS BOARD 32
SCOTTISH STUDIOS & ENGRAVERS LTD., Glasgow 44
SCOTT, PETER, & CO. LTD., Hawick 68
SIEGWART FLOOR CO. LTD., Glasgow 70
SCOTTISH WIRE ROPE CO. LTD., THE, Bishopbriggs 88
SUNBEAM ELECTRIC LTD., Glasgow 150
SCOTTISH NATIONAL GLASS & GLAZING CO. LTD., THE, Glasgow . . 154
SMITH & McLEAN LTD., Glasgow 160
SLOAN'S RESTAURANT, Glasgow 164

TURNER, RUTHERFORD, LTD., Hawick 70
THORBURN, WALTER, & BROS. LTD., Peebles 72
THOMS & BELL, Glasgow 148
TERRITORIAL ARMY, THE 158
TRAILL, DAVID, & SONS, Grangemouth 164

VINDANDA LAUNDRY LTD., Lenzie 28

WILSON, G. L., Dundee 106